THE HAUNTED WEST

RHETORIC, CULTURE, AND SOCIAL CRITIQUE

SERIES EDITOR
JOHN LOUIS LUCAITES

EDITORIAL BOARD
JEFFREY A. BENNETT
CAROLE BLAIR
JOSHUA GUNN
ROBERT HARIMAN
DEBRA HAWHEE
CLAIRE SISCO KING
STEVEN MAILLOUX
RAYMIE E. MCKERROW
TOBY MILLER
PHAEDRA C. PEZZULLO
AUSTIN SARAT
JANET STAIGER
BARBIE ZELIZER

THE HAUNTED WEST

MEMORY AND COMMEMORATION AT THE BUFFALO BILL CENTER OF THE WEST

Greg Dickinson, Eric Aoki, and Brian L. Ott

THE UNIVERSITY OF ALABAMA PRESS

Tuscaloosa

The University of Alabama Press
Tuscaloosa, Alabama 35487-0380
uapress.ua.edu

Copyright © 2024 by the University of Alabama Press
All rights reserved.

Inquiries about reproducing material from this work should be addressed to
the University of Alabama Press.

Typeface: Minion Pro

Cover image: Gertrude Vanderbilt Whitney's *Buffalo Bill—The Scout* at the
Buffalo Bill Center of the West in Cody, Wyoming. Photograph by Brian L. Ott.
Cover design: Sandy Turner Jr.

Cataloging-in-Publication data is available from the Library of Congress.
ISBN: 978-0-8173-2208-3 (cloth)
ISBN: 978-0-8173-6157-0 (paper)
E-ISBN: 978-0-8173-9526-1

Contents

List of Figures   vii

Acknowledgments   ix

Introduction: Approaching the Buffalo Bill Center of the West   1

1. The Place and History of the BBCW   11

2. Reflections on Theory and Method   22

3. The Ghost of William F. Cody at the Buffalo Bill Museum   48

4. Reverence and Survivance at the Plains Indian Museum   71

5. The Sacred Hymn of the Whitney Western Art Museum   96

6. Constructing the Master Naturalist   119

7. New Modes of "How (Not) to See Guns" at the Cody Firearms Museum   145

Conclusion: Living by the Spirit   183

Notes   195

Bibliography   225

Index   239

Figures

1. Entrance to the Buffalo Bill Center of the West   2
2. Gertrude Vanderbilt Whitney's *Buffalo Bill—The Scout*   3
3. Poster in the entrance hall of the BBCW that represents each of the five museums   5
4. Image of Buffalo Bill projected onto mist at entrance to the Buffalo Bill Museum   49
5. Display featuring the board game the Game of Buffalo Bill (1896)   63
6. Deadwood stagecoach at the BBM   65
7. Display of Cody's show attire from *Buffalo Bill's Wild West*   68
8. William F. Cody's camping tent   68
9. Hallway leading to the Plains Indian Museum   78
10. Entrance to the PIM   80
11. Faux anthropologist's notes in the PIM   83
12. *Seasons of Life* exhibit in the PIM   86
13. Interactive Missouri River home at the PIM   89
14. James Earl Fraser's sculpture *End of the Trail*   108
15. Doug Hyde's *Coyote Legend* sculpture   109
16. Allan Mardon's *Battle of Greasy Grass*   110
17. View of *Buffalo Bill—The Scout* as seen through the window of the Whitney
    Western Art Museum   112
18. Exterior view of the Draper Museum of Natural History   120
19. B. A. Ware's cabin with trail sign   127
20. Wolf exhibit at the Draper museum   137
21. Windmill at the Draper museum   139
22. Tiled floor of "Western" region at the Draper Museum of Natural History   143
23. Robert W. Woodruff Modern Shooting Sports Gallery   159
24. Exhibit featuring female sharpshooters   160
25. The *Cost of War* exhibit   163
26. Wall commemorating prior installation of the CFM   176

Acknowledgments

As noted throughout the manuscript, the three of us have been working on this project for more than twenty years. As such, it has benefited from a great many conversations, relationships, and professional opportunities. So, we would like to take a moment to acknowledge the considerable help we have received along the way and to express our gratitude to all those who made this book possible.

Numerous graduate students have participated in this project over the years. Brian and Greg both taught early drafts of the book in graduate seminars at Texas Tech and Colorado State University. The conversations from those courses shaped our thinking and found their way into the writing. Likewise, several graduate students at Colorado State University provided essential editing and research assistance. We are especially grateful for the contributions of Miranda McCreary, James O'Mara, and Cari Whittenburg. The College of Liberal Arts at Colorado State University supported Greg with two semester-long sabbaticals, during which he revised the full manuscript, and Eric with a sabbatical, during which he undertook significant edits and rewrites. Brian had sabbatical support from Missouri State University, which facilitated the final edits to the manuscript.

At the core of this book are five analytical chapters, each of which engages one of the five museums that comprise the Buffalo Bill Center of the West (BBCW). While we have previously published research on all these museums in other contexts, the work here is original. Nonetheless, we wish to acknowledge the outlets that have supported our previous scholarship on this topic:

- Greg Dickinson, Brian L. Ott, and Eric Aoki, "(Re)Imagining the West: The Whitney Gallery of Western Art's Sacred Hymn," *Cultural Studies ↔ Critical Methodologies* 13 (February 2013): 21–34.
- Brian L. Ott, Eric Aoki, and Greg Dickinson, "Ways of (Not) Seeing Guns: Presence and Absence at the Cody Firearms Museum," *Communication and Critical/Cultural Studies* 8 (2011): 215–39.
- Eric Aoki, Greg Dickinson, and Brian L. Ott, "The Master Naturalist Imagined: Directed Movement and Simulations at the Draper Museum of Natural History," in *Places of Public Memory: The Rhetoric of Museums and*

Memorials, ed. Greg Dickinson, Carole Blair, and Brian L. Ott (Tuscaloosa: University of Alabama Press, 2010), 238–65.

- Greg Dickinson, Brian L. Ott, and Eric Aoki, "Spaces of Remembering and Forgetting: The Reverent Eye/I at the Plains Indian Museum," *Communication and Critical/Cultural Studies* 3 (March 2006): 27–47.
- Greg Dickinson, Brian L. Ott, and Eric Aoki, "Memory and Myth at the Buffalo Bill Museum," *Western Journal of Communication* 69 (April 2005): 85–108.

We thank the editors and anonymous reviewers of these outlets for helping us to develop the ideas and arguments that led to the publication of this larger work.

We began revising our essays for the purpose of this book in the summer of 2012. With these revisions in mind we again visited the BBCW and spent time with the director of the center and the directors of each of its museums. Over our several day visit, we interviewed Bruce Eldredge, executive director; John C. Rumm, senior curator of Western American History and curator of Buffalo Bill Museum; Charles R. Preston, senior and founding curator, Draper Natural History Museum; Emma I. Hansen, senior curator, Plains Indian Museum; Warren Newman, Robert W. Woodruff curator, Cody Firearms Museum; and Mindy Besaw, John S. Burgas curator, Whitney Gallery of Western Art. Each of them spent substantive time with us talking about the center and the museums they oversaw. We are enormously grateful for their generosity of time and insight during our visit. More importantly, we are humbled by the passion and care they—and all of the other curators and directors at the center over the years—have lavished on the center and the associated museums. Regardless of our ongoing criticisms, center staff have consistently supported our efforts.

We workshopped very early versions of several of these essays in the early 2000s communication studies writing group at Colorado State University. In addition to the three of us, members included Karrin Anderson, Scott Diffrient, Kirstin Broadfoot, Andy Merolla, Carl Burgchardt, and a consistently changing cast of writers and thinkers. The essays here reflect the intellectual training we provided for each other decades ago even if the specific arguments we made have been left behind.

While we have been inspired and encouraged by dozens of scholars in the field, we are especially indebted to Carole Blair and Bill Balthrop, who have consistently supported this project and our professional development. We have had extended conversations with Carole and Bill about the project, and their scholarship (along with Neil Michel's work) in rhetoric and public memory studies has been foundational. Bill read an earlier version of chapter 7 and made invaluable comments on it. Two anonymous reviewers at the University of Alabama Press provided extraordinary feedback. They functioned as the very best kind of reviewers, helping us to improve and develop the book that we set out to write. Daniel Waterman, the University of Alabama Press's editor in chief, has been tireless in his support of this book and, more broadly, the growth of the study of rhetoric and public memory studies across the humanities. Of course, any infelicities in our argument are our responsibility.

Finally, in our corporate voice that we have sometimes designated as Aoki-DickinsonOtt, we want to acknowledge and express gratitude for the relationships we have created as we have written this book. Over our years of coauthoring, we have also seen each other through all sorts of changes: we have experienced together the death of a beloved partner, the falling apart and building up of relationships, the shifts in jobs and careers. Together we have moved through assistant professor toward full professor, from junior faculty members figuring out how the academy works to senior faculty members engaged in various forms of leadership (and still figuring out how the academy works). Our time together as writers, colleagues, friends has helped us find our way. Wayfinding is a constant topic of our writing—wayfinding to and through museums, wayfinding to and through the AIDS quilt, wayfinding to and through the multiplicities of the West—and, at the same time our writing together has served as a powerful wayfinding performance for each of us. We hold the deepest gratitude for this journey we have been on together for over two decades of our lives.

THE HAUNTED WEST

Introduction

Approaching the Buffalo Bill Center of the West

THE STUDY OF the Buffalo Bill Center of the West and its five attendant museums has been a career-defining endeavor for all three of us. In addition to the multiple journal articles and book chapters that we have published on this topic over the past two decades, studying this space together has been central to our bonds of friendship. So, it seems appropriate to begin by reflecting on how this long and rewarding journey began. In spring 2002 Brian popped into Greg's office (or perhaps stopped him in the hallway . . . neither of us can recall this detail with certainty) to ask for some advice on a class he was teaching. Brian was holding a brochure from the Buffalo Bill Historical Center, which has since been renamed the Buffalo Bill Center of the West (hereafter BBCW, or the center). "Would this," Brian queried, "be a suitable text for an in-class media lab designed to encourage students to think about whiteness?"

The trifold brochure was typical of those for western museums produced in the 1980s, which is when Brian and his family visited the center during a cross-country family vacation. It featured an image of a lone, proud Native American on the cover; its pages were adorned with images of Buffalo Bill, western art, and the surrounding Wyoming landscape. Descriptions of the size and scope of the center's various collections anchored the images. "Yes," Greg replied, "that would do very nicely." "In fact," he continued, "why don't you, Eric, and I drive up there? Perhaps we could write an essay about this place." Within minutes, Eric had signed on and, in March 2002, we drove the 437 miles between Fort Collins, Colorado, and Cody, Wyoming, to spend time at the center.

We arrived in Cody late on a Friday afternoon, checked into our Comfort Inn (where a plush buffalo toy graced the pillows of each room), and headed west toward the center, less than a mile away. The entrance to the center features a statue of Buffalo Bill tipping his hat to welcome visitors (fig. 1). But the initial narrative and affective tone of the center is more strongly established by a large sculpture,

Buffalo Bill—The Scout, which resides in easy walking distance of the parking lot (fig. 2). An art piece sculpted and installed by Gertrude Vanderbilt Whitney, *Buffalo Bill—The Scout* features William Cody straddling a rearing horse as he scouts a trail across the western landscape. The sculpture anchors the north side of the BBCW complex. As we gazed at the large bronze sculpture of the mythic hero and reflected on our long car ride across the Wyoming landscape, there was little doubt that we had arrived both physically and psychically in the "West."

Figure 1. Entrance to the Buffalo Bill Center of the West. Photograph by Brian L. Ott.

Figure 2. Gertrude Vanderbilt Whitney's *Buffalo Bill—The Scout*. Photograph by Brian L. Ott.

The center was open late that evening for a community event. A small country and western band was performing in the lobby and finger food lined one wall. Most of the center's guests seemed to be locals. They were dressed in fine western gear, many sporting Stetsons, heavily tooled cowboy boots, fringes, and large belt buckles. The three of us, dressed in blue jeans, T-shirts, and sneakers, stood out much like someone wearing Allen Edmond wing tips would stand out on one of the massive ranches surrounding Cody. Wandering through a gallery, one of us stopped to talk to a guest who asked, in a refrain we would hear repeatedly during our trip, "You all ain't from around here, are ya?"

At the time of this first visit, the Buffalo Bill Historical Center (BBHC) was composed of four museums: the Buffalo Bill Museum, the Plains Indian Museum, the Whitney Gallery of Western Art, and the Cody Firearms Museum. But construction on the Draper Museum of Natural History, which would become the center's fifth museum, was already underway. We were impressed; the center was bigger and more complex than we had imagined it would be. How, we wondered, did such a large, carefully curated, beautifully presented cultural center come to be located in such a small, remote place? What would this place have us think and who would it have us be? How might diverse identities of past and present be (re)presented within the center? And what might be the rhetorical consequences of the center's museums?

To answer these questions, we devoted several hours over our initial two-day visit to each of the museums and their gift shop. We wandered the grounds, which contained sculptures of cowboys and Native People, as well as the center's founding installation, *Buffalo Bill—The Scout*. We also spent time exploring the surrounding landscape and the small town of Cody. After two days of exploring, snapping pictures, writing notes, and watching guests traverse the center's spaces, we were convinced we could write a paper that might get accepted to a conference. But when Brian sat down to write the first draft of our essay, he quickly reported he was stuck. He had discovered that he could not identify a unifying thesis that adequately captured the diverse rhetorical inducements of the BBHC. So, he suggested we write about just one of the museums. Since the Buffalo Bill Museum was the narrative anchor for the center, he proposed that we begin there. We agreed on this approach, and he proceeded to draft an essay that after many revisions we published in the *Western Journal of Communication* in April 2005.

Multiple visits and twenty years later, we are still writing about the center. In those years, museum designers completed their work on the Draper Museum of Natural History, rehung and renamed the Whitney Western Art Museum, and reenvisioned and reinstalled the Buffalo Bill Museum and the Cody Firearms Museum. The center also adopted a new name: the Buffalo Bill Center of the West. Center curators, administrators, and board members adopted a new credo in January 2010. This credo recommitted the center to the "Spirit of the American West," which it insisted is "definable and intellectually real," "is central to American Democracy," and is "an iconic image of freedom worldwide."[1] Though adopted years after our first visit, this new credo embodies the original mission of the institution to preserve and promote visions of freedom and democracy, and it redoubles the center administration's long-held conviction that these visions are most fully expressed in the western landscape, enacted through the heroism of the cowboy as embodied in Buffalo Bill, and anchored deep in the nation's soul.[2] Simply put, the BBCW's mission is decidedly rhetorical.

Our goal in this book is to fully engage the BBCW's rhetorical character, taking seriously its own claim to capture, define, and promulgate the spirit of the West. The museum's guiding slogan—"The Spirit of the American West"—provides the central interpretive heuristic for our book and, consequently, its title (fig. 3). As we emphasize throughout the book, the BBCW is deeply entangled with the idea of spirits; spirits of the West, of democracy, and of "America."[3] These spirits, we suggest, ground the ethos of the center and offer visitors symbolic and material modes for engaging the center's vision of America.[4]

Figure 3. Poster in the entrance hall of the BBCW that represents each of the five museums, while subsuming them to the new, unifying theme of the "Spirit of the American West." Photograph by Brian L. Ott.

Ethos, along with spirit, is closely related to a third concept that affords a powerful tool to begin making sense of the center and its diverse rhetorical inducements: haunt. In addition to its more traditional understanding as revealed character, ethos embodies spatial and material rhetorics. Charles Chamberlain notes that the ancient Greek word *ethos* is deeply connected to the word *haunt*. Haunts, he argues, are those places where one fits best. They are places that express or embody the soul's most fundamental tendencies. Just as the once wild horse longs to return to familiar pastures, so, too, do humans often want to return to their moral and physical origins.[5]

For many Native Americans, the West was and remains their homeland, the place from which the entire world and its people were made.[6] For Euro Americans, at least since the mid-nineteenth century, the West houses, signifies, performs, and materializes defining characteristics of what it means to be (Euro) American. The West, as it is imagined by the BBCW and within dominant discourse, is untrammeled by the soul-sapping strictures of civilization and is almost immune to the unmaking of individual and collective identity by the diversity and placelessness of modernity. Instead, the West is a place of heroism, individualism, and a commitment to hard work. It is deeply Anglo-Saxon and powerfully masculine. The West, memorialized and performed by the BBCW, promises to its visitors the fundamental character—the haunt—of white America.

But "haunt" can suggest more than a familiar, natural space embedded deep in a being's or a people's soul. Haunt may also refer to something otherworldly, something that is at once present and absent, and because of this twining of presence and absence, haunt exerts a powerful affective influence. A haunted house, for example, in which the ghostly spirits of dispossessed residents are both there and not there, may elicit fear and anxiety, thereby disturbing the feeling of safety and security typically associated with the home. Haunt, in this sense, involves an unsettling presence/absence, one that fosters and elicits a particular atmosphere in which the present is endlessly disrupted and disturbed by the past.[7]

So it is, we argue, with the BBCW. Offering a vision of America that is familiar, comforting, and secure, the BBCW's mnemonics are also haunting, as the return of partially forgotten and repressed pasts uncannily intrudes on the smoothly reassuring stories the BBCW offers. Building on the dual meaning of haunt, we argue that the BBCW narrates a deeply conservative vision of the United States as the home—the haunt—of democracy and freedom. This vision draws upon the mythic figure of Buffalo Bill to ground, orchestrate, and author its remembering of the West. But that vision is not, regardless of its efforts, univocal or singular. Instead, we contend, the preferred vision offered by the center is necessarily polyvocal, complex, and contested. It is contested and made complex by the multiple voices that enter the center through its displays, narratives, and audiences and participants. On an affective register, the center's polyvocality depends in large part on the ways the center and its narratives, displays, and collections are nearly always haunted by the historical violence of settler colonialism upon which the United States as a white nation was founded and built. It is a haunting that produces an unsettled and unsettling atmosphere, one that oscillates between comfort and discomfort. This oscillation is one that we as critics and participants feel keenly. In the pages that follow, we perform the ways we experienced these oscillations within and across the center's museums.

PLAN OF THE BOOK

In support of this argument, we undertake critical analyses of the five museums that comprise the Buffalo Bill Center of the West: the Buffalo Bill Museum (BBM), Plains Indian Museum (PIM), Whitney Western Art Museum (Whitney), Draper Museum of Natural History (Draper), and Cody Firearms Museum (CFM). To appreciate those analyses, however, we first need to situate our interpretive work in the appropriate historical and conceptual contexts. Chapter 1 is concerned with historicizing the BBCW. Specifically, it attends to the location of the center, to the role of its central authorizing figure, William F. "Buffalo Bill" Cody, in framing the center, and to its construction and continuous development over the past one hundred years. We close the chapter by highlighting the stakes involved in an institution such as the BBCW for how we remember the past and how these memories suture our individual and collective identities in the present and into the future.

In chapter 2, we turn our attention to the central theoretical and methodological concerns of the book. First, we discuss the unique rhetorical characteristics and memory practices of museums, focusing on their role in both *collected* and *displayed* memory. Second, we outline an interpretive approach to memory spaces like museums rooted in what we term *experiential landscapes*. Third, we unpack the concept of *being through there* as our central "method" for analyzing the BBCW and for understanding the complex ways that it engages in a rhetoric of haunt and haunting. We conclude chapter 2 with a longer discussion of haunt as an ethical call on the three of us and the center's visitors to, in Avery Gordon's words, "encounter something [we] cannot ignore, or understand at a distance, or 'explain away' by stripping it of all of its magical power."[8] Chapters 1 and 2, then, provide historical and conceptual (theory and method) frameworks for the interpretive work that follows in chapters 3 through 7, in which we take up each of the five museums in the center.

In chapter 3, we analyze the Buffalo Bill Museum. Redesigned in 2012, this museum serves as an authorizing narrative for the BBCW. The BBM presents William F. Cody as embodying a complex character, and through a representation of his character, offers visitors ways of understanding the ethos of the BBCW. Our performance of the BBM begins to give concrete form to the themes that we explore throughout the remainder of the book. In the BBM, haunts and homes are the material, symbolic, and affective keystones of the museum's reenvisioning.

With these ways of seeing in mind, we then turn our attention to the center's other museums. In chapter 4, we explore the Plains Indian Museum. If the BBM is haunted by the lost home of the West, the PIM is haunted by the internal colonization that nearly destroyed Native American civilization on the plains. The PIM strives to resolve Euro American guilt, we argue, through a rhetoric of reverence. As a rhetoric of celebration and respect and as a distanced observational stance, reverence urges visitors to ignore and repress the violent colonization of Native American lands. And yet, like the other spaces of the center, the PIM's rhetoric is not unified, singular, or linear. Instead, the museum also enacts—in moments—material rhetorics of survivance of Native Americans against all odds.[9] "We are still here" echoes throughout the museum, proclaiming the resilience of Native Americans. In these ways, the PIM offers the ethical tug of haunting we will discuss in chapter 2, the conclusion, and throughout the book.

From the PIM, we turn to the Whitney Western Art Museum in chapter 5. In this chapter, we argue that Whitney performs a sacred hymn, one that resolves

8   Introduction

narratively dissonant images and affectively dissonant spaces through appeals to a western sublime. This chapter, focusing as it does on embodied rhythms, helps us to flesh out the concept of experiential landscapes. We explore the ways the museum speeds us up, slows us down, and urges us to affectively move through dissonance to resolution. But as with the PIM and BBM, the dissonance is never fully resolved: the jangling chords remain in our embodied memories.

In chapter 6, we examine the Draper Museum of Natural History. Emphasizing place over time, the Draper invites visitors to become master naturalists. This ahistorical subject derails critical engagement with the museum and with the ways the Draper imagines the natural world. Much as we focus on embodied movement through rhythm and music in chapter 5, here we explore another form of what we call directed movement, a movement designed to urge bodies to accept a mastering relationship to the natural world.

In chapter 7, we examine the Cody Firearms Museum, the center's most recently redesigned space, which prominently features the return of repressed violence. The CFM's rhetorical effectivity and affectivity turns on a powerful play of presence and absence. In this chapter, we develop the critical heuristic of dissociative contextualization, which serves as the rhetorical mode for the CFM to approach and then dissociate from the violence inherent in firearms.

In the conclusion, we draw together the critical claims made in the previous chapters. We reflect on ethos of the center, attending to the way it functions as a haunt for US identity even as it is haunted by horrors of the nation's past. This allows us to trace the complex and often contradictory narratives and atmospheres evoked by the symbolic and material rhetorics of the place without trying to reconcile them. More importantly, we think hard in the final pages about change. We address both museal change and our personal change, reflecting on how this space changed us as critics, teachers, citizens, and friends.

PERFORMING CHANGE

The final pages of the book are about change because, throughout the book, change is a critical and consistent theme. In the coming chapters, we confront an oddity that arises when writing about material places. Though concrete and solid, museums are constantly changing. The great advantage of studying one site for two decades is that it allows us to engage museal change in a detailed, specific, and embodied way. We have, as we have already indicated, published on each of these museums. But over the decades of our visits, two of the museums have been fully redesigned, requiring us to write entirely new analyses of them. Even in our original essays, we were writing about change, as one of the museums—the Draper—was completed and another—the Whitney—was redesigned before we could publish our analysis. In this same time period, the center has been renamed and rebranded. All of the museums but the Draper have experienced changes in leadership. We reflect on all these changes, reflections that motivate the differences in arguments between our previously published work and the arguments made here.

But the three of us have changed as well. We started the project as untenured faculty, settling into our positions as intercultural, media, and rhetorical scholars at Colorado State University. Today, we are all full professors, and all three of us have had substantial leadership roles in the academy within our departments, colleges, university, and in the discipline. More important for this book, we have changed as scholars. We have become humbler about our ability to make universalizing arguments. We have read deeply in growing literatures in Indigenous Studies, museum studies, and in our home fields of co- and intercultural communication, critical media studies, and rhetorical theory and criticism. And we have even more deeply committed ourselves to teaching our undergraduate and graduate students about the communicative importance of place and space, of memory and movement. All these changes resonate through the book. In many of the chapters, we explicitly reflect on them. We do so partly to alert the reader to our positionality. But we offer these reflections for heuristic reasons as well. Too often, we believe, these life- and argument-altering changes are hidden from view, even though they may be the most important elements of the resulting scholarship and pedagogy.

We hope that in being clear about our own changes and revisions, we offer to students of communication—whether newly introduced to the field or decades-long practitioners—permission to change. And, when appropriate, permission to remain the same.

1

The Place and History of the BBCW

THE BUFFALO BILL Center of the West is located ideologically and emotionally, if not geographically, in the center of the American West. Built on the western edge of Cody, Wyoming, the BBCW takes full advantage of its remote location. Indeed, the lengthy journey through the western landscape required to visit the center and its museums works to prepare visitors to celebrate the spirit of the West. Perhaps visitors arrive from the east gate of Yellowstone National Park, the first and most iconic national park in the country. Or perhaps they travel from the south, as the three of us have for the last two decades, in which case they would drive from Sheridan through Thermopolis and up the stunningly beautiful Wind River Canyon. Other visitors drive to Cody from the north, leaving Billings, Montana, and traveling through the rolling Rocky Mountains along the Bighorn and then the Shoshone Rivers. Mountains border the west (the Absarokas), the south (Owl Creek Mountains), and the east (Bighorn Mountains). The Shoshone River tumbles east out of Yellowstone pausing to fill the Buffalo Bill Reservoir, turns northeast at Cody, joining first the Bighorn River, then the Yellowstone River, and hundreds of miles to the northeast, contributes to the Missouri just before that great river begins its southern trek to meet the Mississippi and eventual spill through the Mississippi Delta into the Gulf of Mexico.

Arid and rugged, the Bighorn Basin was for centuries a throughway for Native American peoples. Yet there is little evidence of long-term settlement in the region by Native Peoples and it was one of the last places in the continental United States that Euro Americans permanently occupied. In fact, white Americans were restricted from settling the Bighorn Basin by a series of treaties with Shoshone and other Plains Indians in the middle of the nineteenth century. By 1878, however, the US government had unilaterally abrogated these treaties. Rumors of extensive mineral caches in the Black Hills by George Custer and others undergirded this illegal land grab and paved the path for mining operations and the building of the Union Pacific, the Burlington, and other rail lines through north-central Wyoming. By the late nineteenth century, Euro Americans began to take up permanent residence in the basin.[1] In fact, the history of white settlement of the Bighorn Basin condenses much of the history of the western United States, a condensation that continues to find expression in the BBCW.

While Europeans first arrived in what became the American West in the middle of the eighteenth century, US westward expansion was primarily a nineteenth-century phenomenon. As Jill St. Germain asserts, "The territorial expansion of the United States between 1783 and 1854 was breathtaking in pace and scope, advancing from the crest of the Appalachian Mountains to the Pacific Ocean and spanning the continent between the Rio Grande River on the south to the forty-ninth parallel to the north."[2] In the first half of the nineteenth century, migrants traversed the Oregon Trail through the Intermountain West on their way to the Pacific Coast and Mormons began to slowly occupy the territory that became Utah. If the first half of the century was a period of territorial expansion and gradual infiltration of the Far West by Euro Americans, it was in the second half of the century that whites began to permanently intrude on Native American lands in the Plains, the Rockies, and farther west. The discovery of gold in 1849 at Sutter's Mill, California, the subsequent admission of California into the Union as a free state in 1850, and the completion of the Union Pacific Railroad in 1869 drove the final occupation by Euro Americans of the western United States. In less than fifty years, nearly all the territory of the United States west of the Appalachian Mountains and north to the border with Canada was colonized. In 1890 the superintendent of the census declared the frontier closed and in 1893 Frederick Jackson Turner advanced his famous thesis that the closing of the American Frontier would radically alter the character—the ethos—of the United States.[3]

As the United States expanded its territorial reach, it had to engage both the indigenous and European people already occupying the land. It dealt with these two populations in dramatically different ways. The United States often simply incorporated Europeans into the nation, acknowledging their ownership of land and offering these residents citizenship. However, for a whole series of political, economic, and cultural reasons, the United States government did not do the same with Native Peoples. Driven by assumptions about Native Americans' status as humans and by profoundly different understandings of land use, political organization, and economic practices, Euro American policymakers found no easy way to incorporate Native Americans into the settler colonial goals of the nation. As white people moved westward, the eighteenth century policies of Indian removal—in which Native Peoples were forcibly moved from their eastern homelands to the western territory recently acquired through the Louisiana Purchase—became unworkable. In place of Indian removal, nineteenth-century policymakers imagined Native Americans as rough-hewn humans who could be civilized. Civilizing Native Americans, the thinking went, rested on transformations that could be wrought through education, the introduction of private property, and conversion to Christianity. While the US government—nominally constrained by the separation of church and state—could not easily engage in evangelization, it could make efforts to educate Native Americans and remake their relationship to the land. One way of managing this transformation was through treaties, the most important of which in the West were those signed at Fort Laramie, Wyoming, in 1868.

These treaties imposed mutual obligations on the United States and the native tribes. For the United States, many of the obligations were material and included payment for lands the United States occupied after the treaties, protection clauses that made the US Army the guarantor of the safety of both whites and Native Americans, and the enforcement of relative peace between whites and Native Americans and among warring Native American tribes. As St. Germain argues, the treaties obligated Native Americans not only to cede control of enormous tracts of land but also to make significant cultural changes; the latter included the enforcement of concepts of land ownership and a restriction of western Native American nomadism. When, in the mid-1880s, the US Army ceased protecting Native Americans from raids by whites and the United States summarily seized the Black Hills, the treaty system fell apart. It is in this context that Euro Americans began to develop permanent communities in the Bighorn Basin of what became Wyoming and Montana.

Even as, at least within the white imagination, the frontier was closing and the Bighorn Basin was being settled by whites, various pundits, intellectuals, artists, novelists, and others were promoting Wyoming as the imaginative and ideological heart of the West. This development was true for both white Wyomingites themselves and for US easterners who were already growing nostalgic for the untamed West that the relentless westward colonization had destroyed. Artists like George Catlin, Frederic Remington, Albert Bierstadt, and Charles Russell in the nineteenth century and novelists like Owen Wister and Zane Grey in the early twentieth ordained the arid Rocky Mountain West—and Wyoming in particular—as the quintessential western landscape. It was, they asserted, a landscape that materially and ideologically captured the West even as the West materialized the most powerful and important ideals of America. The grandeur of the landscape combined with the virtues of the cowboy—understood to be a deeply virtuous man who embodied values of rugged individualism, heroism, and hard work; a man who was white and nearly as grand as the mountains in which he scrabbled together his living—embodied a way of seeing and being. These images, imaginings, and landscapes captured not only the minds of many Americans but, as Jane Tompkins writes, their emotions and bodies as well.[4]

BUFFALO BILL AS THE WEST

Of the storytellers who built the image of the West, none were more important than William F. Cody. Born in Iowa in 1846, which coincidentally was the year that the United States entered the Mexican-American War whose conclusion completed the US continental expansion, Cody was always drawn westward. Born in Iowa, he migrated to Kansas, then to Nebraska, and finally to Wyoming where he claimed an enormous swath of land that became his TE Ranch and where he helped found his namesake town Cody, Wyoming, at the very end of the nineteenth century. Acting as a pony express rider, a wagon master, a cavalryman, buffalo hunter, Native American hunter, guide, and US Army scout, Cody developed deep ties to the western landscape. By the time he was twenty-five, his life had become a synecdoche for westward expansion, as the dime novelist Ned Buntline began to tell his story in highly popular fictional accounts.[5]

Recognizing the public's appetite for narratives of western settlement, especially those involving clashes with Indian "savages," Cody embraced the image of Buffalo Bill and "re-created himself as a walking icon."[6] In 1883 he launched a carnivalesque arena show known as *Buffalo Bill's Wild West*, which blended his life experiences with the exploits of his mythic alter ego, Buffalo Bill, into a master narrative of the frontier.[7] In the show, "fact" and "fiction" became indistinguishable.[8] Though the images of the frontier it presented were highly selective, dramatized, and romanticized, "the Wild West . . . seemed like an invitation into living history."[9] A renowned storyteller and showman, Cody "never referred to his Wild West as a show," and audiences in the United States and Europe saw the performance as a serious attempt to tell the history of the West.[10] By the time it ended its run in 1913, "Buffalo Bill was the most famous American of his time" and "typified the Wild West to more people in more parts of the world than any other person."[11] In telling the story of the frontier, *Buffalo Bill's Wild West* "defined the quintessential American hero" and brought "the essence of the American West to the world."[12]

With its dramatic images of untamed lands and cowboy heroes, the frontier mythology Cody and so many others built is distinctly white and American in character. As Will Wright asserts, the white "cowboy represents the American idea, not just American history."[13] The cowboy—and his perfected Other, the Indian—are central characters in the frontier myth, a myth that Richard Slotkin argues is the "oldest and most characteristic myth" of the United States.[14] Fundamental to the myth of the frontier is conflict and violence. This narrative depends on a centuries' long "savage war" in which the forces of civilization violently expelled or exterminated the forces of savagery (usually the Indians). This violence was justified on the belief that the civilized and the savage could neither cooperate nor coexist. The conflict between civilized whites and savage Indians and its justifications not only made sense of the violent expansion of

Euro Americans across the West but also served to help negotiate other deeply embedded tensions, including tensions over slavery—and race more generally—and class.[15] Buffalo Bill imagined himself (and was imagined by others) as standing "'between savagery and civilization all of my days.'"[16] His show, which nightly replayed the civilizing of the West by the cowboy, performed this myth in decidedly popular ways, bringing the West to the East (and, not incidentally, to Europe and even to the West itself). In a technologically savvy show, supported by the nation's most advanced communication technologies and drawing enormous audiences in urban centers far removed from the wilds he represented, Buffalo Bill brought together "old and new, nature and culture, the past and the future. He straddled the yawning chasms between worlds, and in so doing rose to greater heights of fame than any American could have dreamed. He became the nation's brightest star."[17]

CODY, WYOMING, AS THE WEST

Just as few characters capture the frontier myth better than Buffalo Bill, few landscapes materialize the frontier better than Wyoming. Wyoming's centrality as a frontier landscape depends in part on its geography. A land of vast distances, overwhelming mountain ranges, and astonishing natural beauty in places like Yellowstone National Park and the Grand Tetons, the landscape has long been a source of inspiration for images of the West. What is more, Wyomingites and easterners alike have actively turned Wyoming into an idealized western landscape and into the site of faultless US identity. Bill Cody was one of these people. In the late nineteenth century, he built his TE Ranch, which would host many large hunting parties over the course of the next twenty-five years, on the outskirts of what became Cody, Wyoming.

For Cody and Easterners like the clothier Robert Abercrombie and the insurance executive William Robertson Coe, Wyoming's landscape and way of living embodied a final bulwark to shore up fundamental US values.[18] Relatively unpopulated compared to Montana and Colorado (both of which offered far greater mineral wealth), from the 1880s Wyoming was a ruggedly rural—and seemingly empty—landscape onto which easterners could map their fantasies about a better America. It stood, they believed, in stark contrast with all that was wrong with urbanizing, modernizing America of the East. Drawing on deep "yearn[ings] for a purer, nostalgic, more 'American' space . . . the primitiveness many of these easterners perceived in Wyoming made the state the antithesis to an East they believed was overly cultivated, crowded, and corrupted."[19] In this imaging, the West (and Wyoming) is an idealized haunt and home that we briefly outline in the preface, a place where the soul can find rest, where the body can be at ease. This underlying understanding of the West as a powerfully comforting home supports nearly everything else we will experience in the BBCW.

Cody, Wyoming, brings together the narrative force of Buffalo Bill as the civilizing cowboy and the mythologized landscape of the West. Though Cody's high hopes of making a fortune from an irrigation and land-development scheme came to naught—indeed, he was near financial ruin when he died in 1917—the town of Cody was relatively prosperous by the early twentieth century and has continued to flourish. While an oil discovery outside of town and the location of an oil development company in Cody was one part of the town's success, the greatest part of its success rests on its image as a western town founded by Buffalo Bill and committed to his vision of the West. As important as Cody was in the founding of the town and as the grist for the town's narrative, Liza Nicholas argues that it was the imaginative and organizational prowess of Caroline Lockhart and Gertrude Vanderbilt Whitney that turned Cody into a tourist destination and a distillation of the western mythology.

Though Buffalo Bill was the town's most famous citizen, Caroline Lockhart, daughter of a wealthy Kansas rancher and an experienced journalist, came to Cody as a young woman and steadily built the town's subsequent image as an ideal western town. In 1904 she arrived in Cody drawn to the town partly by experiencing the *Wild West* during one of its eastern tours. Settling in Cody, she assumed the editorship of the Cody *Enterprise*—the town's newspaper, founded, not surprisingly, by Bill Cody—and wrote novels, stories, and nonfiction essays popular with thousands of readers in the East. During her years in Cody, she tirelessly endorsed the town and the region as a quintessential western place, was a powerful promoter of the Cody Stampede, and constantly insisted that Codyites dress in image-appropriate western ware. By 1924, the year Gertrude Vanderbilt Whitney's statue was installed, "Lockhart's vision of the West had become increasingly dominant, and westerners accepted regional distinctions previous generations had sought to diminish. Together, then, the East and West had 'discovered' 'The West.'"[20] In short, Cody successfully constituted itself as western both to itself and to others.

In fact, Cody, Wyoming, did so successfully enough to become a locus of significant eastern largess. When the Wyoming legislature appropriated $5,000 for a memorial to Buffalo Bill soon after Cody's death, several prominent Cody residents founded the Buffalo Bill Memorial Association and claimed the money. They immediately began looking for a sculptor to produce the memorial and, with the help of William Robertson Coe, settled on and courted Gertrude Vanderbilt Whitney. Whitney was an eastern woman of enormous wealth. Heir to the enormous Vanderbilt estate and married into the wealth of the Whitney family, she was deeply interested in the development of American art, organizing a sex-inclusive and important art studio in New York and founding the Whitney Museum of American Art. She was also a powerfully effective artist. As she was already one of the most famous sculptors of the twentieth century, Whitney's interest in creating a distinctly American art made her an obvious choice to create the Buffalo Bill Memorial. After conversations with members of the Buffalo Bill Memorial Association, Whitney realized that this commission offered her the chance to sculpt a quintessentially American sculpture.[21]

But the $5,000 appropriated by the Wyoming legislature was barely seed money for the estimated $50,000 necessary to sculpt, transport, and install the memorial Whitney planned. Whitney, Coe, and others founded the Buffalo Bill American Association, composed of wealthy and influential easterners—including John J. Pershing, General Cornelius Vanderbilt, and Winthrop Brooks of Brooks Brothers—who were eager to leave their imprint on the West and, more importantly, use the West to imagine a particular America. The Buffalo Bill American Association "effectively utilized and promoted the West and taken-for-granted 'western' symbols as instruments by which to impart and secure its own vision of America, a vision in which westerner and easterner came together in a shared sense of American exceptionalism and Anglo-Saxon anxiety."[22] By 1924, with the support of these easterners (but in particular with the financial contributions of Whitney herself) *Buffalo Bill—The Scout* was completed and installed on land that Whitney procured for the memorial. Together, then, Lockhart writing from Cody and Whitney sculpting and fundraising in the East began to produce Cody, Wyoming, as synecdochic for Wyoming and the West, a condensation of powerfully compelling images of "self-sufficiency and 'freedom.'"[23]

THE BUFFALO BILL MUSEUM AS THE CENTER OF THE WEST

The fundraising for, installation of, and narrative produced through *Buffalo Bill—The Scout* serve, in many ways, as the founding story for the Buffalo Bill Museum, which, over the next eighty years, grew into today's Buffalo Bill Center of the West. At its founding, the museum was little more than a local institution. Housed in a small log building designed as a replica of William Cody's TE Ranch house, it comprised an odd collection of Buffalo Bill and western memorabilia, taxidermized animals, historic firearms, the putative scalp of Cheyenne Chief Yellow Hair, and a display of locally produced art.[24] From the beginning, though, the museum organizers had national aspirations. Whitney's founding gift was soon dwarfed by the support of Coe, who became the institution's most important eastern supporter.[25] Born and raised in England, Coe believed that Americans took their traditions for granted. He focused his attention and considerable financial resources to educate Americans in these traditions and saw the Buffalo Bill Museum as a powerful site for this pedagogy. Located as it was in a state that Coe believed was still "fresh with the pioneer spirit," he believed that the museum could "tell the deep cultural stories about the West."[26]

Funding for the expansion of the site came from a wide range of other sources. Cornelius Vanderbilt Whitney, Gertrude Vanderbilt Whitney's son, gave a large gift that enabled the building of the Whitney Gallery of Western Art (now the Whitney Western Art Museum). In the 1960s sales from Buffalo Bill's commemorative rifles manufactured by Winchester funded the building of the BBM wing of the center. Promoted by Fred Garlow—Buffalo Bill's grandson—as he toured the United States and Canada dressed as Buffalo Bill, the rifles were priced at $129.95, with $5.00 per rifle going to the museum. Revenue from the sales of the rifles totaled approximately $825,000, enough to build the BBM wing.[27] As the firearm collection expanded into its own wing, the Winchester Company donated a large collection of Winchester firearms to help build out the Cody Firearms Museum.[28] From its founding, then, the supporters of the Buffalo Bill Museum strove to transform this local institution into a museum of national import.

To meet this goal, the BBM embarked on an ambitious expansionary project. Opened in 1958, the Whitney Gallery of Western Art was the first material manifestation of this desired growth. Situated just south of *Buffalo Bill—The Scout* with its enormous, peaked windows looking out onto the sculpture, the Whitney inaugurated the use of the land Gertrude Vanderbilt Whitney purchased years earlier as the location for the growing institution. In 1968 the Buffalo Bill Museum moved from its original log cabin to join the Whitney in a newly formed center.[29] Named the Buffalo Bill Historical Center in 1969, the institution continued to grow. In 1975 the Olin Corporation's Winchester Arms Collection came to the center on a long-term loan. In 1981 the center opened the Winchester Arms Museum in the lower level of the BBM and, when the Olin Corporation permanently donated the collection, built a new wing for its "encyclopedic firearms collection," dedicating the Cody Firearms Museum in 1991.[30] In 1979 museum designers completed the Plains Indian Museum, which houses "a remarkably rich artifact collection."[31] A year after the dedication of the PIM, the center opened the McCracken Research Library, which houses the William F. Cody Archives and holds important manuscripts, photographic and ephemera collections, and, just as importantly, supports the center's desire for legitimacy as a scholarly institution as well as a place of popular memory.

Promoters of the BBHC wanted to grow the institution's reputation as well as its size. By the middle of the twentieth century, the center had clearly accomplished its goal: it was, in fact, a nationally known museum complex. With the building of the Whitney and the newly installed BBM, the institution soon consolidated its position as a leading interpretive site of the US West. In 1959, for example, just after the opening of the Whitney, Ed Christopherson reviewed the gallery for the *New York Times*, asserting that its collection and display of western painting and sculpture makes "a magnificent documentation of the dramatic subject." He noted the importance of the Gertrude and Cornelius Vanderbilt

Whitney gifts to the museum and asserted that *Buffalo Bill—The Scout*—which the gallery's large windows look onto—is one of the finest equestrian statues in the world. And, in a theme reprised in numerous articles about the center, he wrote that "it is fitting that the collection should be shown here in this northwest Wyoming town, because Cody is the pure West. Cowboys, Mountain Men, Indians, trappers and the covered wagon pioneers all frequented this place."[32]

Less than a decade later, on July 4, 1968, when the BBM moved to its new facility next to the Whitney, the *New York Times* was on hand for the opening. Recording that the larger than usual holiday parade "involved no real Indians but several Whites wore Indian make-up and costumes," the *Times* explained that the museum celebrates individualism and free enterprise, values that, according to the event's main speaker, Buffalo Bill "himself exemplified."[33] In 1979 the *New York Times* also covered the dedication of the PIM, for which celebrated author James Michener led the ceremonies. In the 1980s a travel writer exclaimed the Buffalo Bill Historical Center and its museums were "awe-inspiring" and a "wild west show" of their own. Four years later, another writer announced that the collections, taken together, "are a remarkable homage to the spirit of the West."[34]

By 2012, when the reinstalled Buffalo Bill Museum opened, the center—and the newly designed BBM—were important enough to warrant a full-page review by the *New York Times* cultural critic Edward Rothstein. Noticing its representational struggles—namely that the firearm museum is too mired in details to create a cohesive narrative and the PIM is "suffused with romantic genuflection"—Rothstein nevertheless writes that "the center is among the nation's most remarkable museums, repaying close attention."[35] Like so many previous authors, Rothstein clearly locates the BBCW in its material and cultural landscape. Indeed, he introduces his review with a long digression suggesting that the best way to understand the BBCW might be through a local, small gun museum or by watching the staged gunplay outside of Cody's Irma Hotel. Or, Rothstein writes, "for more authentic fare, take a 10-minute drive out of town for the 'Cody Nite Rodeo,' and watch cowboys rope cattle or ride bareback on bucking bulls."[36] Visiting these sites raises a powerful issue of authenticity and of the struggle to locate the West between memory and myth. Cody, Rothstein continues, "is cowboy country. For real. And cowboy country, too, for show."[37]

Few writers, however, have been this skeptical of the importance and authenticity of the center's western landscape. In 1987 Jim Robbins asserted that the center's remote location is aesthetically powerful. "It is somehow easier," he writes, "to understand what motivated Western painters like Bierstadt, Remington, and Russell after you have just driven through the mountains and meadows of the nation's first and largest park."[38] Not to be outdone, Richard Bartlett, author of the center's official history, writes that "perhaps no other region in the United States is still so untarnished by modern times, still so genuinely western" than Cody and the Bighorn Basin.[39] It is in this sense, then, that the BBCW, Cody, and the Bighorn Basin are wrapped together in meanings that appear to be at once deeply local and powerfully general. More ambitious than a local history museum, the BBCW's "particular focus . . . disclos[es] something universal."[40]

This relationship between the local and the universal is built into the center and depends on claims the BBCW and others make of and about the West. The BBCW locates itself in a specific geography, a particular culture, and a carefully defined set of values that asserts its deep differences from the larger world. In its extended credo, the center asserts that its fundamental inspiration is "forged by nature as it created magnificent landscapes and abundant wildlife—a vastness where pioneer forefathers and mothers, and Native Americans joined in a moment of history, originally interpreted and mythologized by people such as William F. 'Buffalo Bill' Cody."[41] Bringing together nature, history, and culture the BBCW claims to preserve and protect US values of optimism and individualism that allow people to confront "frontiers of all kinds."[42]

Its role in continually reasserting these values is crucial since, but for the effort of deeply committed individuals who fund, study, and propound truths about the West, its spirit can die. The credo asserts that "the Spirit of the American West is, tragically, not eternal; it can wither and die."[43] What might cause this tragic death? The answer is simple: corrosive, media-saturated, globalized culture distracts people, keeping them locked indoors, tuned only to "self and cell."[44] This is a world, the credo asserts, of "mass indifference," which has lost its commitment to "classical minimum standards of learning in American history, art, and science, with huge consequences."[45] The authors of this credo clearly articulate the powerful ways material, cultural, political, social, and symbolic resources weave together in the center's efforts to (re)produce the "ethos of hardy individualism" and in so doing, produce an ethos of the West, of democracy, and of citizenship.[46] Out of the sacralized landscapes of the West and its earliest interpretations by westerners like Buffalo Bill, the BBCW creates a stockade against the corrosive effects of late modernity and builds an enduring sea wall against the debilitating tides of the twentieth and twenty-first centuries.[47]

As should be clear, the BBCW locates itself on a powerfully important and acutely risky frontier between a quickly receding past and a rapidly approaching but deeply feared future. The modern world presented in the BBCW's credo is uncanny, filled not with the positive spirit of the West but the haunting of disturbing ghosts.[48] The BBCW stands against these tragically frightening ghosts. The values necessary to ward them off and to make a good life can be found in the life of the cowboy and, specifically, Buffalo Bill. The map to a secure future can be found in the rocks and trees of the Bighorn Basin. The affective aesthetics necessary for meaning can be discovered in western art, the deep history of Plains Indians, and the industrial splendor of deadly weapons. Embodied by Buffalo Bill and imagined through cowboy aesthetics, the proffered spirit is in its most basic form a longed for and haunting white masculinity. The future, in short, must be founded on the western past as imagined and materialized by the BBCW.

But what, exactly, are the contours of this institution's bulwark? What are the textures of this dam? What are the concrete and specific contents materialized, imagined, and performed by the BBCW's appropriation of the material, cultural, historical, and symbolic resources of the West? What atmospheric elicitations are present in each of the BBCW's museums, and how do they evoke the haunting "Spirit of the American West"? And what are the rhetorical consequences of these appropriations? Answering these questions will depend on careful, critical analysis of the BBCW and its museums. Such an analysis cannot proceed, however, simply on the terms of the BBCW's credo. Nor can we engage the BBCW's mnemonics as though the center were a self-contained text. What should be clear at this point is that the BBCW engages its visitors in deeply held and carefully shaped memories. It does so through a diverse array of symbolic and material inducements, which function as structured invitations to particular meanings and affects. In the next chapter, we explore the uniquely rhetorical qualities of museums and proffer the concept of *experiential landscapes* as one mode of understanding and engaging the complexity of the rhetorical processes at play.

2

Reflections on Theory and Method

FEW PLACES, IF any, tell the story of the West—and, consequently, the story of what it means to be "American"—more powerfully than the Buffalo Bill Center of the West. The center's rhetorical power, as we suggested in chapter 1, is due in part to its location, the mythos surrounding its authorizing figure, and the historical persons and forces that contributed to its construction and development. But as important as these factors are, the BBCW's uniquely compelling character as a site of public memory is also a product of its central mode or medium of communicating, namely through the five museums that constitute the center, each of them a world-class museum in its own right. Museums are, after all, not only extremely popular modes of engaging the past: they are also particularly persuasive modes.

Indeed, history museums are perceived by the public to be the most trustworthy source of information about the past. In interviews conducted by Roy Rosenzweig and David Thelen, individuals expressed a belief that history museums provide relatively unmediated access to the past—a judgment that does not appear to vary by sex, ethnicity, or class. Artifacts, objects, images, and narratives within museums are perceived to be "credible" and "authentic" and thus reliable markers and faithful reminders of what really occurred. Because the artifacts collected and displayed are generally perceived as authentic and objective, visitors to such institutions also report feeling particularly connected to the past.[1]

In short, history museums are decidedly rhetorical; they encourage particular meanings, understandings, sensibilities, and feelings about the events, places, and people of the past *and* invite visitors to enact particular models of being and subjectivity in the present.

The perceived truthfulness of history museums, their capacity to affectively make the past feel present, and their size, scope, and complexity pose unique challenges for rhetorical critics.[2] Nonetheless, by attending to the diverse symbolic and material appeals of history museums, critics are well positioned to understand the suasory force of these institutions, as well as other sites of memory.[3] Historians are equipped to argue about the factual accuracy of museums, art critics and art historians are trained to evaluate the aesthetic dimensions of artifacts and their contexts, and scholars of critical theory are prepared to trace the political and economic forces in creating museums.[4] But only scholars of rhetoric are trained to highlight the ways that museums make demands on audiences.[5] Rhetoric's central concern with the ways communicative performances tangle with audiences allows critics to investigate how museums foster and promote a shared sense of the past and affirm and encourage particular performances of individual and collective identity.

In this chapter, we attend carefully to the aforementioned processes by, first, reflecting on the rhetorical qualities and characteristics of museums, especially as these relate to *collected* and *displayed* memory; second, developing the concept of *experiential landscapes* as an interpretive tool for investigating memory sites and attending to their symbolic and material inducements; third, offering *being through there* as a way of engaging the experiential landscapes and museums specifically; and fourth, exploring *haunt and haunting* as a constellation of affective rhetorical modes that fully engage material places, the bodies that visit them, and the cultures in which the places and bodies are located. We conclude with a short reflection on how haunting animates the BBCW and, thus, how haunting undergirds our understanding of the institution's specific narrative and affective appeal. We contend that a rhetorical approach to museums attuned to materiality, bodies, affect, and the multiplicities that arise from these attunements is particularly well suited to fully engaging with the ways museums invite visitors to adopt particular values and perform specific identities.

THE RHETORIC OF MUSEUMS: ON COLLECTED AND DISPLAYED MEMORY

Rhetorical places can take a wide variety of forms. The list of places rhetorical critics and others in the humanities have investigated is large and growing, and the interest among rhetorical scholars in space and place is vibrant. While each concrete place relies on embodied, material, affective, and symbolic modes to do rhetorical work, it also has specific forms in which they are designed and through which they become consequential. Similarly, museums are rhetorical institutions created through specific museal practices. There are, of course, dozens of museum-specific practices that define the difference between a museum and other kinds of culturally relevant spaces, and, to add complexity, there are differences in practices among the kinds of museums located at the BBCW. For our purposes, however, we suggest that four major practices—collection, preservation, exhibition, and representation—lie at the heart of the creation of the BBCW and its constitutive museums. Collection and preservation form what we call *collected memory*, while exhibition and representation form what we call *displayed memory*.[6] Together collected and displayed memory animate the museum's rhetorical invitations to public memory.

A short research story may well illustrate the principles of collected and displayed memory and how understanding these practices prepares us for understanding museums as rhetorical performances. In 2019 the BBCW opened the fully redesigned Cody Firearms Museum. As we will argue in chapter 7, the new museum strives to contextualize firearms in their place and time. A major component of the redesign is a set of displays organized around the theme of the costs of war. In the center of these displays is a large wall embellished with wartime photographs surrounding a video monitor that offers moving images from US involvement in various armed conflicts. Twelve photographs surround the monitor. The display does not tell visitors the subjects of the photographs, nor does it name the photographers or the archives in which the photographs are preserved and from which the images were selected.

In August 2021 Greg emailed Danny Michael, the Robert W. Woodruff curator of the CFM, asking for more information about the photographs. Michael wrote back that the chosen photographs were "largely sourced . . . from commercial and news archives."[7] With that information in hand, we hired Miranda McCreary—a doctoral student at Colorado State University—to gather whatever details she could about the images. The latter, she learned, are drawn from a wide variety of archives, including those of the BBCW, National Geographic, Getty Images, Rijksmuseum, and other sources. Having determined the location and digital copies of the original photographs, we noticed that the photographs as printed on the wall are all edited versions of the source images. They are cropped; color images have been made black-and- white; and the coloration, tint, and tone of black-and-white source images are altered.

To the visitor, the wall is a glossy and smooth reproduction of twelve images offering little interpretive resistance. However, the images are material evidence of the rhetorical work that goes into creating a museum. The photographs themselves are already particular visions of moments in time influenced by the photographers' subjectivity. A wide-ranging set of collection, preservation, and archival practices determined the accessibility of the image to designers. The choice of these twelve images from the nearly infinite number of photographs about war is also, of course, shaped by the preferences, values, beliefs, and attitudes of the designers and curators, as well as by institutional needs. These innumerable practices and decisions constitute collected memory. Meanwhile, the displayed memory is, again, the result of countless and now largely invisible choices. The order, size, color, tone, tint, and cropping of the photographs, together with the lack of explanation about the images beyond the display's title, all point to the non-necessary and, thus, rhetorical decisions that constitute displayed memory. While most visitors are likely not consciously aware of these practices, they nonetheless contribute to the museum's structured rhetorical invitations. Our analysis in chapter 7 engages the rhetorical invitations of this display. In the coming pages, we consider the museal practices that helped create it.

COLLECTED MEMORY

Museums engage the intertwined practices of collecting and preserving, which we take to be at the heart of collected memory. As collectors, museum curators seek, locate, acquire, archive, and ultimately legitimate certain artifacts (both material and discursive) and not others.[8] Since museums "constantly select and discard from the limitless realm of material memory," the appeal to memory is always selective, incomplete, and partial.[9] To be collected means to be valued, and in the case of museums, it means to be valued institutionally.[10] Traditionally, museums have collected primarily material artifacts, which, unlike oral discourse, can concretely anchor the transient character of memory.[11] Objects are not simply representations of the past, they are tangible and indexical fragments of the past; thus, they solidify memory, asserting that a particular past happened. In short, objects stand as embodied testaments to a particular memory.[12] The BBCW's collection of domestic artifacts from William Cody's family life, its collection of Plains Indian materials, its archive of western art, natural history items, firearms, manuscripts and the like, all selectively value certain elements of the West. This selection inscribes these elements' status as worthy both of collection and of attention either in the displays (as we will talk about in more detail) or as part of an archive accessible to curators, catalog authors, museum designers, and scholars. Of course, the performance of collecting ascribes value to the material elements collected, preserved, and retained. And, at the same time, the things themselves shape and frame the collection as the obdurate materiality of items can demand—or at least invite—claims on those interacting with the things. A shirt ripped by a bullet and stained with blood has a powerful indexicality to the body that was also torn and wounded.[13]

At the same time, because institutions do not and cannot collect everything, many—indeed most—artifacts and their indexed experiences are necessarily excluded. Museums and archives are, therefore, complex sites of both collecting and discarding, of presence and absence. While collecting and discarding are not directly mappable onto remembering and forgetting (which are themselves not a dialectical pair), museum collection practices are part of complex memory processes that have the potential to cleanse, absolve, or relieve visitors of painful, conflictual histories.[14] Just as things can demand responses, the absence of things—of, for example, the material record of Native American, African American, and women's activities in the West—also demands and requires an embodied turning away from the material traces of the activities. It is vital, therefore, that critics attend to the materiality of museums and to the precise ways in which visitors experience and interact with tangible artifacts.

This curatorial process always already depends on selection and rejection from a field of possibilities. These possibilities are themselves woven with power and interest, as often the objects available are determined by donors whose interests are not necessarily those of the institutions or the publics. The CFM, for example, exists in the first instance because of the donation of a large archive of guns from the Olin Corporation. Further donations from the sales of a Remington rifle helped build the center. And, as we noted in chapter 1, the first nationally recognized item in the center's collection was *Buffalo Bill—The Scout*, whose form and donation speak directly to Gertrude Whitney's desire to find and produce American art.

Perhaps the most contentious issue in donations and collections are the human remains often collected by scientists of colonizing countries and held in museums at great distance from burial grounds.[15] In the United States—and indeed around the world—collecting objects has often been part of the colonial project, with colonizers stealing or inappropriately acquiring human remains and sacred and deeply meaningful material objects.[16] Examples of this looting are innumerable and include the looting of Egyptian burial sites, the British theft of the so-called Elgin marbles, and the collection of indigenous objects from any of the places colonized by Europeans.[17] History and natural history museums, university anthropological and archeological archives, and private collections serve as the repositories of these items. Museums and universities long justified their collections as modes for the study and preservation of human history.[18]

But many have resisted these collection practices from the very beginning. For decades, those from whom objects and remains have been stolen have been arguing for their return. In the United States, recovery of patrimonial objects and human remains was and is a cornerstone of the Indigenous human rights movements from Alaska to California, Hawai'i to New York, and beyond. Many of the Indigenous materials were taken by settlers, archeologists, anthropologists, and amateur collectors without permission. Others were sold to collectors by people who did not have the right to sell the objects. For Indigenous people, the repatriation of human remains and patrimonial objects is a struggle for basic human rights. In fact, some Indigenous people have likened the efforts to repatriate human remains and objects of cultural patrimony to the African American struggle for voting rights.[19]

In 1990 the movement for repatriation resulted in the passage of the Native American Graves Protection and Repatriation Act (NAGPRA). The National Park Service—which has been entrusted with overseeing NAGPRA—describes the act this way: "Federal law has provided for the repatriation and disposition of certain Native American human remains, funerary objects, sacred objects, and objects of cultural patrimony. By enacting NAGPRA, Congress recognized that human remains of any ancestry 'must at all times be treated with dignity and respect.' Congress also acknowledged that human remains and other cultural items removed from Federal or tribal lands belong, in the first instance, to lineal descendants, Indian Tribes, and Native Hawai'ian organizations. With this law, Congress sought to encourage a continuing dialogue between museums and Indian Tribes and Native Hawai'ian organizations and to promote a greater understanding between the groups while at the same time recognizing the important function museums serve in society by preserving the past."[20] From its inception, the NAGPRA required museums and other official collections to communicate with Native American and Native Hawaiian organizations about the nature of their collection, including any human remains or culturally significant objects. This communication was the first step in ongoing negotiations about the disposition or potential repatriation of the remains or objects held in the collections.

The BBCW and the PIM were, of course, directly impacted by the passage of this act. Emma Hansen (Pawnee), the longtime curator of the PIM, oversaw the museum's response to the NAGPRA and communicated with over three hundred Indigenous groups about the PIM's holdings.[21] As recently as 2019 the PIM and the Blackfeet Tribe of the Blackfeet Indian Reservation in Montana negotiated the return of a Beaver Medicine Bundle, which had been part of the Paul Dyck private collection. Dyck had purchased the Beaver Medicine Bundle from an individual in 1965. The Dyck collection was loaned in 2007 and then given in 2008 to the PIM. In 2008 PIM curators contacted the Blackfeet Tribal Offices about the Beaver Medicine Bundle, and tribal officers confirmed that it was part of Blackfeet ceremonial practices. In 2017 "tribal members in their capacity as Elders for the Beaver Medicine Bundle and Sweat Lodge identified NA.800.360 as a Beaver Medicine Bundle. John Murray sent two letters on behalf of the Blackfeet detailing knowledge of the Beaver Bundle based on past and current ceremonial practices, oral traditions, tribal and personal histories." In 2019 the PIM officially concurred that the Beaver Medicine Bundle had patrimonial significance and affirmed that "relationship of shared group identity that can [be] reasonably traced between object of cultural patrimony and the Blackfeet Tribe of the Blackfeet Indian Reservation of Montana"; consequently, the PIM agreed to repatriate the Beaver Medicine Bundle.[22] Collected memory, then, is contested by these deep historical, ethical, and spiritual considerations.[23] The field of the possible is itself already fraught with political, moral, ethical, and material issues, on top of which collection from this field adds its own layers.

Closely related to the practice of collecting is preservation.[24] For many museums, the collection and preservation of artifacts and artworks form the primary mission of the institution.[25] While the BBCW clearly prioritizes its representational practices over collection and preservation, preservation is nonetheless a central theme permeating the center. The McCracken Library serves as the research archives of the BBCW, preserving and offering resources to the center's constituent museums and to scholars. Meanwhile, each of the five museums contains and conserves enormous archives of artifacts beyond those materials displayed. Preservation of artifacts pertaining to Buffalo Bill's life and times, to the cultural practices of Plains Indians, to artwork of and about the West, and to the vast array of firearms manufactured in the last five hundred years is central to the BBCW's work.

Holding, classifying, archiving, preserving, and making available these items to scholars helps to secure the center's reputation within the world of museums and cultural institutions. What is more, none of the museums of the BBCW display all or even most of the materials collected by the institution, and so much of the center's work revolves around preservation of the collection. But decisions about what to collect and preserve point to the fundamental role that museums play in constructing public memory. In choosing to collect and preserve some art and artifacts and not others, institutions legitimize the things that are selected and delegitimize—potentially even eradicate all traces of—the materials that are not selected. Selection establishes the basis of collected memory—the memory that derives purely from what is included in the archive.

Together, collection and preservation form the backbone of collected memory as we employ the term. Objects that have been accorded social and cultural importance through inclusion in the archive provide the material resources for collected memory. Consequently, collected memory is closely tied to social authority, to who gets to decide what is collected and preserved. As Derrida explains, "There is no political power without control of the archive, if not memory. Effective democratization can always be measured by this essential criterion: the participation in and access to the archive, its constitution, and its interpretation."[26] If the object collected is deemed an artifact of the West, then it becomes at least a potential material anchor that "narrates a history of the West."[27] At the same time, the practice of collecting and preserving nominates the object to become a material index of the West. More than a set of analytical practices, the practices of collected memory are material. Collected memory includes the material practices of gathering, storing, preserving, and archiving the material detritus that will and can mark the West. Collected memory is also material in that selected and preserved items become material anchors of the center's proffered/proposed/displayed memory, as we discuss in what follows. Yet, there are also material consequences of the collected memory, for the collected materials enable and forestall particular understandings and embodied engagements with the West's past.

Displayed Memory

Just as the practices of collection and preservation form the basis of collected memory, the practices of exhibition and representation form the basis of what we term *displayed memory*. Like collection and preservation, exhibition and representation weave together symbolic and material action, and the practices of displayed memory rely in part on the materials of collected memory. This merging creates and is enabled and constrained by museal space; indeed, displayed memory may be best thought of as a set of spatial practices. This delineation should not surprise us since, as Barbie Zelizer writes, "space has always helped define the boundaries of memory."[28] As we demonstrate in the rest of this book, the building design and the spatial location of the museum as well as the placement of objects and testimonials within it work to orient visitors toward the past in particular ways and do so with the purpose of creating a compelling and seemingly authentic experience.[29]

This effort to produce authenticity is, for us, rhetorical. Understood rhetorically, authenticity is not a characteristic that adheres to a person, thing, or experience. Instead, it is a claim made for the purpose of producing a material and cognitive sense of realness. An authentic experience has an embodied, sensory component even as the modes of mediation of the experience seem to disappear from the experience.[30] In an apparent paradox, simulated environments in museums make this very kind of claim. By enriching the materially embodied experience of a museum—the smell, sound, and look of a fire, for example, or the bullet-torn shirt—the museum strives to bring the referenced experiences, materialities, and pasts into the present and the presence of the visitor. Meanwhile, enriched embodied experience affectively pushes the modes of mediation into the background, helping bodies believe they are directly engaging in the experience. The materiality of the museum's inventional modes underlies this engagement. Material, symbolic, and spatial, the museumgoers' bodies and the museums' bodies intersect to create compelling rhetorical interactions.

In museums, at least two factors weigh in understanding exhibitions and the efforts to create a compellingly real performance. First is the matter of site specificity, which deals with the relationship between the site of the museum or gallery and the space unconfined by the gallery. Museums are fashioned by the contents and materials of their physical locations, be these industrial or natural, and thus it matters where memory is activated.[31] Museums are constitutive elements in a larger landscape, a landscape that, as Blair and Michel argue, offer "rules for reading" the museum and suggest specific subject positions for visitors.[32] As we have suggested in the previous chapter, the BBCW's location in Wyoming is central both to its existence and to its pedagogical force. Upon entering the center, visitors are already prepared to learn the lessons of the conquering of the West. We return to the question of site specificity throughout this book.

A second concern with exhibition is that of installation, which refers to the practice of placing an artifact in the "neutral" void of a gallery or museum. The removal of an artifact from its original context and its subsequent placement within a museum necessarily alters the artifact's meaning.[33] In a museum, an artifact's meaning and affective force are shaped by how the visitor arrives at it, by how movement through the museum is organized and directed, and by the associations and dissociations fostered by juxtaposition with and proximity to other artifacts.[34] As our analysis of the center's museums suggests, the order of the exhibition creates and draws on particular trajectories, providing visitors with embodied meaning-making strategies that help them navigate the space.

Regardless of how visitors begin their way into the BBM, for example, they are invited into the space by a mediated ghostly image of an actor as Buffalo Bill, projected onto a foggy mist. As they enter the BBM, they experience narratives of William Cody's family life. Visitors are introduced to Buffalo Bill's career as a showman only after learning that Buffalo Bill was a real scout and a conflicted family man and that this personal history served as the foundation for creating the *Wild West*. The ordering of the museum, then, asserts that the story Buffalo Bill tells in his *Wild West*—and, by extension, the story the BBM tells—is but a telling of the way it really was. In a similar way, the Whitney gallery systematically leads visitors between discordant and harmonious images, moving them inexorably toward a grand window that looks onto *Buffalo Bill—The Scout*. In our experience, the various spaces throughout the museums structure movement and in so doing structure the museums' proffered memories.

Along with exhibition (e.g., site specificity and installation), representation constitutes the fourth key practice of museums and is the second key dimension of displayed memory. Museum curators and designers interpret artifacts and render them meaningful through various modes of display. The representational strategies of museums vary greatly, from curiosity cabinets and life-size, dioramic environments to automated voiceovers and video presentations. The placards, curator's notes, brochures, and exhibit catalogues scattered throughout museums further shape the meanings of the artifacts on display. Historically, the display of artifacts in museums has been about separation, spectacle, and surveillance, as visitors have "gazed" at artifacts preserved and protected behind rope barriers and glass walls.[35] Increasingly, however, museums seeking to foster "lived experience" with artifacts have featured fully immersive, interactive environments.

The United States Holocaust Memorial Museum in Washington, DC, for instance, seeks to "encourage its visitors to reflect upon the moral and spiritual questions raised by the events of the Holocaust as well as their own responsibilities as citizens of a democracy" by having visitors adopt the personas of Holocaust victims and survivors as they move through the museum.[36] Using simulated environments, modern museums often claim to offer visitors a more authentic experience of history. It is in search of this authentic experience that the Draper fills its display on the Yellowstone forest fires of 1988 with the smell of smoke and that the PIM contains a reproduction of a Missouri River house warmed by a realistic-looking and -sounding fire.

Collected and displayed memory offer us basic tools for conceptualizing the modes by which museums come to be museums. Both the collection of the materials that will be displayed and then the display of (nearly always only a part of) the collection are extraordinarily complicated. Daily, banal decisions about individual material things intersect with large ethical, political, and aesthetic discussions—highlighted perhaps by the shifting practices produced by the NAGPRA and the social movements that led to its passage—to create the museum visitors experience each day. Few visitors reflect on all the decisions necessary to create the museum they are experiencing; we know we did not attend to these decisions before we began to study museums. Our job, then, is to use our understanding of the kinds of decisions and practices that lie behind a display, a museum, or a history center, without letting that understanding dominate our analysis. We want, instead, to think hard about the experiences the BBCW invites, to imagine the values, attitudes, beliefs, and actions the museum structures for its visitors. The next section begins to theorize the ways in which the particular forms of museums engage with visitors as whole, fully embodied, people.

THE RHETORIC OF MEMORY PLACES: ON EXPERIENTIAL LANDSCAPES

Having reflected on the rhetorical strategies of museums along the axes of collected and displayed memory, we wish to now broaden our interpretive lens by considering the matter of place. Museums, after all, are *places* of public memory; patrons travel—often great distances—to visit them and experience them in fully embodied ways (though, of course, museums often created complex virtual displays during the pandemic). Since at least the late 1980s, scholars in rhetorical studies and other disciplines have taken an interest in space. Adopting the all-too-familiar trope of "turning," scholars in the humanities and social sciences have broadly acknowledged a spatial turn, while some scholars have argued specifically for increased attention to space in particular disciplines.[37] While the attention to space and place is relatively recent in some fields, these concepts are woven into the very history of rhetoric. As Blair, Dickinson, and Ott note, place has a deep heritage in rhetorical studies, especially as it relates to memory.[38]

Place appears very early in the history of Western rhetorical theory: here, topos may be the most obvious example. In Greek rhetorical theory, topos is used to conceptualize rhetorical invention, offering topoi both as places arguments can start and the directions (or trajectories) an argument can take. Even as topos is useful for thinking about rhetorical invention, it is also a powerful means for thinking about spatial invention. Henri Lefebvre, discussing the ways space is always qualified through embodied gestures and their traces and marks, writes, "In the beginning was the Topos."[39]

Other rhetorical terms are also freighted with spatiality. For example, topos links argumentative invention to the canon of memory, leading many to comment that memory is conceptualized spatially.[40] Memory can combine architectural mnemonics with the inventional strategies implied in topos. In the introduction, we suggested that ethos and its earlier term haunt have been spatialized by contemporary scholars like Michael Hyde and Charles Chamberlain.[41] Thus, the elements of rhetorical invention, the rhetorical canon, and the modes of proof all rely on understandings of place.

Drawing on these ancient traditions but also motivated by contemporary concerns, rhetoric scholars have engaged in a return to questions about the places and spaces of rhetorical action. A number of rhetorical critics engage places of memory like memorials and, to a lesser extent, museums. In fact, much of the work on place in rhetorical studies has focused on these more or less official sites of memory. Cities, suburbs, places of protest, and parks have also drawn sustained attention from rhetorical critics, though they often struggle with fully engaging the place-ness of rhetoric, that is, with its materiality, its temporality, and its embodied inducements.[42] It is in partial response to these difficulties that we offer the neologism *experiential landscape*, the entitling elements of which we now unpack.

Experiential

On its own, the term experiential landscape explains little since its two constituent terms—experiential and landscape—are complex and fraught with challenges. A full exploration of both deserves and, indeed, has received book-length treatments. And yet, brief discussions of these terms and the ways they weave together moves us toward a richer understanding of the imbrications of museums, memory, and materiality. We start with experience. While the problem of experience is deep and wide, for the purposes of this project we briefly identify four major axioms of experience that help us understand museums as experiential landscapes: (1) experience requires sensations of things, whether these be material objects and actions in the world or motions, affects, emotions, and cognitions in ourselves; (2) experience is temporally complex, folding together past, present, and future in an instant; (3) experience is embodied and emplaced; and (4) experience is indistinguishably individual and social.

Accordingly, first, experience is a way of testing out and making sense of the world—that is, of things.[43] The earliest meanings of the word *experience* are closely connected to experiment and capture the idea of testing the world by pushing up against the world's thingness with the senses and feeling the world push back. It is not quite correct to assert that there is a world external to us, one that we perceive in some relatively uncomplicated way or that impinges itself on us. Instead, it is best to understand experience as a transaction, interaction, or engagement between us and the world. In real ways, we extend into the world even as the world integrates into ourselves. As Alva Noë argues, the "world shows up" to us, but it does not do so automatically in the way that an image appears on a screen. Instead, "it shows up as a situation in which we find ourselves."[44]

Noë suggests that experience depends on "sensorimotor understanding," an understanding that weaves together the intellectual, sensing, and moving body with the world, which itself comprises variously sensing, sensible, and moving bodies.[45] This constitutive entanglement of self and world can be thought of as an entanglement of things, where things are conceptualized as relatively composed, organized, and lively matter.[46] Like items in the natural world or the mix of artifacts, elements, and items that make up museums, our bodies and selves are complexly organized things. Experience depends on the constantly transformative sensate bumping together of these lively and organized things. In this testing, the world is transformed, though it never fully reveals itself as we, too, are transformed.

Seeing a chair reveals to us something about sitting, about bodies (like ours) that sit, and about things organized for and by sitting. Bringing this observation to the specific topic of museums, we can begin to understand how the things that form museal collections and exhibitions are woven into our experiences. We depend on the thing of the collection as energetic triggers for our experience. Meanwhile, we bring with us previous experiences with the kinds of things that populate museums and these previous experiences help activate the possibilities latent in the things themselves. Likewise, experiencing a museum or a "Center of the West" coconstitutes the center and the experiencing body, linking the center and the body in an affective, material, and meaningful relationship.

Second, the entanglement of things that comprises experience seems to always only occur in the present. In fact, experience weaves together past, present, and future. For example, as the body begins to move to accomplish a task—say, picking up a knife to begin preparations for dinner—it draws on deep wells of embodied memories of previous efforts at picking up objects. This memory is stored, partly, in the brain but also in the body as part of the proprioceptive and kinesthetic systems that make movement, balance, and orientation possible. These embodied memories often fulfill their function without rising to the level of consciousness, instead functioning through the decision-making processes built into the body. What is more, much of what rises to the level of consciousness includes those sensory inputs that have already been processed by the body's memory, and the body decides what ought to be considered within the conscious, higher level cognitive domains. Thus, the meaning—that is to say, the consequentiality and usefulness—of experience is created through interactions between the present and the past.[47]

Just as importantly, as we experience and act, we are also projecting into the future. Drawing both on the immediate present and our memorized past, we imagine immediate and more distant futures. Dedicated softball players, for example, predict with remarkable accuracy where a well-hit ball will land even as they understand and begin to calculate the movements and decisions of the relationship between the moving ball and the moving body implied by the complexly interacting trajectories and velocities. In a very real sense, the player is experiencing the future by weaving together the past and the present. Understanding experience as testing—as in "to experiment"—the future is woven back into the present as the subject constantly tests predictions against the present while experiencing the present is extended into the future. In this way, then, our bodies organize and shape movements, twining past, present, and future even as they process meaningful encounters with things that are shaped by and shape us.[48]

This knitting of time, however, does not just include these immediate performances where one draws on the past to predict the very near future of catching a ball or slicing a carrot. Instead, when visiting rhetorical places like museums, we are often imagining a more distant future and weighing the experiences of the present displays against that imagined or hoped for future. Elizabeth Weiser, in her book on national museums, records this kind of longer-term futurity as she explores museums designed to help visitors think hard about what the nation in the future might entail.[49] In these instances, the experience is more clearly social (a topic we explore later in this chapter) and the temporality even more complex than that of the well-trained baseball player.

Third, this temporally complex experience is also emplaced. As Nöe argues, we perceive "what is available from a place."[50] This emplacedness of experience is not static; instead, there is a place-based transaction between the experiencer and the experienced such that the experiential event and the experiential place produce each other. Indeed, it is powerful to think of "perception as a movement from here to there, from this place to that. We ourselves (whole persons) undertake our perceptual consciousness of the world in, with, and in relation to the places where we find ourselves."[51] The movement from here to there is imaginative as well as embodied, emplaced, and material.[52] We test the world, moving around to see what might be obscured, hidden, or too complex to understand from any one place. Like the softball player running toward the outfield fence, we use all our senses. These include the five senses with which we are familiar but also a full range of proprioceptive senses that help us catch the ball, stop before slamming into the outfield wall, and throw the ball back toward second base all in one fluid engagement with worldly events while we employ, experience, perceive, and make meaning of the world we live in.[53] Or, from an alternative point of view, "places (along with bodies and landscapes that bound, and sometimes bind, them) are matters of experience."[54]

Fourth, we have written about experience as an interaction among things, as a weaving of past, present, and future, and as emplaced, but it is also always radically individual and social. In fact, the first three propositions—experience as relations among things, temporally complex, and embodied and emplaced—lay the foundation for understanding experience as a folding of the individual and social. Any experience is always singular. It is a very specific testing, weaving, and folding that relies on a once-in-a-lifetime confluence of things, times, and places. But, at that same space-time, each experience is always social. The wovenness of things that constitutes our experiences already means that our sensing selves are extended into the world of other things, including other humans, animals, and agentic material elements of our daily lives. To be embodied and emplaced already means that experience is relational, as emplacement and embodiment are defined by directional relations among bodies and the (often temporary) boundaries that designate this or that body.

LANDSCAPE

The social and emplaced nature of experience leads directly to our conversation about space and spatiality. No less perplexing a term than experience, *landscape* is notoriously ill-defined. As with our discussion of experience above, we do not pretend to cover the topic fully; indeed, such a project would be nearly impossible. But we can trace what we take the meaning of landscape to be for our project and, more broadly, as a rhetorical concept. For our purposes, we want to briefly discuss four major characteristics of landscapes that help us understand museums as experiential landscapes: (1) landscape is a particular way of theorizing and engaging spatiality; (2) landscapes are open rather than closed; (3) landscapes draw on diverse cognitive, cultural, and material apparatuses; and (4) landscapes afford very specific viewing positions.

Our first principle urges us to conceptualize landscape spatially and, in so doing, engage the dynamism of the center and its surrounding environs. This approach to landscape may seem counterintuitive. For many, landscape is conceptualized as a genre of painting or photography and, thus, as the subject matter for various modes of representation. As Doreen Massey argues, many theorists in the nineteenth and twentieth century viewed representation as homologous to stasis and a very specific (and incapacitating) understanding of space. In this view, space as representation is opposed to time or temporality. Massey summarizes the argument of these philosophers this way: "Space conquers time by being set up as the representation of history/life/the real world. On this reading space is an order imposed on the inherent life of the real (Spatial) order obliterates (temporal) dislocation. Spatial immobility quietens temporal becoming. It is, though, a most dismal of pyrrhic victories. For in the very moment of its conquering triumph, 'space' is reduced to stasis. The very life, and certainly the politics, are taken out of it."[55] Landscape understood as a specific tradition of painting or photography easily partakes of this understanding of space. In fact, we explore—sometimes obliquely and sometimes directly—the efforts some representations within the BBCW make to create stasis, to stop time, and to tame the critical movements possible within space-time.

But landscape can indicate a more active sense of space, time, the built environment, and the people who make, inhabit, and use that environment. Geographer Sharon Zukin, for example, writes that "landscape . . . represents a microcosm of social relations."[56] For the anthropologist Amy Mills, "landscape is both a work and an erasure of work. It is therefore a social relation of labor, even as it is something that is labored over."[57] Here, the term is used to signal the work necessary for creating the built environment, the work that that environment embodies and hides, and the ways landscapes can position the environment's users. As Mills writes, "The landscape should be viewed first as a medium through which identity politics are articulated and negotiated. It is also, however, unlike other cultural media, a constitutive player in this process because of its materiality and representative power."[58] From this point of view, landscape becomes more than representation—more than a picture on a wall. Rather, it is seen as the material and symbolic thing in which the vagaries of identity are created, enacted, performed, and hidden.

Quite distinct from being conceptualized as a static slice through time, landscape as we are using it shares much with Massey's understanding of space. Space, for Massey, is "constituted by interrelations," is imagined as the "sphere of the possibility of the existence of multiplicity in the sense of contemporaneous plurality; as the sphere in which distinct trajectories coexist; as the sphere therefore of coexisting heterogeneity," and is "always under construction."[59] This understanding of space directly rejects the distinction between space as static and time as spontaneous and agentic. Instead, space and time are woven together as space-time, where space is a "simultaneity of stories-so-far" and is the realm of movement, which itself always interlaces space-time.[60]

But landscape is not simply homologous with this understanding of space. If it were, we might as well use the term "space." Instead, landscape also partakes of an active understanding of place where, to use Massey's language again, "places are collections of those stories, articulations within the wider power-geometries of space. . . . Their character will be a product of these intersections within the wider setting, and what is made of them."[61] As integrations of space and time, places can be thought of as "spatio-temporal events," where trajectories come together in temporary and always shifting temporalities and spatialities.[62] Landscapes are very much like this, places thought of as spatiotemporal events that make possible, that reveal, that hide, that remix powerful trajectories, and where, crucially, contradictory trajectories (space-time movements) coexist. Again, if we were adopting this understanding of place, there would be little need for us to reinvigorate landscape.

Instead, landscape encodes a particular kind of place and a particular way of thinking about the twining of bodies, built environments, spatial imaginaries, and the constant work to which Mills and Zukin attend. Our version of landscape recognizes the ways landscapes can, as Henri Lefebvre writes, present "any susceptible viewer with an image at once true and false of a creative capacity which the subject (or Ego) is able, during a moment of marvelous self-deception, to claim as his own."[63] Landscape can, in fact, be representational in this way. The landscape paintings in the Whitney often strive to obscure and "assign to oblivion" the "concrete reality, its products, and the productive activity involved" in making the West.[64] Likewise, the BBCW's mission to celebrate the spirit of the American West seems to serve a similar purpose—to steady and secure the western landscape into an apparently natural or real set of relations. The center is filled with images of western landscapes; these images strive to make static the chaos of time. They do so by appealing to visitors' embodied experiences of natural landscapes as well as to their mediated understandings of those landscapes from popular culture. In this book, however, we are determined to activate these seemingly static landscapes.

While recognizing *landscape* as containing within it this ahistorical impulse, we see it as imbued with the vagaries of historically, materially, and symbolically particular and changing performances. Our expression *experiential landscape* works directly to address these vagaries. Reflecting the recognition that the experience is always an interaction among bodies woven into and constitutive of space, we present experiential as always already spatialized, agentic, and temporally specific. By using *landscape*, we refuse to leave landscape as a representational practice that only ever encodes and covers power. Instead, by spatializing landscape, we remind ourselves and others that western experiential landscapes are constituted by relationships, are continuously infused with multiplicity, and are constantly under construction even as landscapes are also drawing on and linked to pasts and position users in specific ways. Our final landscape principles take up these considerations.

Namely, because landscapes are constituted by relationships, infused with multiplicity, and are always under construction, it is best to think of museums and memorials as diffuse material and symbolic performances rather than as discrete texts. "A discrete text is," according to Barry Brummett, "one with clear boundaries in time and space. A diffuse text is one with a perimeter that is not so clear, one that is mixed up with other signs."[65] Whereas traditional objects of rhetorical study such as public speeches have relatively clear beginnings and endings, historical and cultural sites are part of the texture of larger landscapes. As Lefebvre writes, "a spatial work (monument or architectural project) attains a complexity fundamentally different from the complexity of a text, whether prose or poetry," a complexity captured well by "texture." "We already know," he writes, "that a texture is made up of a usually rather large space covered by networks or webs; monuments constitute the strong points, nexuses or anchors of such webs."[66]

The textural experience of museums and memorials does not begin at their entrances, even as the museum may well serve as a strong, nodal point that can anchor experiential webs. Visitors must travel to these sites, which are often surrounded by other historical or tourist sites. It is typical, then, for visitors to occupy many sites in the broader context of a family vacation or school fieldtrip. The experiences and meanings of the larger landscape (and of attendant sites) spill over into specific sites.[67] To approach a museum as a discrete text, whose boundaries are clearly delineated by the structures produced by the museum's designers, risks reducing the critic's task to decoding the meanings intended by the designers. This mode ignores how visitors understand, experience, and use actual spaces.[68] Instead, we suggest that the built environment "has a horizon of meaning: a specific or indefinite multiplicity of meanings, a shifting hierarchy in which now one, now another meaning comes momentarily to the fore, by means of—and for the sake of—a particular action."[69] Museums, then, are profoundly open to varieties of meanings and, more importantly, a multiplicity of actions.

Third, in addition to being part of a larger physical landscape, historical and cultural sites are also part of larger symbolic or imaginary landscapes.[70] According to Gaynor Kavanagh, "when we walk through or around a museum [and its surrounding landscape] we weave both our bodies and our minds through these spaces," which he refers to as "dream spaces."[71] In other words, experience of a particular place comprises not just the tangible materials available in that place but also the full range of memorized images that persons bring with them. The city, notes Victor Burgin, "in our actual experience is at the same time an actually existing physical environment, and a city in a novel, a film, a photograph, a city seen on television, a city in a comic strip, a city in a pie chart, and so on."[72] Similarly, the BBCW is part of a "western dreamscape" comprising memory images from western art, tourist guidebooks, poetry, and cinematic representations of the West.[73] Likewise, the five museums that make up the BBCW engage widely varying dreamscapes. For example, the PIM is part of a dreamscape of the four-hundred-year history of non–Native American representations of the continent's indigenous peoples. From the use of feathers and war paint by the rebels in the Boston Tea Party, to New Age communes, and "playing Indian," the creation and dissemination of images of "Indians" are central to American identity.[74] Like the physical landscape, the dreamscape proffers a set of interweaving relations or experiential nodes that can organize though not determine the practices that occur in a space.[75] This principle suggests the need to investigate spaces of memory as intersections of both physical and cognitive landscapes, that is to say, as experiential landscapes.

Finally, experiential landscapes invite visitors to occupy particular subject positions and these subject positions, in turn, shape perceptions.[76] That is, they entail certain ways of looking and exclude or marginalize others. Experiential landscapes create what John Dorst has called "optical regimes," which he defines as "the particular historical constellation of components, both material and intangible, through which human visual experience becomes organized at a given moment."[77] Just as oral discourse interpellates individuals as concrete subjects, experiential landscapes hail bodies, interpellating them.[78] Subjectivity requires precise bodily coordinates, for as Lefebvre notes, "the body is both point of departure and destination."[79] In recognizing and acknowledging the hail, the body locates itself in time and space through and in which the subject comes to perceive the world.[80] Experiential landscapes, then, offer fully embodied subject positions that direct particular ways of looking.[81] These subject positions suggest the appropriate interpretive subjectivity within a landscape.

BEING THROUGH THERE

Thus far, we have offered two arguments about rhetoric and museums. First, we proposed that museums are fundamentally rhetorical. This is so because the museal practices of collecting, preserving, displaying, and representing enact and depend upon contingently held values; serve to support specific imaginations; and engage audiences and users on questions of value, belief, and action. Second, we suggested that the rhetoric of museums can best be understood if approached through the perspective of experiential landscapes, which highlights the material, contingent, interwoven, and multitemporal workings of these institutions. In both cases, we return again and again to a basic premise: though symbolicity is important, even crucial, to the rhetorical work of museums, attending to symbols does not exhaust—or really even begin to engage—museums' suasory character. As such, we urge approaching museums as material spaces filled with concrete things, spaces that are situated in a larger physical and psychic environment, and that appeal to the visitors' entire embodied selves.

What then might be a critical approach that is well attuned to these assumptions? In as much as our approach to interrogating the BBCW's material and symbolic performances employs a "method," which strictly speaking rhetorical criticism rather assiduously avoids, it is akin to Dickinson and Aiello's notion of *being through there*, which stresses an experiential approach to the study of communication.[82] This approach privileges the fully embodied experience of the critic (*being*), movement in space and time (*through*), and the particularities of the space itself (*there*).

First, our study involves fully embodied engagement with the BBCW. As we have already discussed, experience is concerned with bodies and the way they interact with the material and symbolic dimensions of the world around them. What is more, we argued that museums are made up of the things collected and displayed in them. Throughout this study, we take seriously our sensing bodies and, in particular, the meaning and presence effects that the BBCW—its artifacts, designs, and geographic location—invites and induces in us and others. For example, we attend to our embodied experience of sitting in front of a simulated fire in the PIM, our discomfort at being surrounded by beautiful displays of guns in the CFM, our arrival at the musical apex of the Whitney's flow of art and ideology, and our long hours spent in a car getting to Cody, Wyoming, and returning home. We can only write about these experiences by opening our fully sensing selves to them.

The experiencing body—open as it may be to its environment—also carries with it a body of experience. Thus, we bring to the center our complex selves. We come—as we explicitly discuss at some points—as three men having both similar and distinct backgrounds. We share, for instance, academic training in communication studies, though that training is—within this larger context—rather diverse. We also share a long history of visiting the BBCW, as well as a long history of friendship. But there are important differences in our bodies of experience, as well. Two of us are born westerners, the other is from the East Coast. Two of us are white, one of us biracial. Two of us identify as heterosexual, but all of us also enact forms of queerness. Despite our varied selves, our manuscript adopts, for the most part, a "corporate" or, at least collective, "AokiDickinsonOtt" voice. This voice weaves together the many strands of the selves we bring with us to the center, to our scholarship, and to our writing. As is typical of jointly authored scholarship, it risks, of course, erasing vital differences in our experiences of and perspectives on the spaces with which we engage. But when those differences have arisen, we have had lengthy conversations about the BBCW to ensure that our analysis is guided, first and foremost, by our object.

We are committed to the idea that good criticism is object-driven. Simply put, the enterprise of rhetorical criticism is neither author-centered (as autoethnography typically is) nor audience-centered (as reception analysis is). It starts with the premise that places of public memory (like museums) reflect a unique, finite, and identifiable set of symbolic and material resources; those resources are organized in particular ways. The distinctive organization of specific symbolic and material resources (as opposed to the random arrangement of infinite resources) functions rhetorically to create a series of "structured invitations." The structured invitations of a site are unique to that site (and its distinctive organization of symbolic and material resources). Audiences can and do, of course, sometimes resist these invitations. But the idiosyncratic ways in which visitors take up and respond to a site does not alter that the site is structured in a particular way and, thus, fosters a specific set of structured invitations. This process functions much like a dinner invitation. When someone invites a person to dinner, the invitee is free to accept or decline the invitation, but their choice of how to respond does not alter the invitation itself. As critics, we analyze the structured invitations of museums; we do not concern ourselves with the ways audiences actually use or respond to them. Such an enterprise would be in the realm of reception analysis, not rhetorical criticism.

Second, *being through there* also implies movement in space and time. On the one hand, there is the movement of our bodies through the actual spaces of the museums and, indeed, structured movement is absolutely central to the experience of all five museums. At a minimum, movement through space involves both vector (direction) and velocity (speed).[83] Museal design and display practices greatly influence both dimensions. While some exhibits tightly control movement and, hence, experience, other spaces invite more unstructured or self-directed movement. Similarly, while some exhibits slow visitors down, asking them to pause and attend carefully to certain artifacts and displays, others shuttle them along, moving them quickly to another point, location, or space. Obviously, critics of museums need to examine closely how built spaces are structured to influence the movement of bodies. On the other hand, there is the movement of the center, its institutional development and unfolding, through time. Over our decade of visits to the BBCW, visiting at different times of the year, different moments in our careers, and with different interests in mind has helped us locate the center in time. We have watched an evolution of the center, which the center itself does not easily reveal. What is more, conversations with the center's curators and directors help us get behind the public spaces into the temporality of its building.

Third, *being through there* emphasizes the particularities of place. As much as a given experience may be idiosyncratic and as much as a space may change over time, there is—in all spaces—a "there" there. The symbolic and material qualities of a space are unique to that space and, taken together, they function as structured invitations. They urge bodies, regardless of their differing backgrounds and experiences, to see and attend to certain objects and artifacts and to ignore and overlook others. They invite bodies to feel certain emotions and atmospheric intensities and to deny and repress others. They encourage bodies to adopt and perform certain ways of being and to avoid and repudiate others.

Rhetoric, in short, while always participating in recognized forms, genres, and modes of communication, is always also particular. Minimally, a rhetorical critic of museum spaces would want to attend carefully to the design and display practices of various exhibits, from glass display cases to interactive touch screens. Critics should be asking what is remembered and forgotten; exploring where and how exhibits are installed within the confines of the museum; analyzing the spatial, temporal, and technological relationships among exhibits; examining how exhibits depict and represent their subject matter; and investigating what technologies (video, simulated environs, etc.) are employed within exhibits and how those technologies frame their subject matter, engage visitors, and shape visitors' experience.

THE RHETORIC OF THE BBCW: ON HAUNTS AND HAUNTING

In the middle years of our travels to Cody, we noticed that the center's name had been changed from the Buffalo Bill Historical Center to the Buffalo Bill Center of the West. As we entered the redesigned foyer, a new, large banner introduced us to the center's shifting emphasis from Buffalo Bill as a character to the West as a place and ideology. Splashed across the banner was the center's new tag line, "Celebrating the Spirit of the West," which visually and symbolically wove together images from the center's five museums. As we bought our tickets and moved into the center of the foyer, we saw a new introduction to the BBM. A ghostly moving image of Buffalo Bill (played by an actor) projected onto water vapor welcomed us to the museum and the center. We—and various children visiting the museum—ran our hands through the misty Buffalo Bill. Put together, the new name, the rebranded museum, and Buffalo Bill's ghostly appearance invited us to join the center and its museums in celebrating the spirit of the West, to see in these museums something fundamental and essential about the West, to analogize from these core treasured values to the values of being an American, and to move from this specifically contoured American identity to a particular understanding of democracy.

We wondered, then, what would happen if we took the center (and its materialization of ghostliness) at its word. What is this "spirit of the West" that the museum invites us to share? What, we wondered, tweaking the phrase a bit, are the multiple, conflicting, and cacophonous spirits of the West? What if we took the ghostly actor's version of Buffalo Bill seriously to follow him on the "back trails" of the West and search for ghosts otherwise ignored, pausing for the spirit to move us in ways unintended by the space's designers, funders, and curators? What if, in short, we imagined the space as both a haunt and as haunted, as an enactment and embodiment of haunting, and as a representation of the hauntings and haunts that are constitutive of the West? To critically perform the center's haunts and hauntings, we need a better understanding of the relations among haunt, rhetoric, and experiential landscapes. In what follows, we argue that four interwoven relations can help us understand the interconnections between haunt, rhetoric, and experiential landscapes as they are materialized in the BBCW. Specifically, we would like to suggest that, as the BBCW's central rhetorical mode, haunt and haunting is (1) emplaced and embodied (or affectively charged); (2) inclusive of past, present, and future; (3) integrative of comfort and fear; and (4) evocative of some settler colonial performances.

Before outlining these four characteristics, we want to broadly define haunting as we will use it for our project. Haunting is an affective performance and cultural structure, founded on repression. It demands of the haunted person repetition that is, at once, pleasurable and painful. As a cultural structure, it can call us to important ethical and political actions. Three definitional elements of haunting will guide our analysis. First, haunting is a result, a produced meaning, and an affective state directly related to repression. Avery Gordon argues that "haunting describes how that which appears to be not there is often a seething presence, acting on and often meddling with taken-for-granted realities."[84] The repressed emotion, activity, or action returns as a haunting, which often materializes in the form of a ghost. Second, the repressed return is at once pleasurable and painful. Buffalo Bill projected onto ghostlike water vapors is a pleasurable return of the lost entertainer. But it is also a pleasurable return of what for some is the painfully lost cowboy, lost America, and lost world system that Buffalo Bill constitutes and represents. The ghost offers the pleasure of reuniting with the lost even as it reminds us that the lost thing is not actually available to us. Third, haunting involves repetition. Haunting is not a singular event; instead, it is a consistent and constant return to a form that allows us to feel the loss of or approach—without calling forth the lost thing in its full value—that which we have repressed. We return to those moments and places that let us feel the presence of the ghost.

Woven together in haunting, then, is repeated ghostly representation of repressed memories, the repetition of which is both painful and pleasurable. Joshua Gunn writes that "haunting is a semiotics of repression."[85] The ghosts that haunt us, he suggests, can "be understood as representatives of the causes of repetition, as marks of the unmarked," while haunting, he continues, is "a simultaneous experience of the pleasure and pain that ghosts inspire."[86] We gain a certain enjoyment from calling forth ghosts, from approaching the repressed. When we write that the BBCW compels its visitors through haunting rhetorics, it is precisely in this understanding that haunting is painful and pleasurable, the understanding that ghosts are "representatives of the causes of repetition." These basic understandings of haunting undergird and trace through the following four characteristics of haunting that are particularly relevant to our book.

EMPLACED AND EMBODIED

Importantly for our project, haunt and haunting has a powerful spatiality. Some of the earliest instances of haunt refer explicitly to place. As we noted in the introduction, Charles Chamberlain directly links the Greek term and idea of *ethos* to an even older idea of haunt. In Homer, Chamberlain finds the *ethea* of the horse—its natural pasture and river—against which the manager is an attempt to domesticate the horse. The horse's natural place is a matter of habituation, the places and practices to which it "has been and is accustomed."[87] He writes about how the haunt was thought of as a founding, formative, or ancient place where an animal or a soul was most comfortable. The captured horse longs for the wild expanses where it was born, in a desire for familiar haunts. The longing for a comforting, ancient home undergirds the still-used phrase "old familiar haunts." This sense of haunt captures a mnemonic, material, embodied, and affective relationship to place. Haunt speaks not only of a place to which we might wish to return but also of the ethical or values-oriented drive this place encodes. As Chamberlain argues, the meaning of *ethos* develops from haunt into the ethical centeredness of an individual or a group, a centeredness that links directly to a sense of place and belonging.[88]

As we have been discussing, however, haunt is always two-sided. Just as we can connect haunt to welcoming, homelike spaces, so to we can link it to the uncanny, or the unhomely.[89] The uncanny as an affect arises when a familiar place or setting becomes suddenly unfamiliar. This is the performance of the haunted house, that moment when a space that ought to offer comfort and intimacy suddenly turns scary and deeply disturbing. Repressed ghosts show up in this space, turning an old familiar house into a space that is disturbing because of the return of seemingly forgotten events, relationships, or moments. Haunts as comfort and as uncanny rely on each other. Familiar haunts nearly always hide, ignore, and turn away from disturbing relations: they can only be comfortable when the troubles of and in the place are ignored. Meanwhile, the uncanny haunt is precisely the space/time of these repressed memories' return.

There is little material or conceptual distance between the understanding of haunt as emplaced and haunt as an embodied or affectively charged. Places are haunts not because of some inherent quality of the place. Instead, a weaving of the material place and a person's embodied memories of the place create the affective cluster we are calling haunt. Our familiarity with a place, our understanding of a place's role in our identity as individuals or as parts of cultural groups, and the way one place cues us to remember other places lodged in our embodied memory are all part of haunt's affective charge. In short, an experiential landscape may well feel haunted, may well feel like an old familiar haunt. This feeling is an affective and embodied response to the material and symbolic forms of the body's place and of place's bodies. The body and its memories imbue the place with hauntedness, and yet the place and its particular form is a nearly necessary precursor to triggering this affective charge.

Inclusive of Past, Present, and Future

Haunt and haunting is a specific mode by which experiential landscapes weave past, present, and future. Haunt and haunting demand pasts that are deeply encoded in individual and collected memory. The warmly remembered past of the familiar haunt founds the comforts of a present place. This remembered past also motivates the longing to, in the future, return to these remembered comforts. Bill Cody's character projected onto misty water speaks this very haunting, as he urges us to—in the coming moments and in more distant futures—follow him on the back trails of the West to his familiar home and to his identity-supporting landscape.

Similarly, the ghostly haunt functions by way of the return of the repressed. The haunted house feels uncanny, out of sync, and odd, and it triggers this affect by bringing the repressed past into the present. But haunting, as Gordon points out, creates an ethical demand, a demand of "something to be done."[90] "When it appears to you," she writes, "the ghost will inaugurate the necessity of doing something about it."[91] Experienced in the present, this powerfully affective past can demand a reckoning performed in the future.

Integrative of Comfort and Fear

The affective charge of haunting is not unidimensional. Instead, haunt and haunting has two dialectically related affects: comfort and fear. Like Freud's uncanny, the haunt's place of comfort—like, say, the familial home—is one that is partially constituted by excluded and repressed conflicts, desires, and demands. The familiar past is comforting as long as the deeply embedded conflicts generated by desire are repressed and forgotten. As long as the family's secrets remain secret, the family can be a site of comfort. But families must have—always have—those secrets that, when they return, can disturb the comforting place.

It is not simply that there are two different affects of haunt or two different meanings. Instead, the one meaning—that of comfort—relies on the processes of repression and momentary forgetting that provides the material of fear-inducing haunting. At the same time, the ghostly haunting produced by this return of the repressed is precisely the ethical call to make right the violence of our familiar, familial, communal, and national past.

Evocation of Settler Colonial Performances

Finally, haunt and haunting is a particularly apropos approach for studying the BBCW and its embeddedness in settler colonial discourses. Lorenzo Veracini argues that settler colonialism is deeply mimetic. Like all state formations, those created via settler colonial practices required and require violence. But the settler situation demands that this violence is hidden, ignored, and repressed. The "violent foundations of [settler colonial regimes] must be disavowed," Veracini writes, "a recurring narcissistic drive demanding that a settler society be represented as an ideal political body makes this [disavowal] inescapable."[92] On the one hand, settler colonialism, unlike other forms of colonial practices, sets out to imagine and then create a home and homeland for the newcomers. This home is built into the rigorously mis-seen emptiness of the land to be settled. On the other, this home is always constructed on already occupied land; the home's walls exclude the very peoples the settlers imagine were never there. The concrete and psychological imaginary home, then, is created through and depends on disavowal and a constant turning away from those dispossessed.

These disavowals of the founding violence of the settler colonial nation are the very imaginative and material kernels of which haunts are built. Reflecting on the founding traumas of settler nations, Veracini urges "an appraisal of the imagination and psychology of settler colonialism."[93] Haunting is one mode of thinking carefully about the psychology and imagination of settler colonial forms. Indeed, as Warren Cariou—writing about settler narratives of the Canadian prairie—argues, settler representations of the prairies embodies a "lurking sense that the places settlers call home are not really theirs, and a sense that their current legitimacy as owners or renters in a capitalist land market might well be predicated upon theft, fraud, violence, and other injustices in the past. The driving psychological force behind these Aboriginal hauntings as they are imagined by non-Native writers, then, is as in most ghost stories the return of the repressed."[94] We will sense this "return of the repressed" throughout the BBCW as the violence of settler colonialism is both acknowledged and ignored, its absence shouting loudly in its silence.

We can tarry with these ghosts. We can be with the living and dead Indigenous people who are, as the PIM enacts, still here. As Avery Gordon writes, ghosts are "attached to the events, things, and places the produced them in the first place; by nature, they are haunting reminders of lingering trouble."[95] We are invited to reexperience the repressed violence, to become productively uncomfortable, and, in so doing, to take up an ethical position regarding this otherwise repressed past. The center, then, offers those willing to be so moved a chance to bring these hard moments of the past into the present for the purpose of remaking, of reimaging, the future. It may be that by tarrying with the ghosts in the center we can begin to decolonize our own psyches, to embrace the complexities of the settler colonial landscape of the West. This is a kind of "spirit of the West" the center rejects and, yet, in raising the specter, it makes this other imagining possible.

Taking up the problematics suggested here and in the preceding chapter, in the coming chapters we attempt to materialize the haunts and hauntings of the BBCW, enact the proposed methods for studying experiential landscapes, and reflect on the ways that we as authors, critics, and citizens are woven into and unweave the BBCW's rhetorical invitations. We begin this critical performance with the museum that serves as the center's founding space, the Buffalo Bill Museum.

The requests made on our bodies at BBCW are made affectively compelling through haunts and haunting. If, as we have proposed through this chapter, collection, preservation, exhibition, and representation designate the chief rhetorical practices of museums, and experiential landscapes suggest a useful interpretive lens for investigating sites of memory more broadly, then "haunt and haunting" highlights the specific rhetorical workings of the BBCW. As we suggested in the introduction, the BBCW works in concert with its surrounding cultural, geographic, and temporal enactments to make compelling a deeply conservative vision of America by locating the "spirit of the West" as the nation's cultural and ideological home or haunt. That vision is grounded in idealized images of the West as an untamed and untrammeled frontier anchored in the mythos of Buffalo Bill. In anchoring this vision, the BBCW draws on and reinforces a deep well of white masculinity that permeates American political and cultural formations. White masculinity is the center of the center. But we further suggested that even as the BBCW fosters an atmosphere of safety and security, its vision of the West is haunted by the historical violence upon which the nation is founded. For us, at least, this produces an unsettling atmosphere, one in which the past and its ghostly spirits crack the smooth veneer of the present.

In what follows, the three of us will invite you to tarry with the ghosts that inhabit the center and its museums. We will urge you walk beside us as we feel and see and sense the hauntings of this space and its (and our) experiential landscapes. While it is certainly the case that both whiteness and masculinity are centering forces in the museum, the Spirt of the West is complicated and haunted. Our hope in the coming pages is less to provide a final analysis of the center and its constituent spaces than to perform some of the desired and resistive possibilities the BBCW offers us. In short, we wish for our writing to be heuristic, offering ourselves and our readers more complex and humane ways of seeing, being, and acting.[96]

3

The Ghost of William F. Cody at the Buffalo Bill Museum

Ladies and Gentlemen, permit me to introduce myself. I am William F. Cody. But, more than likely, you know me as Buffalo Bill. I am fortunate to know the West as few people dead or alive have known it. Its strong characters, its colorful history, and its vast landscapes will never be blotted from my mind. All of my life, it's been my pleasure to show the West's beauties, its marvels, and its possibilities to those who under my guidance saw it for the first time. I'm about to take the back trail, looking through the eyes of memory at the West I have known and loved. And it will give me great pleasure to take you with me. I will share some of my favorite tales about the buffalo, the pony express, and the stagecoach. I'll show you some of the humors as well as the stirring scenes of the frontier. And I'll try to vary the pace for I know that travelers appreciate frequent changes of scenery. Now, for Americans, and for all people, the American West is a priceless possession. If in following me through some of the exciting scenes of the old days your interest is awakened, I should feel richly repaid.

—ACTOR VOICE-OVER ACCOMPANYING THE VISUAL IMAGE AT THE ENTRANCE INTO THE BUFFALO BILL MUSEUM.

ON OUR NEXT-TO-LAST visit to the BBCW, we knew we would be focusing on the fully redesigned Buffalo Bill Museum, whose reinstallation was completed in 2012. We had first published on the BBM in the mid-2000s and were curious about the changes wrought by the new installation and intrigued by the ways the BBM would enact the BBCW's newly adopted motto to celebrate "The Spirit of the American West." "We believe," the center trustees wrote, "the Spirit of the American West is central to American Democracy and is an iconic image of freedom worldwide."[1] Desperately in need of a complete redesign, the BBM was reimagined and reinstalled after the center's rebranding effort, an effort that does, indeed, evoke the spirit(s) of the West.

Knowing about this emphasis on the spirit of the West/the West's spirit, we should not have been surprised when we were greeted by a ghostlike, actor-portrayed image of William F. Cody projected onto misting water at the museum's entrance (fig. 4). "I'm about to take the back trail," the actor intones, "looking through the eyes of memory at the West I have known and loved. And it will give me great pleasure to take you with me." Cody's technoghost assures us that the journey will be one into a well-known if almost-lost place and time, a time of our collective and individual past, a journey to an old familiar haunt. A journey that takes us home.

Figure 4. Image of Buffalo Bill projected onto mist at entrance to the Buffalo Bill Museum. Photograph by Brian L. Ott.

Together with this first impression and projection of the ghost of Cody in all of its technological wonder, the "staged materiality" of the museum quickly places us into spaces of domestic home artifacts, or the reconstructed living spaces of the Cody home.[2] Newly subdued lighting, artistic poster easels detailing domestic tragedy and loss, an infusion of more earthly aesthetic tones within the museum (compared to the high "showman" carnival colors of its prior iteration), and Cody's lingering, ghostly presence evoke an atmosphere replete with reflective moments—melancholic moments where the past can perform its haunting of the visitor into the present. The narratives performed in the BBM focus on Cody's home life, his relationships, and his various efforts to turn the West into a personal, familial, and national home. Compared to the previous iteration of the museum, the new BBM performs a demythologizing account of Cody, making him and his context more complex, more fraught, more challenging, more intimate. Shifting from a carnavalistic form, this memorial to Cody invites us on a journey home.

Home, specifically, serves as the material, aesthetic, affective, and symbolic cornerstone of the BBM's reenvisioning. The museum shifts its attention from Buffalo Bill the showman to William F. Cody the fraught family man, beset by everyday struggles surrounding marriage, parenting, loneliness, celebrity, modern restlessness, and a desire for roots. In pivoting from Buffalo Bill to William Cody, from showman to real man, and from spectacle to everyday life, the museum offers the spirit of the West as an affectively and ideologically compelling home for its late modern audiences.[3] Cody's ghost beckons us, calls us home; in introducing us to his two selves, he reminds us of our own bifurcations, of our own modes of haunting and ghostliness. In a haunting invocation of memory, the spectral figure invites us to (re)turn to the West's back trail and into his houses, tents, and most prized pastures. We accept the invitation.

From the ghostlike image of Cody projected onto water vapor to the *Window on the West* multimedia display that serves as the museum's apogee, Cody is constantly presented as longing for a return to his home(s) and wishing to return to his old familiar haunts. But this home is uncanny. Riven between the Old West and the New West, between a life on the plains and a life in the spotlight, between the nostalgic desire for a simple life as hunter and guide and visions of newfound wealth built on railroads and irrigation, the BBM's Cody is (often unintentionally) haunted by his impossible dreams. As visitors, we travel with Cody through this museum and are invited to experience this same haunting. This call into the haunts of the Old West is woven into a New West of technological innovations that separate us from nature, constantly evolving understandings of intimate and national homes, and rapidly changing social relations. The new museum rejects its older version's emphasis on spectacularized and violent masculinity. At the same time, it imports a seemingly more human but no less traditional imagining of the "Spirit of the American West."

Haunted by its ghostly guide and by (barely) repressed colonializing violence, the reimagined BBM, we argue, harnesses the affective force of William F. Cody's everyday life and struggles to domesticate the West's ghosts in the service of affording its visitors the comforts of a well-understood home, the security of familiar social relations, and the locating power of past and place. Additionally, the newly renovated BBM elicits a call into the darker creases of memory and remembering of William F. Cody, eliciting a somber atmosphere of quietude, reflection, and discernment. In advancing this argument, the chapter unfolds in three stages. First, we revisit the notions of haunt and home as they inform our approach to the newly redesigned BBM. Second, we situate the BBM in an appropriate context of museum design, highlighting key differences between the reinstalled museum and its previous iteration. Finally, we reflect on the multiplicities of haunting and home, and on the evocations of affect and atmosphere(s), that the museum performs.[4]

ON HAUNTS AND HOMES

As we argued in chapter 2, haunt weaves together a living being's soul with its embodied and embedded material landscapes. Home is one of the most powerful of these haunts, but, as we also suggested, home as haunt contains within it its own antonym. Comforting and structuring, home is also the site of the return of deeply disturbing pasts, as it can be haunted by the ghosts of that which we would prefer to repress. The (dis)comfort and (dis)ease of home is often registered as affect rather than as cognition. The longing for home encoded in the haunt is felt as much in the body as recognized by the brain; it is triggered by the full range of human senses.[5] Home is signaled by smells and sights and sounds as much as or more than by any symbolization of or within the home.[6] Sometimes the home and its pasts are welcoming. Other times the home's past returns as images of repressed and repulsive others, acts, and feelings. In this second sense, haunted homes are unhomely and uncanny. The disturbingly haunted home—the uncanny home—is not invaded by an alien spirit but rather houses an already existing spirit the residents had hoped to forget.[7]

The redesign of the BBM emphasizes—even as it attempts to cover over—this haunting. The earlier version/vision of the museum emphasized Buffalo Bill the showman and the *Wild West* extravaganza. As we argued in an essay about the earlier version, the space in many ways replicated the show by making the violent colonization of the West into a spectacle, thus sanitizing for viewers the painful memories of this past, which persist in the violence represented in the enormous posters from the show and a movie William Cody made from it.[8] The reimagined and reinstalled version of the museum, by contrast, more centrally focuses on Cody's story as a story of home and away, of haunts and haunting, and of subdued atmosphere over extravagant spectacle.

But how might rhetorical critics explore the home of Buffalo Bill and the West as a haunted and haunting space? Because we engage the museum as a spatial and material thing composed of and by many material "things"—the detritus of Cody's life, the bodies of the visitors, the design elements produced and staged by the museum designers, the misty William Cody at the entrance—our approach values the material, the aesthetic, and the affective, as well as the symbolic, the representational, and the signifying.[9] For us, understanding rhetoric fully depends upon careful engagement with both matter and symbols, attention to both unqualified affective intensities and qualified processes of meaning-making. It further entails a willingness to understand material things as agentic and coconstitutive of human subjectivity.[10]

Haunt is a particularly useful critical concept in such an endeavor, for the responses to haunts—whether positive, negative, or ambivalent—are registered viscerally by the body before being registered consciously as emotion.[11] Exploring the rhetorical dimensions of material spaces requires the critic's fully embodied engagement with the space, including its aesthetic and signifying elements, sensory and symbolic inducements, vectors and velocities, and spatial and temporal flows.[12]

BUFFALO BILL'S NEW/OLD HOME

As we suggested in chapter 1, the history of the BBM and the BBCW are deeply interwoven, for the BBM was the founding museum of what would later become the BBCW. Yet, the BBM nevertheless has its own history. Understanding this background aids us in better grappling with its current rhetorical invitations. The history of the BBM intersects with two crucial memory movements of the late nineteenth and early twentieth centuries. First, the BBM is a relatively late example of historical house museums and, like the broader movement, depends on women's role in the late nineteenth and early twentieth centuries as cultural preservationists.

From the mid-nineteenth century, Americans have been preserving local and national history through the institution of house museums. At the same time, the earliest form of the BBM weaves together the historical house museum with the log cabin form to create a compelling memory space for the founding of the BBCW, drawing on the American valorization of the log cabin.

Perhaps the most important early house museum was that of George Washington's Mount Vernon. The longtime home of George Washington, the building was falling into ruin by the mid-nineteenth century. In 1853 Ann Pamela Cunningham passed by the property while traveling on the Potomac River and was struck by the home's disrepair. While many had petitioned state and federal authorities to care for the home, which was the site of increasing visitation, no one had taken responsibility for the house's expensive and ongoing upkeep. Cunningham was determined to reverse this neglect and in December 1853 began a campaign to purchase and restore the house before it was lost. Importantly, she organized women of the South and then, following the Civil War, women from around the nation to join her in this preservation effort. The Mount Vernon Ladies' Association—the oldest women's historical preservation and patriotic group in the United States—took on the task of purchasing, restoring, and managing Mount Vernon as a historical house that embodied important national values.[13]

This women-led effort at Mount Vernon intersected with larger discourses about women's role in historical preservation and the building of patriotic values.

In fact, the nineteenth-century preservation movement was, according to historian Patricia West, "enmeshed in the cult of domesticity," and the house museum became a site of "Domestic Religion."[14] The house museum—precisely because of its domesticating aesthetic and affect—drew on the moral power that sacralized the home as an answer to pressing political issues of the era, including "social heterogeneity, political conflict, and the effects of the disestablishment of religion."[15] While the Mount Vernon Ladies' Association was the first such organization, it spawned others, including Daughters of the American Revolution (who formed in 1890 and declared their mission to teach patriotism through historical sites and promote education, particularly of history, in order to teach foreign citizens how to be good citizens and create a uniform support of the American government) and the Daughters of the Republic of Texas who, in the early twentieth century, organized the restoration of the Alamo in San Antonio.[16] Each of these groups and their efforts engaged local places, and yet the material and symbolic performances meshed with national political concerns. As Patricia West argues, "late-nineteenth-century museums would increasingly focus on their ability to promulgate national loyalty in an increasingly polyglot citizenry. The invention of a shared vision of America, set in an immutable past, was a potent middle-class response to the conflict of heterogeneity of the late nineteenth century."[17] Nineteenth century historic preservation, then, offered white women an opportunity to step out of their constraining domestic roles into public spaces, and the places they preserved were platforms for political arguments about nationhood and patriotism.

Mary Jester Allen's efforts in Cody, Wyoming, are part of this lineage. An eastern journalist and William F. Cody's niece, Allen moved to Cody and, in 1926, founded the Buffalo Bill Memorial Association. With the help of Codyites and members of Cody's family and supporters of the Cody Memorial Association, Allen determined to create an appropriate museum honoring her uncle. She and others chose to create a log-house museum that recalled Cody's famous TE Ranch house and referenced a long-held understanding of log houses as the icons of "American progress and self-reliance."[18] The museum opened to the public on July 4, 1927. Allen and her colleagues filled it with a collection of Buffalo Bill and western memorabilia, taxidermized animals, western art, and, most disturbingly, the alleged scalp of Cheyenne warrior Yellow Hair.

As with most of Cody's life, the story of Yellow Hair's scalping is fraught with inconsistencies and inaccuracies. Some, including Cody, asserted that he killed Yellow Hair in hand-to-hand combat in July 1876, as part of the post-Custer conflicts in the Colorado Territory. Others say that Cody shot him dead with a Winchester carbine. Still others assert that Yellow Hair was already dead when

54   Chapter 3

Cody took his scalp. It is not even clear that Yellow Hair was, in fact, scalped. What does seem clear is that on the day of the fight, Cody had dressed in one of his theatrical costumes and, upon the death of Yellow Hair, scooped up the warrior's war bonnet and shouted, "The first scalp for Custer."[19]

What is also clear is that this story and its apparent material remnants served as a founding legend for Buffalo Bill—and in many ways for the post-Custer West. By October 1876 Cody had woven this story into a melodramatic stage show that premiered in New York. While the costumes Buffalo Bill wore during his *Wild West* performances predated his battle with Yellow Hair, they gained significance in the retelling and became—along with Yellow Hair's regalia— authenticating markers of the BBM. These stories that founded Bill Cody's *Wild West* and the accoutrements collected for the show serve as the center's founding narratives and collection. In this way, the institution's origin story is that of settler colonialism, with Cody's "precious possession" of the western landscape predicated on and justified by his violence against Native People.

The log cabin that served as the first version of the center had a similarly fraught relationship with facts and built on and reinforced white colonizing narratives. While rumors of turning Buffalo Bill's TE Ranch house into a museum abounded, its remote location made these plans impractical. Instead, Allen and the Buffalo Bill Memorial Association designed and built a log house in the town of Cody. Constructed with the TE Ranch house in mind, the log house was nonetheless an idealized version of the ranch building it represented. Comparing photos of the ranch house and museum, former curator of the BBM Juti Winchester notes that the museum house was "not a replication as much as it [was] an idealized construction of the place that Mrs. Allen would have had Cody call home."[20]

Building the museum in the form of a log house drew not only on the specific mnemonics of Cody's ranch house but also on a nearly one-hundred-year tradition of linking log structures to essential American values. Indeed, log buildings run through US iconography in the nineteenth century. For example, Whig presidential candidate William Henry Harrison incorporated the log cabin into his successful campaign against Martin Van Buren in 1841. Characterized by Van Buren as an unsophisticated man from the hinterlands, Harrison turned the log house into a sign of his authenticity, with the cabin representing honest, homespun values that contrasted positively for many with the urban and cosmopolitan values of Democratic politicians. By the early twentieth century, the log house was a well-understood manifestation of US values. The idealized rebuilding of Lincoln's log cabin birthplace in 1911, the popularity of Lincoln Logs toys, and log tourist cabins throughout the rural United States in the 1920s all served as material performances of an essentially American understanding of self-sufficiency.[21] The log structure museum inherited these rural, down-home values, reinforcing the cowboy values the BBM sought to perpetuate. For the next forty years, this log structure housed the BBM and Allen remained its guiding spirit.

After completion of the Whitney gallery in 1959, the Buffalo Bill Memorial Association continued its successful fundraising program, this time to build a new home for the BBM connected to the gallery. Fred Garlow, one of Cody's grandsons, promoted the Buffalo Bill Memorial Remington rifle during a North American tour to which he drew large audiences by reprising his grandfather's stories. As noted previously, $5 of the $129.95 purchase price went toward building the new BBM; the effort raised $825,000.[22] Meanwhile, William Robertson Coe, an Englishman turned US patriot, continued to provide large donations to build a museum that not only celebrated the life of Buffalo Bill but also offered a space to reinforce what Coe took to be the central values of America—values he believed were best embodied in Wyoming and were at deep risk of being lost. On July 4, 1968, the half-completed BBM joined the Whitney gallery and Whitney's *Buffalo Bill—The Scout*, creating an increasingly large and complex memory machine in the "frontier town of 5,000."[23] When the BBM fully opened in 1969, it—along with the Whitney—was christened the Buffalo Bill Historical Center.[24]

By the early 2000s, when we first visited the BBM, the center had grown to four museums and the fifth—the Draper Museum of Natural History—was under construction. The BBM we visited in those years emphasized Cody's central place in constructing and telling the story of the cowboy and the US frontier. In this version of the museum, the BBM accepted Cody's claim that Buffalo Bill's *Wild West* "was an invitation into living history" and "defined the quintessential American hero."[25] According to Cody, the nightly performances reenacted a historically accurate and authentic telling of the West's history. Just as the *Wild West* focused on the real history of the West, the previous museum's iteration focused attention on the show, though it also included information about William Cody's life before and after the show's long-running successes. Despite the museum's declaration that it represented Buffalo Bill's *Wild West* and in so doing offered a clear vision of the West and its cowboy hero, we argued that the museum's practices of collection, display, and representation privileged "images of Whiteness and masculinity, while using the props, films, and posters of Buffalo Bill's Wild West to carnivalize the violent conflicts between Anglo American and Native Americans."[26]

The museum, as it was then designed, materially and symbolically placed Buffalo Bill and the narrative structure of Buffalo Bill's *Wild West* at the center of America's authentic story. Throughout the BBM, visitors were urged to identify with Buffalo Bill as a hero, to imagine themselves as part of a lineage founded by cowboys like Buffalo Bill who settled and civilized the Wild West.

56 Chapter 3

If they accepted the museum's rhetorical invitations, visitors could enact a renewed understanding of America's Manifest Destiny. And, yet the BBM could not ignore the violence of western settlement. Instead, it used Buffalo Bill's own strategy to address the violent colonization of the West, that is, the museum carnivalized the violence, rendering it as mere entertainment, dramatic and spectacular to be sure, but shorn of any critical engagement with actual history and its material consequences.

HAUNTING DOMESTICATION

In many ways, the new design reverts the BBM to its roots as a log cabin house museum. While the log house itself is absent (though the building still exists and serves as the visitor center for Cody, Wyoming), the impulse to preserve Cody's memory in a house-like form reappears in the new version. Like the originating, repressed, and (in)authentic log house of the first BBM, the new design accepts Cody's invitation to return with him to a comforting past. At once new and old, the rhetorical problem of expressing a laudatory spirit of the West while also acknowledging the spirit's violent manifestations remains. In the reimagined version of the BBM, the rhetoric shifts from carnivalization to haunting. In short, the new BBM largely replaces Buffalo Bill with William Cody, effectively transforming the showman into a real man beset with the problems and opportunities men of the West faced.

The shift from Buffalo Bill to William Cody is materialized through concrete practices of (re)placing and (re)locating. While the physical dimensions of the BBM remain the same as when they were first constructed in the late nineteen sixties, the BBM as constructed through the materialized movements is substantially altered. This change results in and is created by shifting Cody from a mythmaker to a backcountry guide, and from an Indian hunter into a ghost searching for a home in which to finally find rest. His years on the road with the *Buffalo Bill's Wild West* show are shown to be a popular and humane representation of the civilizing of the West that took an enormous toll on Cody as it removed him from the securing relations of the lived West. The violence embedded in *Buffalo Bill's Wild West* and in his life as hunter, scout, and Indian killer is repressed and represented in the mourning of the losses Cody is shown to have experienced. The focus of this new museum, then, is not the rough-and-ready show but instead is an uncanny, always repeated, and never fully successful return home.

The museum performs these haunting repressions, returns, and replacements through contemporary museum design practices that emphasize familiar performances over objects and utilizes technology to create intimate and interactive relationships between museum goer and display. Importantly, these same design principles underlie the museal practices in three of the BBCW's four other museums: the Draper, the PIM, and the Whitney. By intersecting this new museum with the more recent designs of the other museums, the BBM draws and announces the intimate and domestic relationship among humans, between humans and nature, and among the variety of ways of performing a western identity.

For example, the Draper opens by offering visitors to join scientists and park rangers on a hike from high-mountain tundra through alpine meadows, down into high-country plains. A similar trail appears in the BBM in Cody's introduction to the museum urging visitors to join him on the back trails. Likewise, the emphasis early in the BBM on Cody's family life filled with both joy and sorrow replicates the early familial teepee scene in the PIM, and the struggles of Cody's life journeys interlock with the PIM's *Seasons of Life* multimedia exhibit at the apex of that museum. Finally, the bison family diorama that greeted us in the lobby of the center when we first arrived in the early 2000s has moved into the BBM; and, as it did in its early setting, reminds visitors that the subject position they will occupy in the BBM will be one of family and home. In these material museal practices, the BBM weaves itself more deeply into the BBCW's larger mythic narrative. In so doing, Cody becomes less exceptional and more representational; the museum is now less a hagiography of a celebrity and more a generous exploration of a prototypical western man. In situating Cody's personal and familial narratives and his desires within the BBM, the museum prompts the visitor to bridge past and present, memory and myth, and real and ideal in domesticating and humanizing "Buffalo Bill" and his place in the West.

In shifting the representational balance from showman to everyman and from the celebrity spectacle of *Buffalo Bill's Wild West* to naturalizing aesthetics, the museum asks the visitor to engage the constructions of the man, William F. Cody, while taming the highly masculinized, iconic representation of Buffalo Bill within the redesigned and newly evoked atmosphere of the BBM. Finally, by foregrounding Cody's desires for simpler early day practices and ways of being that resonate with the everyday (and overstressed) individuals in contemporary global society, the museum weaves the visitor into Cody's haunts, urging us to become the contemporary embodiment of the "Spirit of the American West."[27]

As we settle into the newly redesigned BBM, the familial bison diorama greets us. The bison, like the taxidermized animals in the Draper, are dead and safe. However, in their imposing size, they remind us of the impressive bison herds that roamed grasslands of the West. From the perspective of the BBM, they serve (as noted on a placard) as "a Window on Buffalo Bill's West." As Buffalo Bill was known for his exploits in killing American bison, this seemingly pacific window on Cody's West introduces us to the complex weaving of family, nature, and haunting. Of course, the vast grasslands of the Southern and Northern Plains were the pastures on which the bison belong; it was their haunt. The largest extant mammal in North America, the American bison was a central node in the plains ecosystem, integral to the complex weaving of bison and human relationships over the course of hundreds of years.[28]

The introduction of horses to the Plains Indians in the early seventeenth century by the Spaniards in New Mexico began a radical remaking of the relationship between humans and buffalo. In the one hundred and fifty years or so between the Apache's successful inclusion of horses into Plains Indian culture—including migrations, hunting, and war-making habits—the relation among bison, horses, and Plains Indians took on deep cultural as well as material and ecological meanings. For Euro Americans and Plains Indians alike, this relationship was central to "Indianness."[29] For Plains Indians, this relationship was one that should and could be fundamental. For white Americans, unmaking the affiliation was a crucial component of westward expansion. Turning Plains Indians into farmers and remaking religious practices such that the religious importance of bison—and the landscape more broadly—was replaced by a Christian God was key to Euro Americans' understanding of Manifest Destiny. Meanwhile, the destruction of buffalo herds in the nineteenth century was deeply correlated with the destruction of Plains Indians during the same time period.[30]

In 1804, when Lewis and Clark began their exploratory journey from St. Louis to Oregon, the bison herd may have numbered seventy million, though some scholars put the number much lower given the widespread drought across the plains and, subsequently, the lack of food for bison.[31] Regardless, the population of bison on the plains was enormous and seemed inexhaustible. In the early years of the nineteenth century, white European hunters began to slaughter buffalo for the hide trade, and by 1830 the herd was less than half its size. By 1870 observers estimated that there were seven million bison on the plains, and in the 1880s the herd "had been reduced to a few wandering bands with possible extinction looming large. Their reduction illustrated human arrogance, wastefulness, and lack of insight."[32] In the middle of this unprecedented slaughter, Cody claimed to have killed 4,862 buffalo over eighteen months, providing meat for railroad crews.[33]

But, as David Nesheim argues, Cody's role in the destruction and then preservation of North American bison is "complex."[34] Even as Cody was central to the destruction of the buffalo—both as buffalo hunter and as part of the Euro American colonization of the plains—his storytelling placed the buffalo as a central icon of the West. Borrowing his name from the animals and placing the buffalo hunt as a key drama in his thirty-year-long show helped cement the relationship of buffalo and the American West. Preservation efforts, which began as early as the late nineteenth century, were motivated at least in part by the buffalo's iconic place in the US psyche, a place partially created by Cody and the yarns he spun year after year around the country and the world.

The bison diorama enters material representation into this complex context.

As taxidermized animals, these buffalo do not simply represent the North American bison Cody once hunted. Instead, they are material remnants of these animals. As John Dorst argues about another taxidermy scene in the BBCW, the skin of the taxidermized animal remembers. It remembers the organic performances that led to the body that is now on display. What is more, these stuffed bison skins also remember the dynamic co-performance of dead animal and living taxidermist. The skilled and artistic body of the taxidermist draws from the dead bison's shape a shade of the animal's once powerful life, as the taxidermist breathes lifelike substance into these animals.[35]

But even as the skins remember their lives through the skill of the taxidermist, the diorama works hard to shift our attention from the dead/live buffalo toward the western landscape and then to Buffalo Bill. In titling it "Bison on the Kansas Prairie: A Window on Buffalo Bill's West," BBM designers position the diorama as an invitation to understand Buffalo Bill's West. As a window on his West, the bison family and its organization is understood as a synecdoche for the material, social, and symbolic organization of the West. Crucially, though the diorama's materiality appeals to nature, the gathering of the buffalo in what appears to be a nuclear family is unlikely to have occurred in extant buffalo herds, as adult cows and bulls run in separate herds. Additionally, once cows wean their calves, gathering among members of the herds is essentially random and not in the least familial.[36] The diorama, then, does not reflect or select the social habits of bison. Instead, the family grouping of the bison deflects attention from bison habits while materializing and naturalizing very specific understandings of human relationships, namely traditional familial relationships, in the West. In short, the bison are domesticated; they are driven from their haunt, remade into an image of the Euro American imaginary. To the extent that the bison are a materializing synecdoche of the West, their domestication in the diorama is also a domestication of the western landscape. Organized through a Euro American domestic imagination, the bison family synecdochically reduces the complexity of plains life to the nuclear family.[37]

Within the BBM, this domestication of the western landscape is overseen and authorized by Cody. In a nearby diorama, Cody lies down on a sandy hill. Binoculars in his right hand, dusty hat laid aside, his long, dark hair disheveled and almost covering his eyes, the young scout surveys the bison, the museum, and its visitors. This Cody, visitors learn, is twenty-one years old, married, and has a child. He lies atop a hill in north-central Kansas. The placard reads that it is late in the summer of 1867, and "The Kansas Pacific Railroad is extending its line westward. Cody has been contracted to supply buffalo meat for construction workers . . . [and is] providing meat for United States Army personnel stationed at nearby Fort Hays." The quintessential lone male on the Great Plains, Cody oversees the civilizing forces that will turn the Old West into the New

West. On the lookout for hostile "Indians," searching for bison to shoot for meat and sport, exploring land to develop into wealth-generating ranches, and creating stories to tell easterners, Cody invites museumgoers to submit to his gaze. We are asked not simply to follow Cody on the back trails but to also imagine ourselves as domesticated—tamed—westerners. At the same time that we are asked to take on his gaze, we are also asked to imagine the West as domesticated, as bent to the will of Euro American masculinity. The space urges visitors to perform their selves in this complex set of relations and, at the same time, become the gazers demanding of the West and its inhabitants submission to these rules.

Left out of these two dioramas is a hauntingly absent Other. The near annihilation of the bison was a crucial element in the hoped-for annihilation of the Plains Indians. The killing of the bison—along with the destruction of plains' habitat by sheep and cattle—was a central component in forcing Plains Indians away from their traditional hunting patterns and into subservient relationships with whites. "In an effort," Roxanne Dunbar-Ortiz writes, "to create Indigenous economic dependency and compliance in land transfers, the US policy direct the army to destroy the basic economic base of the Plains Nations—the buffalo."[38] Emma Hansen—curator emerita of the Plains Indian Museum—writes about the great sadness Plains Indians experienced as an entire way of life with its economic, environmental, and spiritual expressions came to a crashing end as the buffalo were destroyed.[39] The people of the Plains Nations occupy the negative and empty space between the representations of the young Cody and the buffalo family, their lives and lifeways haunting the exhibit.

The haunting relations among bison, Plains Indian, the Great Plains, and Cody registered in these two dioramas provide the fundamental characteristics that mark the rest of the BBM. The less dramatic displays of Cody memorabilia and the signs that accompany them return again and again to these themes. In the opening display, for example, Cody is offered as a "Man of the West, Man of the World," who represents many of the forces that lead to "the Changing Face of America." To understand this man, his world, and America, however, is to understand the tensions rooted in Cody's own identity. As one museum sign announces, "MANY KNOW BUFFALO BILL, the icon whose Wild West Show brought the West to the world. Long after the Wild West's final performance, it still affects how we envision the West and America itself. Yet hardly anyone knows the individual behind the performer. Buffalo Bill was real, but so was William F. Cody."[40]

The two dioramas and the museum at large remind visitors that beneath the family and the showman was the West. Throughout the BBM, these two men— Buffalo Bill and William F. Cody—are drawn back to the region and its simplicity. The West, Cody asserts, is "my home country and that's the place I love." He goes on to say, "Do I want to go back there? You just bet your life I do."

Along with other BBM displays humanizing the man, the discourse of Cody's expressed desire to return to the land housing nature's wildlife becomes central to the journey in the BBM. These discourses do the work of carrying forth Cody's call as an everyday man who discovered his place on the global stage and secured his legacy in the American West.

With the bison family/young Cody dioramas functioning as the museum's early drama, visitors are well introduced to the contradictions and complexities of the West as imagined in the BBM. They are invited to move through and perform these contradictions in a complex weaving of time and space in the exhibits that surround the dioramas and present the narrative of Cody's domestic life. While nominally organized temporally as a tracing of Cody's path from youth to old age, the exhibits move spatially as well, as Cody initially moves west from Iowa to Nebraska to Wyoming and then travels again and again from west to east as he seeks fame and fortune first on theater stages in New York and then in open arena shows that traveled the globe. As visitors wind more deeply into the museum, they are also drawn more intensely into Cody's oscillations between east and west, public and private, success and failure.

Visitors are guided through these space/time shifts by somber-hued translucent windows. These are darkly colored, deeply saturated, and earth-toned (and thus draw on the visual resources of the Draper and the PIM), in contrast to the relatively bright overall lighting in the museum. These translucent windows further sharply contrast with the previous museum's design. Against the older museum's light palate and focus on the *Wild West*'s carnivalesque forms, these darker tones connect the displays to a stronger emphasis on western landscapes, provide a more serious emotional tone, and suture Cody more deeply into personal, social, and material contexts.

The window designs are complex, incorporating half-toned images of Cody in western landscapes overlaid by etched script. Weaving together photographs and explanatory words, the windows continuously shift attention between the symbolic and the visual, creating affectively complex signs where the words and photographs tug on mind and body at once. The windows pull visitors into materially performing identification with Cody in his natural settings and linguistically construed historical contexts. Meanwhile, the panels' translucence draws visitors through the windows to the exhibits beyond and beside the signs, urging viewers to place Cody and his landscapes into the three-dimensional museum world that surrounds them. The windows unceasingly draw viewers' vision into and through themselves, creating an embodied experience of the museum and its vistas. This embodied experience, however, has both a sense of immediacy—as viewers engage what is directly in front of them—and a certain remove, as they are asked to peer through, around, and behind displays and are directed to materially and affectively ponder the proffered social and ethical relations. In short, the windows are imbued by a dreamlike characteristic: they materialize the space as a spirit-filled vision.

The movement through these standing windows performs the temporal, spatial, and personal flows and contradictions of Cody's life. As visitors, we perform with the museum the weaving together of a life in the West (scouting, guiding, killing Indians and buffalo, marrying, grieving the loss of children, always longing for a home), as well as a life about the West lived in a global context (becoming a character in novels, plays, and finally imagining the real West in *Buffalo Bill's Wild West*). In the show, the stories of his embodied life in the West (the killing and scalping of an Indian) are replayed in the arena. Yellow Hair's real death haunts the staged deaths of American Indians, and the lived West weaves with the desires performed in the *Wild West*. These conflicts, contradictions, and repressed returns guide the movement through these early stages of the museum.

The compelling dioramas and their (repressed) family dramas are surrounded by far more subdued and less involved displays of furniture and other detritus from Cody's family life. Placed against dark green wallpaper, the heavy wood furniture and carefully framed portraits invite visitors to imagine that they are in a spare rendition of one of the Cody residences. A placard early in this section informs us that Cody's familial life with Louisa was "turbulent." "She desired a settled life," a placard reads. "He wanted freedom. 'I was on the plains; my home was on the saddle,' he later recalled." In fact, the sign continues, "Will's career—and his restless spirit—began to take him away," from his home, his four "adored" children, and his wife.

This western narrative of feminine domestication and masculine freedom is complicated by the early death of three of Bill and Louisa's four children. Absent for all four births, when he learned by telegram that his son Kit was mortally ill with scarlet fever, Cody rushed home from a dramatic performance and held Kit as he died. Six years later, ten-year-old Ora died. Although Bill and Louisa were discussing divorce by then, the death briefly drew the couple together. The heartbreak of these losses and the death of Arta in 1904, Bill's constant traveling, and the consistent and nearly irreconcilable differences between the couple marked Cody's familial life as one of loss and conflict. "Separation bred loneliness, anger, mistrust," reads one sign. Another notes, "The tragic deaths of their son and two daughters brought heartbreak and despair. Could any marriage endure such hardships?"

The early parts of the museum, then, move visitors from the shimmering projection of William Cody inviting us to wander with him on paths of memory to compelling and dramatic installations figuring young Cody as a hero of the West and finally into the difficulties of life and death in the Cody nuclear family. Visitors are, in short, woven into the contradictions between Buffalo Bill

Figure 5. Display featuring the board game the Game of Buffalo Bill (1896). Photograph by Brian L. Ott.

and William F. Cody. They observe the quiet, private life that Louisa desired, while viscerally engaging in the rambling western life that appealed to Buffalo Bill. Visitors are invited to live with Cody and these difficult passionate commitments to home: home in the untamed West, home in front of the crowds, and home in the (re)productive nuclear family.

But the uncanniness of Cody's home populated with the ghosts of dead children and a dying marriage quickly shifts into a children's playground. As museumgoers move from the dark-hued familial exhibits, they wander through large, steel images of Cody outfitted in his show costume on a rearing horse, nearly naked Indians firing arrows into the air, and a yellow stagecoach sitting in the midst of this warlike scene. After the realism of the dioramas and the somber stillness of the familial scenes, this playfully interactive exhibit can seem strange and disorienting. As these are clearly not authentic relics from Cody's life, one searches for clues to make sense of these colorful and dynamic objects.

Near the end of this odd exhibit are two installations that shed light on its mystery. Visitors learn that in the late 1890s the game maker Parker Bros. produced a popular tabletop game, the Game of Buffalo Bill (fig. 5). The pieces preserved in a glass-box exhibit clearly served as the models for the sculptures that visitors are free to wander through. In other words, museumgoers find

64   Chapter 3

themselves in the middle of life-sized reproduction of a board game many children owned over one hundred years earlier. The original game featured paper and cardboard cutouts based on *Buffalo Bill's Wild West*. The cutouts were inserted into American Tobacco cigarette packs and could be arranged into dramatic acts that reproduced in cardboard and paper the performances of westernness (re)produced in the show.[41] As designed, game players moved the small pieces about a table-top game board. In the museum, the game parts have morphed into life-sized interactive museum elements. Firmly bolted into the floor, these installations invite visitors to move themselves around the game markers and in this way join Buffalo Bill in becoming westerners.

Understanding these steel cutouts as representations of game pieces provides the interruptive frame necessary to bring the rest of the area into focus. In contrast to the domestic displays, the life-sized Buffalo Bill game pieces, theater stage and stagecoach (fig. 6), and the Irma Hotel wheel of fortune game wheel materialize (familial) play and produce a mischievous, inventive, and immersive space that aesthetically and rhythmically counterbalances the somber mood of the earlier family man section. Beyond just wandering through the pieces and staring at the Parker Bros. game, visitors can climb into the stagecoach used for years by Cody in his *Wild West* and watch a documentary about the show in which the stagecoach appears. They can view "Irma's Wheel of Fortune, ca. 1905," which hung in the Irma Hotel bar just down the street from the BBCW, and they can spin a reproduction wheel that narrates how Cody's "luck turned out!" This wheel informs visitors of gamelike facts in the life of Buffalo Bill and his performance. But the wheel also weaves Cody's life as showman into his familial life, informing museumgoers that in 1887, "While in England, Cody becomes romantically involved with Katherine Clemmons, an American actress with little talent. As her manager, Cody invests $50,000 in her short-lived theatrical career. Their relationship ends in the mid-1890s." Interlacing public and private life, serious and playful pursuits, business opportunities, and relationship drama in a way that involves visitors' moving bodies complicates Cody's life as western synecdoche. Offering him as hero and jester, portraying him as a wayward and committed family man, and imagining him as extraordinarily successful and deeply ineffective in his public and private lives respectively, the museum seems perpetually haunted by the densities of Cody's life.

Indeed, this area is a complex weaving of time and space and of authenticity and reproduction. We touch and wander around the giant game pieces, which were installed just after the turn of the twenty-first century and are based upon actual game pieces made immediately before the turn of the twentieth. The stagecoach in which we can sit serves as a key material enactment and signifier in Cody's show in the nineteenth and early twentieth centuries. The documentary running on a loop attempts to authentically represent the show itself.

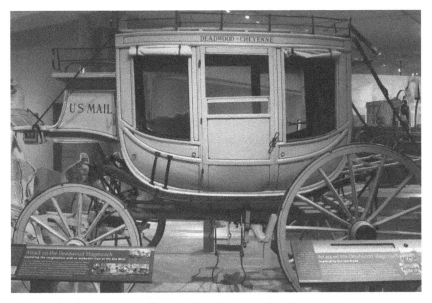

Figure 6. Deadwood stagecoach at the BBM. Photograph by Brian L. Ott.

Meanwhile, the material objects that certify the truthfulness of the museum may in fact be reproductions of real historical objects (game pieces made into museal sculptures) even as the historical objects (the stagecoach) are themselves reproductions of reproductions. The games and fantasy life embodied here situate visitors in childhood, urging a return to a youthful and enthusiastic performance of a dominant/nondominant game of Cowboys and Indians. It is no mistake that the darkness of domesticated Cody is woven into ghostly invitations and compelling dioramas and is left (nearly) forgotten in the melancholic joys of playing Cowboys and Indians alongside Buffalo Bill.

THE WINDOW OF THE WEST

Museumgoers are led, finally, to the BBM's climax by the flickering lights of the *Window of the West* multimedia exhibit. In this digital window, visitors are reminded again that one of the museum's rhetorical conceits is that of the windows. After entering the BBM by passing through Cody's ghost, which shimmers in the misted water, visitors pass by the (dead and never existent) American bison family, which serves as a window to Cody's West. Now at the museum's apex, museumgoers are invited again to look through a window into the West. Here the museum asks visitors to fully merge their vision with Cody's. No longer only a particular vision or a specific way of seeing, the *Window of the West* creates a majestic, sublime representation of the West that—as sublime reproductions do—urges visitors to imagine their own limits within it.

This mediated window is a mirror of the cathedral-like window toward which one is drawn in the Whitney gallery. In that museum (which we discuss in chapter 6), visitors are drawn by a materialized rhythm through representations of the West that urge them to acknowledge and then reject the violent colonial conquering of the West by Cody and his compatriots. For all of the diversity of representations of the West in the Whitney, the final resounding chord is materially and visually created through the massive, peeked windows looking out onto *Buffalo Bill—The Scout*. In the Whitney the discordant tones of the West are resolved in this window, which reverently positions Cody as the American Scout who, like many of the cowboys scattered through the gallery, can eventually lead us home.

While the Whitney's window looks out onto an actual landscape, its focal point is a representation of Cody as scout and cowboy, seer, leader, and westerner. The window in the BBM, on the other hand, is entirely simulated; the landscape comes to us through amazing photography and videography that draws on centuries-old US aesthetic traditions of representing sublimity. Together, the windows weave technology, space, time, and vision to consistently situate visitors as viewers of a West that is bigger and grander than themselves even as it pulls them into these landscapes as a deeply longed-for home. Meanwhile, the aesthetic echoing of the two museums' real and metaphorical windows only adds to the interplay of myth and reality, using, for example, technologically mediated representations of outdoor vistas woven with real-time vistas looking onto the landscape of the West.

From the art-easel placard of the *Window of the West* titled "William F. Cody's West: A Window into His Soul," visitors learn that while on the road with his show, "William F. Cody increasingly yearned for the West that was wild. 'How I long for the glorious mountains and sage-brush,' he wrote in 1912. 'I cannot be truly happy away from there.'" Noting his "special relationship with Nature," the placard reads, "In Nature, Cody felt he encountered God. Nothing stirred Cody's soul more than the majestic landscapes of the West he knew and loved." In listening to the actor's voice-over accompanying the *Window of the West*, we notice that it captures sentiments of being overwhelmed by the growing cities and the fast pace of Cody's show, as well as a deep longing for a return to quieter days, magnificent landscapes, and singular adventures. Over stirring strings and accompanied by photographs and paintings of the Rocky Mountains, the putative Cody intones:

> I want to ride my horse on the plains, not in the arena . . .
> . . . I want to look my mother Nature in the face again . . .
> . . . and shake hands with her in her home.
> To me, this is the most poetic spot on earth . . .
> Toward the land of the setting sun lie the real wonders of the universe . . .
> . . . the marvels wrought by the hand of the Great Supreme . . .

They are the haunts of mystery and silence.

I hear the wind sighing through the pine tops . . .

   . . . moaning as if loath to leave this enchanted amphitheater of mountain . . .

   . . . I am in the home of Nature's God, in His resting place . . .

   . . . and I never want to leave . . .[42]

Understanding that the West was his deeply desired haunt, Cody makes nature into his mother, transforms the mountains and the Great Plains into his home, and weaves his soul into the whispering pines and the moaning winds. Indeed, like the winds that freshen the mountain top, Cody is "loath to leave this enchanted amphitheater of mountain." This exhibit is filled with longing, teems with nostalgia, and is dedicated to an exploration of home in a deeply existential sense. If the cathedral windows of the Whitney urge a reverential understanding of both Cody and the West, in the BBM a haunting engagement with the land returns in force. Visitors are in the presence of God and have been led to this blessed haunt by the wise storyteller, William F. Cody.

Meanwhile, in creating this new, domesticated version of Cody, the BBM also performs the West for its visitors. In place of a West primarily devoted to carnivalized and dramatized conflicts between Euro Americans and Native Americans, understood as a place of consistent and heroic action, this New West is offered as a securing and stabilizing home. In urging visitors to join him on the back trails and by focusing on his (admittedly troubled family life), this version of Cody offers a West that is a familiar home, a well-known landscape, and a lived-in place. While this West still offers opportunities for heroism, it is the heroism of the scout and the guide and the self-sufficient family man rather than that of the larger-than-life showman. And, so in this museum, Buffalo Bill is replaced by William F. Cody, and the *Wild West* is replaced by the haunted/haunting West.

REMEMBERING BILL

There are more exhibits in the museum, including Cody's *Wild West* attire (fig. 7), the tent that he called home when he traveled the world performing his show (fig. 8), an exhibit about his last great hunt with Prince Albert of Monaco, and a map of all the towns Cody visited with the *Wild West*, which allows visitors to see if he traveled through or near their hometowns. And, at the very end, visitors are asked to write in a few lines about what they think Cody's legacy is. But by the time one has reached the *Windows of the West*, the BBM has performed its rhetorical brief. We have come to know a complex Cody; we have been invited to see Cody as standing in for the West with his private and public lives woven into our understanding of nation; and we have been urged to identify with Cody and, in so doing, perform with him the "history, promise, and enduring spirit of the American West."[43]

Figure 7. Display of Cody's show attire from *Buffalo Bill's Wild West*. Photograph by Brian L. Ott.

Figure 8. William F. Cody's camping tent. Photograph by Brian L. Ott.

Introduced as a flickering ghost, Cody returns throughout the museum as a haunting reminder of what he/we have lost. His longing to return home to the plains and the mountains expresses his deep desire for a natural world untrammeled by the travesties of the modern condition—in short, the Spirit of the American West. This spirit, the BBCW asserts, "is, tragically, not eternal."[44] The spirit—and its potential loss—haunts us. As visitors wander the BBM, they are drawn into a haunting dream; they are pulled home, but a home disturbed by the return of the repressed, by Cody's dead children, of course, but also the return of the bison and Indians killed, by a West long since destroyed, and by a West that never actually existed.

As Derrida asserts, acknowledging, welcoming, and providing hospitality for the ghosts of repressed pasts and (un)imagined futures is a work of justice. "If I am getting ready to speak at length," he writes, "about ghosts, inheritance, and generations, generations of ghosts, which is to say about certain others who are not present, nor presently living, either to us, in us, or outside us, it is in the name of *justice*."[45] The memories and hopes and possibilities of others call on us, they demand—if in sotto voce—attention. They remind us of those things we want to forget but which we forget only at the risk of perpetuating injustice. Hospitality lays demands on the host and the (ghostly) guest. And so, the BBM is haunting. It urges visitors to return to where their spirit can best live, but in so doing it also reminds them of ghosts of the past, present, and future. If one listens carefully, their iridescent voices call us toward justice despite the BBM's best efforts to expunge these ghosts.

In our most recent visit to the BBCW, we were fortunate enough to speak with the curators of all five museums, as well the center's director. In those conversations, we learned that the center itself was in a state of rebranding, a rebranding that sought to unify its five museums under one clear mission and message: to become the preeminent site in the world for studying and understanding the American West. Central to that rebranding effort was the center's new slogan, "Celebrating the Spirit of the American West."

It is in the broader context of this rebranding effort that the redesign of the BBM must be understood. Buffalo Bill is, of course, the authorizing voice not only of the museum that bears his name but of the entire center. And it is for precisely this reason that visitors must be reminded that behind the world-famous showman and the dime-store novel character Buffalo Bill was a real person, William F. Cody. It is William Cody, not Buffalo Bill, who returns from his grave to tell us that "the American West is a priceless possession."

In personalizing and humanizing a mythic icon, the BBM allows visitors to experience the "spirit" of the West through the eyes of the individual the center tells us embodied it best. Visitors perform this work thanks to their own embodied movement through the museum. The reason embodied movement is so central to the rhetorical workings of the BBM is that it locates museumgoers in history, in the story of the West not as told but as lived by the person who best reflects it, who in the face of great personal hardship could still appreciate its natural beauty, who in traveling all over the globe to tell its story wanted nothing more than to return to this space of national provenance, and who believed that the American West reflected a particular character of person.

What the renovated BBM does by demythologizing the story of "Buffalo Bill" is effectively mythologize the story of an entire country. The story of the American West as experienced at the BBM is one of hardship and hope, of rugged individualism and hypermasculinity, of Manifest Destiny and American exceptionalism: it is fundamentally the story of what it means to be American. As Roland Barthes has observed, myth transforms history into nature.[46] The BBM takes the life of William F. Cody, substitutes it for the history of the American West, encodes it with the ideology of American exceptionalism, invites visitors to embody that ideology, and then says there is no story here at all, just an essence, a core way of being in the world, in a word, a "spirit" . . . a spirit that, in being celebrated, continues to haunt us.

4

Reverence and Survivance at the Plains Indian Museum

IN 1836 THE history painter George Catlin embarked on his final journey westward to paint North American Indians in their natural, unspoiled settings. Catlin, who was concerned that the "noble" albeit "uncivilized" Plains Indians were a "vanishing race" soon to be lost to history and to the march of progress, had dedicated his adult life to documenting their customs, ceremonies, and everyday life in his paintings.[1] "His mission," writes western art critic Brian Dippie, "was to preserve a visual record of the western tribes before civilization came calling and ruined them forever."[2] In his lifetime, Catlin traveled more widely in North America than any other artist, producing more than five hundred paintings. Today, his self-titled "Catlin's Indian Gallery" is regarded as one of the most important "pictorial representations of Indian life made in the era before photography."[3]

Catlin's desire to preserve the rich culture and history of the Plains Indian— to, in his words, "champion" and "speak well" of a people "who have no means of speaking for themselves"—was not without its pitfalls, however.[4] In "speaking for" the Plains Indian, Catlin's art reflected a European bias, fusing classicism and romanticism.[5] In his field notes, Catlin wrote, "The native grace—simplicity, and dignity of these natural people so much resemble the ancient marbles, that one is irresistibly led to believe that the Grecian Sculptors had similar models to study from."[6] More than a century and a half since Catlin undertook his final western expedition, his paintings now seem to embody the crass stereotype of the "noble savage." Yet, though this perspective has fallen out of favor, Catlin's preservationist desire is felt no less strongly.

In fact, stereotypical renderings of Plains Native life like Catlin's are repeated often enough by museums and museum designers that for many Native Americans, museums are sites of worry, anxiety, and distress. As Amy Lonetree

(Ho-Chunk) writes, "Museums can be very painful sites for Native Peoples, as they are tied to the colonization process."[7] Collections and displays of Native Peoples' art, artifacts, clothing, and the archeological record of Native American life in the nineteenth and twentieth century often circulated around white beliefs regarding the near-term disappearance of Native Peoples. Emma L. Hansen—the curator of the PIM who oversaw the redesign of the 2000 opening— argues that Euro American scholars, collectors, and museum curators collected stories, art, and artifacts and retold the stories and displayed the material culture as though these were "representative remnants of those 'dying' and 'disappearing' cultures."[8] Tinged with nostalgia and offered as examples of a vanquished people, these nineteenth- and twentieth-century displays served the purpose of settler colonialism by making the dispossession of Native Peoples an already accomplished fact that was then justified through the meanings ascribed by Euro Americans to the cultural materials displayed.

The PIM collection started, not surprisingly, as the collection created by Bill Cody. "Unlike the ethnographic assemblages of large North American and European natural history museums of the late eighteenth and early nineteenth centuries," writes Hansen, "the Plains Indian Museum's collection originated with the Northern Plains clothing and accoutrements of Native American performers in Buffalo Bill's Wild West shows that toured from 1883 to 1913."[9] The collection began, then, in a very different way from that of collections held elsewhere, which focused more on clothing and other items used in hunting, battle, and everyday life. At the same time, the collection originally served the purposes of the *Wild West* show, which was one of the powerful institutions to build the image of Plains Indians as locked into narrow narratives of warlike, buffalo-oriented, and disappearing savages. As Ryan Burt writes, "Buffalo Bill translated Native violence—long disseminated in the nineteenth century via 'blood and thunder' dime novels—into a visual language" that helped constitute "Indian" for many Euro Americans.[10] The initial collection practices of the PIM—what we term "collected memory" in chapter 1—are rooted in the practices of colonialism even as they allow the PIM to focus on the clothing and accoutrements of Plains Indians' everyday lives in ways that other museums are unable to do.

But neither the collection nor the museum's display mode are determined by its respective early history. "Over the years," Hansen writes, the PIM "has developed through acquisitions of major private collections and, more recently, works representing the creative output of contemporary Plains Native artists."[11] What is more, as the BBCW began to plan the first installation of the PIM in 1970 and then its redesign in the 1990s (the current museum opened in 2000), the museum sought active participation from Plains Natives. The PIM board was and continues to be populated by several individuals of Plains Indian identity/

background, and the redesign launched in 2000 was led by Hansen, a member of a Plains Indian nation.

In fact in 2017, Rebecca West—who succeeded Hansen as the curator of the PIM and then became the BBCW executive director and CEO as of spring 2021—narrated the development of the PIM as in opposition to older forms of displaying and narrating Plains Indian life. As West told the story at the Buffalo Bill Centennial Symposium held at the BBCW on the one hundredth anniversary of Bill Cody's death, the BBCW had displayed the Plains Indian materials it had collected in "curio style" for decades. On November 3, 1976, the board decided that it was time to move away from this display mode to a museum organized around exploring living, changing, and diverse Native American peoples of the plains. West calls the decision by then BBCW director Peter Hassrick to design a new museum in direct consultation with Native Americans "earth-shattering for 1976."[12] West places this decision in the context of American Indian Movement (AIM) and the occupation of Alcatraz. "There was a great fear of the power of the Native movement," West narrates, "and in fact there's a bit of ugly history, in the center's history, where Dr. Harold McCracken actually had the National Guard on call to ensure that some of the Indian members of AIM or who else, I am not sure who he was afraid of, would [not] come into the museum and take over and perhaps take some of the artifacts."[13] Nonetheless, the center formed the PIM advisory board to oversee the museum's development and included Plains Indians on the board, including the Lakota artist and scholar Arthur Amiotte.

As it began the redesign process in 1994, the PIM more deeply engaged Plains Indian board members to create a museum that recognized how difficult museums can be for Native Americans. Using the collected Native American artifacts, the new design displayed artifacts in an effort to narrate "the story of the survival of the Plains people and their most important traditions."[14] Housing "one of the country's largest and finest collections of Plains Indian art and artifacts," the PIM is also an exemplar of contemporary museal practices, practices principled on a "humanities perspective" and multicultural sensibility.[15] The aim of the a multiyear, multimillion dollar renovation and "reinterpretation" process was to "position the Center as one of the leaders in the museum field in educating the public about Native peoples of the Great Plains."[16] To achieve this goal, the PIM advisory board insisted that "whenever possible the voices of the Plains artists, historians, educators, traditionalists and leaders . . . guide the interpretive process."[17] Of the fifteen board members overseeing the redesign, nine were Native Americans and Emma Hansen led the redesign team.

Completed in June 2000, the renovated PIM is a technological marvel, complete with interactive touch screens, automated audio recordings, wall-sized video displays, and fully immersive, living environments. With the aid of "interactive and experimental exhibits," the design team sought to avoid the cultural

74   Chapter 4

biases of the past and to allow avowed Plains Indian people to speak for themselves.[18] The present chapter explores the weaving of the narratives in the museum, the enabling of those narratives through the collected materials, and the material practices of display.

In our earlier work on the PIM, we argued that the museum works to absolve white visitors of the social guilt regarding western conquest through a rhetoric of *reverence*.[19] Reverence, we suggested, exercised a double articulation, evoking both a profound sense of respect and a distanced, observational gaze. This double articulation, which combined the ideologies of admiration and difference, performed the symbolic function of transcendence.[20] The social guilt associated with the violent colonization of the West was assuaged by a discourse of reverence, reflected in the museum's "atmosphere" and, more specifically, its "moods" and "synesthesia" of seriousness and warmth, which erected a new social hierarchy in which respect for and celebration of difference became the valued social virtue.[21] In moving through the PIM, we maintained, visitors were invited to avoid and even forget the sins of colonization by participating in a discourse of reverence—a discourse that celebrates the Other without identifying with it.

Or so we argued in our previous analysis of the PIM. After conducting considerable research on the museum, both its history and the space itself, we were convinced that while the museum is thoughtful, careful, professional, and compelling, it nonetheless served the ends of supporting colonial discourses and offered many ways for visitors (or, at least, white visitors) to avoid looking directly at the hard truths about the relationship between white America and Native America.

In the intervening years, however, the literature on Native American museums has grown dramatically and the literature about the PIM has shifted as well.[22] What is more, reviewers of the present manuscript pushed us to think more carefully about the museum as a site of survivance and rhetorical sovereignty. Just as museums change, so to do those of us who write about them. In our reappraisal of the PIM, we recognize that our assessment of the museum was overdetermined. As we demonstrate, the museum does offer a rhetoric of reverence that can help visitors absolve themselves of colonial guilt. This reverence or absolution is how the three of us, as differently positioned as we are, have responded to the museum each time we visited. At the same time, however, this rhetoric of reverence offers us opportunities to experience aesthetic and affective resources of survivance and to affirm rhetorical sovereignty. As we have engaged with literatures in survivance and Indigenous sovereignty, spent more time with writing by museum curators and board members, and reexamined our own assumptions, we can feel these alternative appeals. In short, the museum's rhetorical invitations are more complex than we initially understood.

Our revised thesis, then, is this: the PIM develops a rhetoric of reverence that manages the museum's complex invocation of memory to absolve white guilt, while also offering audiences affective, aesthetic, and material appeals to survivance. To explore this complexity, we begin with a short discussion of the intertwined aesthetic practices of survivance and rhetorical sovereignty. We then weave these understandings with our concept of experiential landscapes laid out in chapter 2 to think about the multiple affective and symbolic invitations of the museum. We conclude the chapter by reflecting on the productive and disheartening complexities of the PIM as a dwelling place.

SURVIVANCE, RHETORICAL SOVEREIGNTY, AND EXPERIENTIAL LANDSCAPES IN THE PIM

Refusing to settle on a single definition of survivance, Gerald Vizenor (Chippewa) writes that "the nature of survivance creates a sense of narrative resistance to absence, literary tragedy, nihility, and victimry. Native survivance is an active sense of presence over historical absence, the dominance of cultural simulations, and manifest manners. Native survivance is a continuance of stories."[23] He continues, "Native stories have secured a singular humane practice of the cultural tease, that potential parody and tricky *tease* of situational commerce, communal ceremonies, the concerted caricature of strangers, mockery of dogged academics, and the transformation of animals in stories."[24] He further writes, "Natives by communal stories, memory, and potentiality create a sense of presence not an inscribed absence."[25] For Vizenor and others, survivance is a way of seeing, theorizing, and performing Native presence in spite of the nearly overwhelming efforts to dispossess Native Peoples of their culture, land, and time.

At least three principles arise from these invocations of survivance. First, survivance is an aesthetic practice. It is a way of telling stories, using language, and creating art. Vizenor, for example, writes poetry, analyzes the poetry and fiction of other authors, and engages with the visual rhetoric of Native painters. In rhetoric and communication, scholars have focused on the symbolic action of survivance, attending to documentaries, novels, and museums (taken mostly as symbolic structures) and drawing on aesthetics of wit, trickster rhetorics, and parody to create aesthetically compelling Native narratives.[26]

Second, the aesthetics of survivance resist dominant narratives and, in so doing, build Native identities that create ways of being that honor Native values and practices while undermining/resisting/opposing/thwarting white ways of being that are often taken for granted. For example, Vizenor distinguishes between accountability and "communal responsibility." Individual accountability is an undergirding principle of a white, capitalistic mode of imagining the relationship between the individual and society. In contrast, Native stories emphasize "original, communal responsibility, greater than the individual, greater than original sin, but not accountability, animates the practice and consciousness of survivance, a sense of presence, a responsible presence of natural reason, and resistance to absence and victimry."[27] Survivance uses mimicry, parody, and what Vizenor calls "natural reason" to play on and remake white discourse. Most fundamentally, troping white discourse insists on the presence of Native Americans.

While troping white discourse insists on Native presence, so, too, does survivance's connections to place. Building on place-based natural reason and emphasizing commitments to communal responsibility creates aesthetics that resist colonial ways. Arguing that rhetoric needs to speak of indigeneity, Tiara Na'puti (Chamorus) writes, "We know ourselves as a people belonging to place, a people of the land that we have called home for more than 4,000 years. Our kinships are forged through ancestry or systems of poksai (to nurture/welcome)—so there is no such thing as being part Chamoru. As Chamorus, we understand ourselves as having full responsibility to ocean, land, and people."[28] The aesthetics of survivance, then, emphasize the natural reason created by connection to place, foster communal responsibility to "ocean, land, and people," and trick and turn colonial white discourse, discourse that was and is determined to dispossess Indigenous people of ocean, land, and communal responsibility.

Third, the aesthetic practices of survivance are a rhetorical mode of creating Native sovereignty. In his groundbreaking essay "Rhetorical Sovereignty: What Do American Indians Want from Writing," Scott Richard Lyons (Ojibwe/Mdewakanton Dakota) argues that writing—and language more broadly—is a powerful mode by which American Indians claim sovereignty. Just as practices of survivance consistently call on land, place, nature, and mutual responsibility, so, too, do American Indian practices of rhetorical sovereignty. Lyons emphasizes that "it is precisely this commitment to place that makes the concept of rhetorical sovereignty an empowering device for all forms of community. While most Indians have a special relationship with the land in the form of an actual land base (reservations), this relationship is made truly meaningful by a consistent cultural refusal to interact with that land as private property or purely exploitable resource. Land, culture, and community are inseparable in Indian country, which might explain Native resistance to such policies as the Dawes Allotment Act of a century ago, which tried to transform Indians into bourgeois whites by making them property-holding farmers."[29] Likewise, Lyons argues that rhetorical claims to sovereignty engage and utilize the discourses of white colonists even as that language is shifted, turned, troped, and thus, remade into a language useful in claiming sovereignty. "As the inherent right and ability of peoples to determine their own communicative needs and desires in the pursuit of self-determination, rhetorical sovereignty requires above all the presence of an Indian voice, speaking or writing in an ongoing context of colonization and setting at least some of the terms of debate. Ideally, that voice would often employ a Native language."[30] Rhetorical sovereignty and survivance weave together to create agency as well as material and symbolic place in the context of dispossession.

But how might rhetorical sovereignty and survivance mesh with experiential landscapes? Rhetorical sovereignty and survivance are characteristics of the communicative practices of the creators of those practices. As we argue in the opening chapters, however, the ability of a museum to direct meaning-making and world-making invitations grounded in visitor response depends on the rhetorical resources museumgoers bring with them. More specifically, understanding the invitations of the PIM to survivance or rhetorical sovereignty will at least partially depend on whether users have the rhetorical resources available to understand the aesthetic claims the site makes. None of the three of us, for example, identify as Native American or Indigenous. Over the years, we have read literature on indigeneity. We have been guided by students and faculty across our institutions and by the literatures themselves. In so doing, we have begun to appreciate in new ways the PIM's appeals to survivance and its invitations to rhetorical sovereignty. The discussion of the PIM that follows will reflect these changed perspectives, adding complexity to our cognitive and embodied experiential landscapes.

As we incorporate these new insights, we are also mindful of the invitations the PIM extends to those whose value systems, affective predilections, or education predispose them to welcome absolution for their white guilt. The PIM offers equally compelling and carefully constructed invitations to a reverent relationship between the audience, the museum, and its subject. This intersection mitigates white guilt and reduces affective and symbolic engagement with the dispossessive practices of settler colonialism. These invitations hook into predispositions and tropes of white relationships to Indigeneity that, as we argue, articulate Renato Rosaldo's "imperialist nostalgia" whereby audiences revere and mourn that which colonialism has actively worked to destroy.[31] Our discussion of the PIM will reflect our ongoing engagement with the museum as a site that, at least partially, eases contemporary audience's affectively charged concerns about settler colonialism and the troubling ways white folks have displaced Indigenous peoples over the last two and a half centuries.

The affective and emotive, material and symbolic weaving of the complex rhetorics of survivance and white innocence is one way that our bodies and minds engage the museum's haunting. Haunting, as we have been arguing, affectively engages in a relationship between presence and (seemingly) absent, present and (seemingly) past. In the PIM, we can further engage the complicated ways museal display practices intersect with experiential landscapes—that is the materials and opportunities audiences bring with them—in performing haunting. The distanced respect characteristic of reverence that organizes the museum's invitations to survivance, sovereignty, and innocence articulates well with haunting. Both are affectively loaded invitations, lacing present and past, presence and absence. As the museum offers survivance to audiences ready to see and feel these invitations, this very same offering can serve as a rhetorically salient reverence that separates some audience members from colonial dispossession. For example, moments like the assertion that "we have always been here" in the reconstruction of a Missouri River house can trigger the ghosts/the haunting of those people and places lost to the flooding of the Missouri Valley. These hauntings encode ethical and uncomfortable claims on many audience members, inviting them to remember that which was lost and to knit it together with the present.

REVERENTIAL DISTANCE AT THE PIM

As we have described in earlier chapters, visitors entering the BBCW find themselves in a tall, spacious, and light-filled atrium. The atrium's design easily orients visitors (from left to right) to the gift shop, the Draper Natural History Museum, the BBM, the Whitney Western Art Museum, and the Cody Firearms Museum on the far right. Much harder to see is the location of the PIM. Visitors must proceed down a long hallway located between the BBM and the Whitney gallery that physically and visually separates the PIM from the rest of the center (fig. 9). Getting to the PIM means moving through a wide, relatively unused space to a coffee stand. Passing by a short hallway with restrooms on the right and a light-lunch-oriented café on the left, we finally arrive at the naturally lit passageway to the museum.

Figure 9. Hallway leading to the Plains Indian Museum. Photograph by Brian L. Ott.

The hallway itself is brightly lit, as its walls are windows that look onto sculpture gardens on either side. The last part of the walkway gently rises to the darkened entrance of the PIM. The play of light and dark and the movement of slight ascent make the PIM entrance invisible from the atrium while also creating a sensory moment, a feeling that this space and experience is distinctively set aside from the rest of the center. Before entering the museum, then, our bodies are already conditioned with rules that will guide our experience here. The Plains Indian people are at once celebrated in their own museum and distanced by this long hallway. The spatial relations among the atrium, the other museums, and the PIM combine the conflicted logics of reverence and the challenging rhetorics of survivance. The presence of a special museum dedicated to "Plains Indian cultures, traditions and contemporary lives" fosters an attitude of respect, admiration, and appreciation.[32] This special place emphasizes the set-aside nature of indigenous lives but also the remarkable courage required to survive and thrive in the face of the violence of settler colonialism. The location of the PIM in its own building, separate from the white- and Old West–centered museums immediately off the atrium, invites a sense of distance.

Through our analysis, we illustrate that this sense of distance operates along the axes of culture, nature, and history. When understood within the larger landscape, we are encouraged to embody an anthropological, technological, and amnesiatic mode of looking that sees the Plains Indians as culturally, naturally, and historically distant—as Other. These modes of looking can reassure the visitor that while the Plains Indian is to be revered, such reverence will not necessarily disrupt the stable and centered identity of white people in the United States. And yet, these embodied modes of looking are not airtight. The museal resources used to create them also offer important mnemonics for embodied experiences of survivance and sovereignty. In the final section of our analysis, we will make more explicit how the modes of reverence can also serve rhetorics of survivance, an emphasis that can disrupt the fully distanced mode of reverence and begin to unmake settler colonial relations within the museum.

CULTURAL DISTANCE AND ANTHROPOLOGICAL LOOKING

The experiential landscape of Wyoming locates the visitor as an awestruck observer of sublime nature. The PIM draws on but revises this subjectivity, inviting visitors to become anthropologists—the professionals who specialize in studying, understanding, and explaining Others.[33] This subject position is materialized before entering the museum. As they move toward the museum's entrance, visitors traverse the passageway leading from the center's atrium toward the PIM and come to embody an anthropological way of looking.[34] The special claim of anthropology is to travel to other parts of the world, investigate the Others there, and bring the knowledge back home.[35] The long hallway works analogously by having visitors travel not only across the vast distances of the Mountain West but also from the center of the center to the PIM. In its physical relation to the rest of the BBCW, the PIM works to situate Plains Indian experience as the distant and distinct Other of US national memory and identity. This Other serves as the margin necessary for centering white American identity. Thus, even before entering the museum itself, the visitor is led through spatial, visual, and embodied rhetorics to an understanding that Plains Indian culture is on the borders of the meaning of the West and, in turn, of the United States (fig. 10).

Figure 10. Entrance to the PIM. Photograph by Brian L. Ott.

The visitor quickly discovers a technologically and visually sophisticated space that embeds one in an all-encompassing experience. The use of light, sound, interactive displays, and explanatory material made the museum the most engrossing space in the BBCW twenty years ago. The subsequent design of the Draper and the redesigns of the BBM, Whitney gallery, and CFM all draw on the PIM as a museal model. The PIM elicits atmospheres by offering a strengthened "vantage point of the experiencing individual and underscore[es] what it means to be mindfully present in spaces" as well as fostering interplay "between mindful physical presence and the body, between sensitivity and activity, between the real and reality."[36] Lighting and sound are crucial to creating the atmosphere of the museum. The lighting of the space is soft and warm. The flooring is dark, the high and open ceiling is painted black, and the ambient lighting is low. In contrast with this generalized darkness, streams of bright light, like intense rays of sun, focus on specific displays, drawing our attention and bodies to the highlighted foreground. At the same time, the larger darkness hides the rest of the museum, its visitors, and displays. This effectively reduces the experience to the individual visitor (i.e., isolated anthropologist) and to a visitor's interaction with the (high)lighted display. This reduction is also an intensification of experience and, as such, is a visual and embodied metonymy. Metonymy, Burke argues, substitutes "the corporeal and the tangible" for the intangible states materializing and intensifying that which might otherwise be abstract.[37] By visually limiting distractions, the museum deepens and substantiates the visual force of each element a visitor encounters.

The second crucial element in engaging visitors through one of the "most important generators" in the "realisation of atmospheres" is the use of sound.[38] Upon entering the museum, we can hear the low murmur of recorded voices. All but one of the major displays using Native voices provides oral histories of the elements on display. At the teepee immediately to the right of the entrance, for instance, a woman's voice describes the traditional home, explaining the basic and differentiated gender roles of Plains Indian families. Similarly, in the nearby display regarding Plains Indian modes of travel, voices explain the importance and difficulties of migration in precontact Plains Indian culture.[39] In yet another display dedicated to American bison, men's voices detail the rituals of the buffalo hunt and the sacred stories that tell of the relationship between humans and buffalo. The voices emanating from the displays make present to the visitor traditional Plains Indians ways of living. These recorded voices, unintelligible from a distance, draw visitors into close, multisensory contact with the displays. The visitor can easily assume an intimate modality of reverential listening to Native American coded voices that slip in and out of presence as information is imparted. Taken together, the lighting and the sound foster an intimate, concrete, and fully embodied experience. The distance between past and present and between object and subject is narrowed to the thin and permeable skein of the visitor's skin. The museum's technology invites a closing of the distance between our current selves and the museum's historical and present subjects, placing the Plains people into a relationship of agency and embodied presence with us.

While the sound- and lighting-scape produce an embodied sense of intimacy, the museum also constructs a world that is culturally distinct from that inhabited by most visitors. Most of the dwellings represented or reproduced bear little resemblance to contemporary homes or architecture, at least for us and likely for many other visitors. The domestic, hunting, and clothing artifacts displayed are coded as primitive and consist of natural—that is apparently unmanufactured— materials. Even more important, the accent of the voices in the recordings sound distinctly like nondominant English. Meanwhile, the ways of life and religious myths that the voices narrate are historically and cultural distant. Thus, the PIM locates Plains Indians in a different place and time. This difference, however, is framed as one that can be understood and studied using the tools of anthropology. The museal narratives, with Native voices and with the intensification of the focused lighting, play a central role in inviting the anthropological positioning. As visitors listen to the voices, they are invited to become lay ethnographers interacting with an interlocutor. The stories the interlocutor shares reveal to the visitor/anthropologist the intricacies of lost traditions.

As visitors gaze into the museum's first teepee, for instance, a woman's voice describes the roles of women in the home. Seeing an actual teepee—its naturalistic setting, sandlike floor, and casual arrangement of domestic utensils—reinforces an anthropological mode of looking. The voice—coded as Native American—details the practices of cooking, cleaning, childcare, and everyday life that occurred in this domestic space. Meanwhile, the lighting has narrowed the visitor's experience to this teepee while the surrounding context (of the museum, of the center, of the West) is shadowed. The ubiquity of teepees in the collective imagination affirms the exhibit's authenticity, while the voices of Plains Indian people invite visitors to imagine they are gathering firsthand knowledge about Plains Indians. The Native voices, the life-size materialization of the teepee stocked with cookware and toys, and the intensification of the embodied experience position visitors as anthropological observers of a complex, compelling, and distinctly other culture.

The teepee is a familiar image in popular culture, so most visitors immediately recognize it as a symbol of Plains Indian life. Visitors who arrive at this exhibit having previously toured the BBM may bring with them an additional understanding of the teepee based on the images of teepees in films of Buffalo Bill's *Wild West* arena show—and as we have discussed, the foundation of the PIM's collection rests on the artifacts used in that performance. In these short films, which play continuously in the BBM, the teepee serves to signify an uncivilized Other. In an all-too-familiar scene, as (re)presented in the films, Indians kidnap a white woman and Buffalo Bill must ride into the Indian village to rescue her. To the extent that the teepee in the PIM activates this memory image from the media in the BBM, it contributes to the image of a distanced and even savage Other. But, even if this memory is not at play, the space in the PIM invites visitors to listen to and gaze upon the Other as a compelling, even fascinating, but distanced object of knowledge.

This anthropological vision is reinforced when visitors move from the teepee to the display cases along the wall. Here the space is designed like a more traditional museum. Artifacts representative of the culture are displayed behind glass; they are named and interpreted. The main interpretative tool looks like an anthropologist's notes. To the right of each wall-mounted display is a book with laminated pages. The visitor can turn through these books and read about the items on display. The books' design elements—the typography, arrows, illustrations, and layout—appear handmade. The seeming spontaneity of the notes emphasizes that an observer created them as part of a research project whose purpose is to understand and explain Native life (fig. 11). The title page of each book tells the visitor that these are "curator's notes" for the displays. This titling would suggest that reading the notebooks as part of an anthropological vision is incorrect. However, the curator and the anthropologist work hand in hand. The curator, using the knowledge and materials of the anthropologist, designs the museum displays for the public. Both curator and anthropologist are professionals at interpreting the exotic.

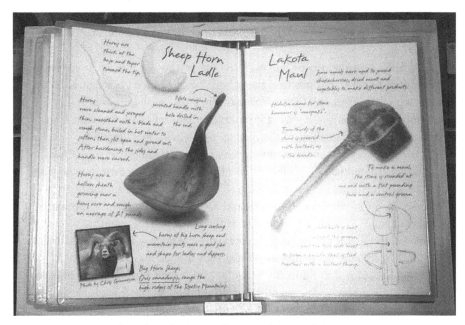

Figure 11. Faux anthropologist's notes in the PIM. Photograph by Brian L. Ott.

Most importantly these notes invite the visitor to identify with the anthropologist or the curator instead of with the culture under examination. In flipping the pages and reading the notes, the visitor is asked to become the professional analyst. The hand-produced field notes are not the explanation; rather, they present the data from which the analyst produces the final elucidation. As visitors turn the pages, they engage additional parts of themselves. They touch the pages and move them, reading the information they contain. They shift their attention to the display cases to which the pages refer, moving eyes and bodies. These books provide a social scientific augmentation to the directly experienced voices and artifacts. The interpellation of the visitor in this space is not only a mental operation; instead, the museum engages the subject's body, shifts its attention, and does its work visually, aurally, and haptically.

Visitors are invited to generate their own knowledge of distant Others from the notes in the books, the artifacts on display, and the voices in the recordings. This knowledge allows the visitor to gain a reverential appreciation of the past and its Others, all the while maintaining a nuanced distance from those studied. The presence of Plains Indians is acknowledged—even celebrated—in the museum, but the acknowledgment is accomplished from an almost insurmountable distance. The museum invites the visitor first and foremost to identify with (and even to become through performative enactments) the scientist and the curator. Identifying with the professional (read: white) analyst helps the visitor keep the native Other at a distance and thereby hold the tragedy of colonization at a distance as well.[40]

Further, by making Plains Indians into Others whose way of life is so clearly premodern in belief and practice, the colonizing of the West is refigured as the civilizing of the West and Plains Indians. While the museum never makes this argument explicitly, this civilizing discourse remains at least an option for visitors. In her critical analysis of the Birmingham Civil Rights Institute, Victoria Gallagher argues that the latter museum uses a rhetoric of progress to mute the contestatory potential of representations of civil rights.[41] The Birmingham Civil Rights Institute is not the only museum to use this discourse. In his magisterial analysis of memory in US culture, Michael Kammen argues that the ideology of progress underlies much of the struggle with memory in this country.[42] What is more, the discourse of progress articulates with the larger discourse of Manifest Destiny, a macro discourse that we have already argued underlies the BBM.[43] In short, we are primed to fill in the narrative gaps in the PIM with a rhetoric of progress. As we argue subsequently, the museum does little to disrupt the predisposition to read the history of Plains Indians through the lens of progress. In fact, the rhetoric of progress is most strongly reinforced by the consistent depiction of Plains Indians as a simple people tied to the land and embedded in the rhythms of nature.

The foregoing analysis, we believe, is essentially correct, at least coming from a positionality like the one that the three of us share with many of the visitors. But there is more to this embodied experience of the museum. Speaking at the Buffalo Bill Centennial Symposium, Arthur Amiotte (Oglala Lakota)—a founding member of the PIM advisory board in 1976, a member of the National American Indian Museum and the Little Bighorn Memorial boards, an internationally recognized artist and scholar, and the great grandson of Standing Bear who performed in *Buffalo Bill's Wild West*—narrated the importance of the BBCW to him. Before his association with the center, Amiotte knew—through the telling of family stories—of his family's "association with the Buffalo Bill experience." "To discover a place that had archives," he continues, "that had objects, it brought together, it created an impetus for me to want to pursue this." The center "was an epiphany that I wanted to spend a lot of my time and to try to do as much as I could."[44] For Amiotte, the PIM as an expression of the collections of the BBCW offers powerful resources for him to begin to fill in the missing elements left to him from the oral history. The story of his family's relation to the "Buffalo Bill experience" was "passed through the sieve of oral tradition out of which, through which, it was strained, parts were left out, parts were forgotten, parts were diminished and it was not until I reached an age of reason with a modicum of education that I had to go back and rediscover" the fullness of the stories.[45] For Amiotte, the BBCW and its Plains Native archives is a rich resource for his own storytelling, his own modes of survivance.

As Vizenor argues, survivance is an aesthetic and often narrative practice that weaves memory and presence. "Natives, by communal stories, memory, and potentiality create a sense of presence not an inscribed absence."[46] Even as from one perspective the anthropological gaze places a respectful and reverential distance between us and those represented in the museum, for audience members like Amiotte the stories narrated here hook into already living memories, creating a presence in place of an absence and intimacy rather than a distance. We can feel this intimacy too. We can toggle between our sense that the museum wishes us to hold Plains people and their lives at a respectful temporal and material distance *and* the museum's pull to understand its subjects with more complexity, resisting the trope of disappearing and static Native cultures.

NATURAL DISTANCE AND TECHNOLOGICAL LOOKING

Through the arduous journey that brought them to Cody and perhaps through their sojourns in the sublime landscape of Yellowstone, visitors are already conditioned to imagine their PIM experience as one that will reveal to them the mysteries of a natural people. Likewise, as visitors move from the center's main atrium through the sunlit hallway to the PIM, they can see (through the glass walls on both the left and the right) sculptures of Native Americans situated within gardens of grass, shrubs, and trees. Beyond the sculptures, the rising, empty slopes of the Rockies visually associate Plains Indians with a rugged, untamed western landscape. Large, glass doors on both sides of the passage allow visitors to enter the gardens and relax in the natural surroundings. Nowhere else in the BBCW—not even in the Draper—is the outside as at once visible and accessible as it is during the passageway from the atrium to the PIM.

While representations of Plains Indians embedded in nature abound in the PIM, the rhetoric is perhaps most explicit in the high-tech, multimedia *Seasons of Life* gallery that dominates the apex of the museum (fig. 12). We can enter from either the left or the right side of this three-level gallery. We are surrounded by images of Plains Indian life, but the most arresting vision lies before us. In the center of the display is a teepee like the one that has already been interpreted at the start of the museum; on the right are two female figures engaged in domestic activities; on the left a man crouches on the cliffs above the teepee. He appears to be hunting. The wall behind this scene is lit to suggest the last remnants of sunlight as day falls into night. Opposite the display are a horse and rider, perhaps returning from hunting or gathering, or perhaps finishing a migratory journey—narratives already told in the other galleries of the museum.

Figure 12. *Seasons of Life* exhibit in the PIM. Photograph by Brian L. Ott.

Running on a continuous loop is a multimedia presentation composed of slides, video, and voice-over. The visuals are projected onto the wall behind the teepee and rock formations. During the presentation, lights brighten and dim onto elements of the display as the narrative/narrator emphasizes details of the Plains Indian life. The narrative formally moves visitors through the "seasons of life" as experienced by Plains Indians before the arrival of white people. It connects Plains Indian life to that of nature, explaining the different activities that people engaged in during the different seasons—hunting, gathering, preserving, migrating, playing, learning domestic crafts, engaging in vision quests, and the like.[47] Structurally, the multimedia presentation embeds Plains Indians not only into nature but also into cyclical time. Randall Lake argues that there are fundamental differences in Native American and Euro American conceptualizations of time.[48] While many Native American cultures assert that time is cyclical like the seasons, Euro American culture emphasizes that time is linear and, more particularly, progressive. This display privileges cyclical time, emphasizing Native American visions of history. In material ways, it tells the stories of Plains Indians from a Native American perspective.

Yet the narrative itself complicates cyclical time as an adequate theory of history. Indeed, as winter approaches and the lights in the gallery dim and the images on the wall turn to snow and ice, the narrative obliquely refers to the invasion of the West by Euro Americans. A women's voice intones, "We were not prepared for the tribulation to come. We thought we would be on the land forever." This language is rich in rhetorical implications. The coming of Euro Americans to the West is named as a "tribulation," euphemizing the violence and conflict that will mark the encounters between Plains Indians and Euro Americans. Further, the narrative points to a competition between linear and cyclical time, in which cyclical time ("we thought we would be on the land forever") is overrun by linear time. Thus, while the gallery privileges cyclical time in explaining Plains Indian culture before the coming of Euro Americans, it also emphasizes the inevitability of Euro American invasion of the West. The gallery enacts the discourse of the vanishing "red man" analyzed by Lake. He writes, "To a degree, the theme of the vanishing red man, like its cousin the noble savage, romanticizes native people and martyrs them to Euramerican greed and racism. Yet, the portrayal of their inevitable doom almost absolves whites of culpability, fixing blame instead on the inexorable march of abstract forces like 'progress.'"[49]

Embedding Plains Indians in nature, then, is not a simple claim that Plains Indians are closer to nature than are Euro Americans. Instead, it positions Plains Indians as distinctly Other than Euro Americans. Plains Indians are natural, caught up in cyclical seasons over which they have no control. Euro Americans, by contrast, are cultured, civilized, and embedded in a progressive history—a progressiveness that is inexorable and will necessarily overrun the naturalness of Plains Indians and at the same time is controlled by human actors. The inexorability of history's progress is crucial, for it can absolve Euro Americans of guilt over the violence done to Plains Indians. The controlled progressiveness is crucial, for it is on this ground that Euro Americans can claim civilization for their own and, again, justify the violence of conquest.

These museal performances strive to offer innocence and at the same time perform compelling resistances. The complicated interaction of natural time—the time of days and seasons—and western linear time underlies the natural reason and natural liberty of survivance. "Native stories of survivance," Vizenor writes, "are prompted by natural reason, by a consciousness and sense of incontestable presence that arises from experiences in the natural world, the turn of seasons, sudden storms, migration of cranes, the ventures of tender lady's slippers, chance of moths overnight, unruly mosquitoes, and the favor of spirits in the water, rimy sumac, wild rice, thunder in the ice, bear, beaver, and faces in the stone."[50] Natural reason does not simply reject the linearity of Western time; rather, it remakes Western time through witty, teasing turns, wrapping together the resources of white ways of performing with ways that honor and bring to the present Native reasoning. The wittiness and teasing of white structures that Vizenor values is less visible, less felt here than in other instances he references. The gallery's complicated story—following the seasons *and* recognizing the oppressive force of Western temporality—offers a compelling (if practical) response to the dominant story. In this space, at least, western settler colonial temporality is not the only way of feeling time. As Mark Rifkin suggests, displays like the *Seasons of Life* gallery can be understood and felt as an expression of "temporal sovereignty" in which alternative forms of temporality gesture to "struggles over Indigenous landedness, governance, and everyday socialities."[51]

This complex discourse of nature and temporality is further reinforced in an exhibit of the low, river homes typical of the Plains Indians living along the Missouri River in the twentieth century (fig. 13). While sitting around a fake but convincing fire, visitors watch and listen to a video and slide presentation digitally embedded in the home's walls that informs them about the loss of tradition and culture caused by damming the Missouri River.[52] Although the dam radically disrupted agriculture and fishing and flooded long-standing Plains Indian homes and communities, the narrative informs visitors that despite this challenge Plains Indians have not been and cannot be eradicated. "We've always been here," a voice says, "we'll always be here." The appeal to cyclical time in the narrative suggests that Plains Indians will survive even as their ways of being are destroyed by the technological needs of modernity. Even in the face of tribulation (read: progress), Plains Indians will endure, for as the voice continues, "this is our land." This assertion of survival can mitigate the guilt of Euro Americans by assuring visitors that progress has not resulted in eradication. In asserting survival through connection to the land, the narrative creates a false sense of triumphalism. At the exact same time, there is a powerful appeal to survivance: no matter what is thrown at Native Peoples in the name of settler colonialism, Native folks survive and even thrive. They do so by continuing to claim their relationship to land and nature and natural temporality.

That the Plains Indians' relationship with nature and cyclical time is represented through postmodern visual technologies is central to this exhibit's rhetorical force. The same technology that preserves and promotes visitors' reverential respect for Plains Indian culture is also directly opposed to that culture. The destruction of the Plains Indian relationship with nature came at the hands of Euro Americans and their technology (an argument made most explicitly in the CFM chapter of this book). At the same time, these technologies are offered

Figure 13. Interactive Missouri River home at the PIM. Photograph by Brian L. Ott.

as the best way to preserve and (re)present that which has been lost. The technology of the presentation itself, then, serves as further proof of Euro American superiority and distance from these "natural" people of the Plains.

The use of Western technology and materials to make critical aesthetic and rhetorical claims is a deep and long tradition in Plain Indian artistic practices. Writing about the Lakota regalia that traveled with and circulated alongside Buffalo Bill's *Wild West*, Emily Burns argues that intersecting Lakota traditions with Western demands was a powerful mode of survivance. "The blending of non-Native commerce and Native art production," she writes, "is layered with nuance and spaces for hybrid meanings and interventions that reveal the agency of Native artists and performers." The artform of Native regalia, she continues, "makes statements about Lakota cultural identity."[53] The use of Western technologies to make claims to survivance, then, is the very kind of trickster practices Vizenor theorizes and explores as the modes of survivance. In a wink and a nod, these high-tech performances serve to help visitors apprehend and feel Indigenous relations to land, nature, and time.

HISTORICAL DISTANCE AND AMNESIATIC LOOKING

The passageway from the atrium of the BBCW to the PIM, which we argue works to foster cultural distance, also enacts a rhetoric of historical distance. As visitors travel through the passageway, they move experientially through time, ultimately arriving at the museum's entrance. Once there, visitors confront a

90 Chapter 4

large wall, stenciled with a black and white photographic montage of Plains Indian warriors astride horses, stampeding buffalo, a wood framed house, and a small inset of text and color pictures of contemporary Plains Indians. The composition of the montage situates the past of the Plains Indians as more dramatic and compelling than the present depiction of the "People of the Plains." With its explicit emphasis on the past, one might expect the museum to also acknowledge the colonizing violence of that past. And, indeed, it is acknowledged in various places throughout the museum. For example, in the exhibits on the buffalo and on Native ceremonies, there is an implicit recognition of conquest through a discourse of recovery. Contemporary powwows (like the one held each year at the BBCW) are represented within the PIM as ways of recovering traditions nearly lost to colonization. Likewise, images of recent buffalo hunts serve as a connection to the nearly lost tradition of buffalo hunting that was central to Plains Indian life and culture. And, as we argued in the previous section, the *Seasons of Life* exhibit euphemizes colonization as "tribulations" and places Plains Indian/Euro American contact within the deep cold and everlasting darkness of winter.

But perhaps the most transparent place where the violence of conquest is simultaneously acknowledged and denied is in the least interesting, least compelling exhibit in the museum, *Encounters*. This exhibit is simply a long wall with a timeline covering the nineteenth century. This timeline is the only direct representation of the century—the one most deeply damaging to Plains Indians. This exhibit is also without multimedia, without interactive displays, without an attempt to create realistic settings, without the Plains Indian voices to tell the story, without so much of the technological and inclusive-voiced visitor enticements used in other areas of the PIM. From our perspective, every effort is made to make this one exhibit uninteresting. Using print and uninspired displays of artifacts, the wall (re)presents the history of conquest during the long nineteenth century. The flat, beige wall outlines historical events, including the killing of the buffalo, the coming of the missionaries with their message of God's saving grace and their smallpox, the boarding schools to which Plains Indian children were sent and in which they were beaten for speaking their native languages. And here is noted the battle of Wounded Knee—the battle that symbolically and materially ended nineteenth-century Plains Indian resistance to Euro American conquest.

At last, this shameful story is summarized, in the visual, aural, and material equivalent of passive voice. Take, for instance, the rifle displayed at the far left and the very beginning of the wall. The placard tells us that the rifle is not special. Instead, it is typical of the weapons used in the West. Further, it is the sort of weapon, the densely printed placard asserts, used by both Euro Americans and Plains Indians. The notice acknowledges, though grudgingly, that it is also the type of weapon that helped the US cavalry defeat Plains Indians again and again, though it does so by naming the rifle as the weapon of choice in the "Plains wars." If visitors come to this exhibit in the PIM having first toured the CFM, then the rifle may be understood as a weapon of war based on the experience of the CFM's exhibit titled *The Cost of War*. Or they may see the weapon as one example of many that the CFM's firearms history section presents as characteristic of the nineteenth-century West. Crucially, when it presents these western weapons, the CFM urges visitors to come to the PIM for a more complete discussion of the use of firearms on the Plains and by Native Americans. The CFM presents these guns and their historical surroundings through a rhetoric of dissociative contextualization, whereby the traumas associated with the guns are ignored through attention to nontraumatic contexts. In the case of the CFM, that context urges us to understand guns as useful tools, technological marvels, objects of play and pleasure. Here, in the PIM, the gun appears as a tool of settler colonialism. We engage the CFM's deferrals in chapter 7.

Perhaps most important visually, however, is that the long *Encounters* wall is confined to a narrow space. Seeing the whole wall at once is impossible, limiting our ability to fully grasp the horrors of those hundred years. Rather than creating an intimacy between the viewer and the display, and instead of offering a relationship of empathy, the forced closeness between the display and visitor obscures the horrors of Manifest Destiny. The visual design of the display ineffectually narrates the conquest, nearly eliminating affective or embodied connection between the present visitor and the past destruction. The wall is particularly tedious when viewed in context of the technological sophistication of the surrounding museum, wherein the reverential relation between visitors and Plains Indians in the rest of the museum is created through stirring narratives, told in Native voices, with moving images, all embedded within fully embodied displays.

At this wall, however, no voices engage the visitor, no touchscreen displays beckon; there are no books to read, and no movies to watch. This wall works hard to not interrupt the reverence the PIM has fostered in every other exhibit. Visitors are invited by the absence of technological sophistication to disengage from this (non)exhibit; and in ignoring this exhibit, visitors may also ignore the history told here. By providing the barest acknowledgment of conquest in the least interesting way, the wall privileges forgetting over remembering.

The exhibit seems all the less significant within the larger landscape of looking created by the BBCW. Down the hallway, visitors experience sublime western art in the Whitney gallery, compelling gun displays in the CFM, engaging display of western natural history in the Draper, and colorful representation of Buffalo Bill Cody in the BBM. Finally, looking at the wall through the eyes of those who have just traveled to Cody from the sublimity of Yellowstone National

Park, the wall is almost nonsensical. The narrative, visual, aural, and haptic force of the PIM's experiential landscape undermines the likelihood of this exhibit compellingly conveying the pain and loss of the nineteenth century. The wall is not so much a gesture toward memory as it is an amnesiatic mode of looking—a mode that is often central to political reconciliation.[54]

As convinced as we are of this understanding of the *Encounters* wall—an understanding reinforced when we recall that the CFM urges its visitors to visit this wall to gain a fuller understanding of firearms and Native experiences—the wall does offer alternative affective responses. What we have been calling a bare, passive-voice, and uninteresting display others can see as starkly compelling. Rather than leading to a deadened response, the display's formal differences can create a heightened response whereby the starkness of the nineteenth-century near-genocide on the Great Plains is mirrored by the starkly uncompromising aesthetics of the wall. The stark and bare display performs a homology with the stark terrors of settler colonial practices of the nineteenth century.

As Amy Lonetree argues in *Decolonizing Museums*, a decolonizing museum practice "must be in the service of speaking the hard truths of colonialism. The purpose is to generate the critical awareness that is necessary to heal from historical unresolved grief on all the levels and in all the ways that continues to harm Native people today."[55] For us, the wall raises crucial questions about settler colonial practices but does not do so in a way that really "speaks the hard truths of colonialism." The passive voice approach allows us to, if we wish, avoid the clear facts—that Euro Americans set out with all deliberateness to destroy Native Americans. The doer of the deeds is left unnamed, the explicit nature of the dispossessive efforts remain unnarrated, and the disastrous consequences are presented in a way that makes it relatively easy for audience members to remember and then forget Euro American maleficence.

This amnesia intersects with the larger discourses about the internal colonization of the US portion of the North American continent. Colonization within the boundaries of its territories allowed the United States to represent its "expansionist motives as essential to nation-building, denying the imperial."[56] This nation-building impulse was justified, in part, by the rhetoric of Manifest Destiny, which claimed that westward expansion was not simply necessary for political or economic reasons but was instead a moral or even religious national duty.[57] Figured this way, colonization carried with it difficult contradictions. Anderson and Domash argue that "the experiences of colonizing internally brings to the fore . . . contradictions inherent in national identities forged from positioning the colonized as both them and us; and from national identities requiring an imagined past, place and people, and yet denying that place and people a presence."[58]

Creating and maintaining US national identity depends on creating stories that negotiate contradictions, "stories that deny and assert the presence and significance of internal 'others.'"[59] These narrative contradictions about US colonization of Native Peoples intersect with larger issues of national memory. Some individuals want to forget the past and particularly those aspects of it that are painful and self-indicting. Others want to remember the past, particularly those who contest dominant discourses of the nation.[60] The PIM is fraught with these contradictions, and it offers a rhetoric of reverence, we argue, in its efforts to transcend these difficulties. In celebrating the culture and life of the Plains Indians, the museum demonstrates respect and appreciation for a fragile past. The museum compellingly gestures toward aesthetics of survivance and offers resources for rhetorical and temporal sovereignty.

The reverential celebration is also regularly offered through a series of distancing materials, aesthetic, and symbolic performances. The museum's anthropological, historical, and technological rhetorical modes offer us many opportunities to distance ourselves both from the traumas of settler colonialism and from the dynamic presence of Plains Indians. In these modes, the museum downplays the role of Euro Americans in the colonization of Plains Indians' land and the destruction of Native Peoples' cultures. Indeed, the very creation of the BBCW's archives depended on an understanding that the center was collecting and preserving relics of a dying past. In forgetting these histories, the museum (re)constructs a Plains Indian culture useful to the creation of a complacent national identity. This complacency has, in turn, contributed to the ongoing mistreatment of Native People in the twentieth and twenty-first centuries.

THE PIM AND NATIONAL MEMORY

As the three of us discussed the revision of this text and worked to engage more deeply with the museum's affordances for survivance, we returned again and again to the long hallway that both separates and joins the BBCW and the PIM. While the PIM invites circular and cyclical movements, the path to get there is decidedly linear. There is an embodied linear-circular-linear transformation that happens in moving from the long straight hall into the circular museum whose apex emphasizes the cycles of life back out to the hallway and from the natural light of the hallway into the museum's subdued electrical lighting and back into the natural light. The natural light out in the hallway is "real time" and the subdued lighting inside the museum is more mystical, dreamlike, and otherworldly. For us, entering and leaving the museum invokes a sense of subdued haunting, of another time, another season, another place (the large contemporary posters that hang in the museum notwithstanding). We asked ourselves this question: Are museum spaces of minoritized identities always subject to less (realness) or more (ghostliness) to them simply because they are not dominant? Is it important that the two darkest, dreamiest spaces in the BBCW are the PIM and the Draper, both of which memorialize the colonization of place and the people in the place? For us, the BBCW's museums express and perform a powerful desire to acknowledge the loss of people, land, and animals while offering to many of their visitors the comfort of placing those losses elsewhere and elsewhen.

The PIM—and as we will discuss in chapter 6 regarding the Draper—presents a prehistory of and for white America. Nations depend upon such histories to ground national identity. Settler colonialism, however, makes this history particularly difficult to tell. On the one hand, Plains Indians' tenure on the land is longer than that of the invading Euro Americans and can therefore provide a deep historical substantiating for the nation. On the other hand, the history of conflict is one that, when measured by contemporary standards, is shameful. The PIM negotiates this tension through a reverential rhetoric.

The museum preserves and celebrates Plains Indian culture by invoking conceptions of time, nature, culture, social relations, and cosmologies that are profoundly different from those of many visitors. In this sense, the museum offers the nation a deep history. But while the museum recounts the rich culture of premodern Plains Indians, it often works to absolve Euro Americans of the violence of conquest. The museum creates a space of memory in which Plains Indian history and culture is placed on view, honored, and valued. It provides this deep past as a part of what it means to be American. In (nearly) ignoring the history of settler colonial dispossession, the past as presented here does not contradict the present; nor does it serve as a critique of American national identity. Instead, it narrates a mythical, nostalgic past. According to Renato Rosaldo, agents of colonization often yearn "for the very forms of life they intentionally altered or destroyed."[61] "Imperialist nostalgia," he adds, "uses a pose of 'innocent yearning' both to capture people's imagination and to conceal its complicity with often brutal domination."[62] As Euro Americans celebrate this deep past, they are cleansed of their sins in the immediate past and present. In celebrating the distant past of Others, Euro Americans can avoid present-day racism and forget the ways the nation is built on the very oppressions it constantly denies. The dual appeal to both respect and distance is evident in the subject position afforded visitors, a position we argue combines a "reverent I" with a "worshipful eye."

And yet the logic of reverence is not always simple and straightforward. Haunting complicates this rhetorical mode. Visitors are asked to stand in a worshipful relationship to Plains Indians and their embodiment of the western spirit. Native Americans are part of the history of the haunt to which we (Euro Americans) wish to return. But Native spirits—disturbed by immoral deaths, improper burials, and loss of their proper homelands—haunt the Euro American home. They can remind visitors that valued homeland, comforting pastures, familiar ways are carved out of the stolen land and built on the bones of dispossessed Native American people. The museum reminds us that the white West is haunted not only by the destruction wrought by settler colonialism but also by the survivance of the very cultures white folks tried to destroy. The thriving force of Plains Natives can be a constantly haunting call to conscience, demanding that we create a home that welcomes Native and white alike.

Earlier in the book, we connected the doubled meaning of haunt—as a welcoming and familiar place and as a place disturbed by the ghosts of repressed memories—and ethos as a dwelling that can "create and invite others into a place where they can dwell and feel at home" while discussing sometimes difficult truths.[63] This effort to create a dwelling place for collective identities depends on mnemonics. Carole Blair and Neil Michel write that "constructions of memory offer particular versions of collective identity to their adherents. Put differently, the way we understand the past at least implicitly underwrites our understandings of who we are or who we should been in the present and future."[64] More than simply offering a set of mnemonics to underwrite who we are or should be, the PIM performs difficult negotiations of conflicting memory structures. Though it regularly resolves the memory conflicts in favor of white absolution, as we dwell in the museum, we are also repeatedly in the affective presence of more complex memory possibilities. The "home" reflected by the PIM opens the possibility of difficult and potentially productive conversations between white and Native People, between settler colonialism and decoloniality. Is this a museum that fulfills Lonetree's museal goal of assisting "communities in their efforts to address the legacies of historical unresolved grief by speaking hard truths of colonialism and thereby creating spaces for healing and understanding"?[65] In our judgement, it is not. But in its hauntings, in its contradiction, the museum holds out the possibilities for speaking these hard truths.

5

The Sacred Hymn of the Whitney Western Art Museum

ONE OF THE central premises of this book is that museums, like memory, are mutable. For instance, when we first visited the center, the Whitney Western Art Museum, which was then known as the Whitney Gallery of Western Art, featured almost exclusively traditional (read: white and male) western artists presented in a relatively conventional way. In 2007 and 2008, however, the Whitney was renovated. The redesign of the museum, which reopened in 2009, offered a fresh, new look; the gallery space was reorganized, the art was regrouped and rehung, and the West was reimagined.

During our prior visits, the Whitney was organized chronologically, tracing western art from the early nineteenth to the late twentieth century.[1] Within this broad historical arc, artworks were arranged according to both artist (George Catlin, Thomas Moran, Frederic Remington, and Charles M. Russell, for example) and genre/medium—wildlife, landscapes, paintings, bronzes, and illustrations. The focus on individual artists and genres reproduced the dominant conventions of art museums across the country, while the temporal structure retold the mythic story of the West—it began with Native Peoples and their lands, traced European settlement (including the destruction of the buffalo and the violent removal of Indians), and ended with the veneration of the cowboy. Thus, the gallery was, for many visitors, familiar in both its form and content.

The redesigned Whitney disrupts both the formal conventions and the narrative content that had previously governed the space. The gallery now organizes the artworks thematically into five major subjects: wildlife, western landscapes, Native Americans, western heroes and legends, and historic events. The result is an eclectic blending of artists, genres/media (paintings, bronzes, marble sculptures, etc.), and time periods within each of the subject areas. This diverse mixing of perspectives, artistic styles, and histories creates conversations both among and within the five themes, producing variously complementary and contradictory renderings of the West.

In its new design, the museum redoubled its efforts to produce a rhetorically resonant atmosphere. As we point out in earlier chapters, atmospheres are what Gernot Böhme called "attuned spaces" wherein the bodies in the space—human, art, and design elements in the case of this art museum—permit, encourage, and produce "specific affective participation in our world."[2] As Böhme articulates, atmosphere urges critics to investigate relationships between human, sensing bodies and the things of the space like movement (fast or slow, this way or that), synesthetic mood (coolness or melancholia, for example), and conventional expectations (elegant or fanciness). As we have been arguing throughout this book, the subject and the object are extended toward or into each other. Museum visitors extend their understandings and embodied expectations toward the art objects even as the objects and spatial design extend toward and even into the viewers' bodies. The museum's bodies and the visitors' bodies interlace and interweave to create the experience of and in the museum.

In this chapter, we take seriously *attunement* as a mode by which human bodies can associate in ontologically complex ways with their environments.[3] Indeed, we take music as a material metaphor for the rhetorical force of the Whitney. In subverting the traditional codes and conventions of art museums, the redesigned gallery reimagines the West and elicits a series of affective dissonances. These dissonances are ultimately resolved, we assert, by situating Buffalo Bill Cody as the gallery's composing force. Indeed, our central contention is that the redesigned Whitney performs a sacred hymn that—in repositioning Buffalo Bill Cody as its orchestrating figure—resolves discordant images and narratives of the West, harmonizes diverse themes into a single vision, and reconstitutes national identity in terms of the western sublime.[4] The sacred hymns we track in the museum raise the haunting specter of repressed memories—the horrors of settler colonialism, the destruction of the western ecosystem by industrialization, and the angry rejection of racial and ethnic others—only to resolve these dissonant images and affects into a dominant understanding of western sublimity. The mood of the space, the attunement of human and museal bodies to each other, is complex but at its root serves as a preparation for a very specific experience of the western sublime.

In support of this argument, this chapter unfolds in four parts. First, we continue our consideration of museum change, with particular attention to the ways the Whitney was the earliest expression of the BBCW's revised name and mission. Second, we deepen our theorization of embodied movements. Our marrying of music and architecture will allow us to emphasize the energetic attunements between human bodies and built spaces. Third, we analyze how the gallery presents and then hides the West's hauntings by creating and resolving a

98 Chapter 5

series of affective dissonances, thereby harmonizing the gallery's major themes. Fourth, we explore how the gallery fosters an experience of sublimity that serves to reconstitute western identity.

THE MUTABLE MUSEUM: MEMORY AND CHANGE

In previous chapters, we engaged questions of museal changing, inspired by the BBCW's changing institutional goals and design and by the ways those changes manifest in the museums that also changed over the time of our study. In the next section, our aim is threefold: to further clarify the role that curatorial processes and museal practices play in the construction of public memory in art museums; to highlight the various forces that influence these processes and practices, thus promoting routine change in museums and their structured appeals to public memory; and to explain rebranding efforts undertaken by the BBCW as they influence both the Whitney and the larger atmospheres of the center. This discussion of museum change will serve as a context for understanding the subsequent analysis of the Whitney.

Forces of Change

As social institutions, museums are susceptible to a wide array of cultural, social, political, and economic forces. Sometimes these forces arise from within an institution and other times they are exterior to it. But regardless of where they originate, these forces can powerfully impact the museal practices of selection, preservation, exhibition, and representation and, hence, collected and displayed memory as we discussed in chapter 2.

Economic factors, for instance, can profoundly constrain collected memory. Most art galleries have limited financial and spatial resources, which restricts the amount of art they can collect, preserve, store, and display. Indeed, the acquisition of new collections often necessitates the elimination of older ones (or, just as consequentially, their movement from display into storage). Another difficulty for collection and preservation is the development of innovative art forms that are more ephemeral and fleeting.[5] How would a museum collect, for example, Cristo's temporary installations and what are the best ways to archive digitally produced art?

In much the same way that economic forces influence collected memory, social and cultural forces influence displayed memory. As museums strive to stay fresh and interesting to audiences, their practices of exhibition and representation are influenced by the emergence of new technologies and changes in aesthetic taste. As we have already seen, recent museum designs utilize interactive touch screens and spatial aesthetics that eliminate the distance between visitors and displayed artifacts and artworks. Since the practices of exhibition and representation produce distinct ways of seeing their objects, revisions to these practices can produce new—often unintended—ways of seeing and think-ing. But perhaps the most powerful factor in generating museum change is so-cial and political change. As Blair, Dickinson, and Ott explain in *Places of Public Memory*, memory is always "activated by concerns, issues, or anxieties of the present."[6] As the central concerns of society change, social institutions such as museums can be implicated in and influenced by this evolution.

Consider how social and political reformations have altered museums around the globe. The overthrow of apartheid in South Africa, for example, prompted radical changes in its museums.[7] Responding to a new social and political land-scape, South African museums began a process of deep revision that according to Dubin, "constructed new ways of thinking and doing and understanding."[8] The South African example suggests that change is dialectical—that as the mu-seums change to reflect new social and political realities, they simultaneously affirm and produce social and political changes. Since the latter are often driven by changing public sensibilities, publics can also exert tremendous influence over the character of museums. We have already witnessed this push and pull in the Buffalo Bill Museum, where changing attitudes about the West and about Buffalo Bill underscored the need to revise the BBM in a way that made Wil-liam Cody more complex, more attuned to deeper moods, more human. And we will see these cultural influences, including the impact of prevailing public senti-ment, in our analysis of the CFM in chapter 7.

As should be evident by now, a wide variety of factors contribute to routine changes in museums. That museums change regularly can pose serious chal-lenges for researchers studying these institutions. For one thing, changes to a museum are often not readily apparent to researchers who have not been to that museum in the past and carefully documented its previous design. In fact, when a museum undergoes significant change, it often hides or physically destroys traces of its past incarnation.[9] Rarely do museums reflect on the fact that their current collected and displayed memory is only one option among an infinite array of possibilities. As we will discuss in chapter 7, the CFM is at least a partial exception to this rule. Throughout that museum, the design reflects on the pre-vious form of the display. Unlike the CFM, the Whitney does not reflect on the changes it has made or on the choices that make up the new design. Despite the challenges—or rather, because of these challenges—there are benefits to exam-ining museal change, not the least of which is that changes to the museum often reveal much deeper changes to society and to our sense of self.

WHITNEY WESTERN ART MUSEUM AND THE
REBRANDED BUFFALO BILL HISTORICAL CENTER

The Whitney, as it now stands, is in its third major incarnation. The Whit-ney Western Art Museum was officially dedicated in 1959, though Gertrude

Vanderbilt Whitney, for whom the museum is named, "actually started the museum's art collection" with the completion of *Buffalo Bill—The Scout*, in 1924.[10] The Whitney was redesigned in the 1980s and, again, in 2009—its reopening timed to correspond with the gallery's fiftieth anniversary. The redesigned Whitney needed to embody the BBCW's new name and newly adopted credo. In fact, the Whitney redesign is the first redesign completed within the context of this newly developed understanding of the center's self-identity.

As visitors enter the main BBCW entrance hall, an enormous poster introduces them not to five distinctive museums but to the center as a whole, informing visitors the institution is devoted to "Celebrating the Spirit of the American West." The shift in emphasis from the five museums to the center and its overarching theme is repeated on the BBCW website. The website introduces the center, presents its trademark slogan, and describes its five themes (not museums): Buffalo Bill, Yellowstone's natural history, Plains Indians, firearms, and western art. These same themes are evident in the images that comprise the welcome poster in the entrance hall, but the overlapping and softly blurred edges of the images create, upon first glance, the appearance of a single image. This practice of subsuming difference to a single unifying theme is, as our subsequent analysis demonstrates, central to how the redesigned Whitney works. Indeed, the five major themes of the Whitney, while not exactly the same as those of the BBCW, map closely onto the themes we experience in the gallery. Just as importantly, the Whitney strives to create an overarching mood for the museum, of which the specific art objects become particular notes in the larger attunement that is the Whitney.

THE MATTER OF MOVEMENT: RHYTHM AND HARMONY

Throughout the book, we have consistently stressed the importance of embodied movement—what we termed *"being through there"* in chapter 2—in understanding the rhetorical force of built environments. One of the primary motivations for our thinking carefully about movement is to bring the body fully into engagement with museums. In discussions of the body in rhetorical, communication, and cultural studies, it is often treated as stationary and as a site of signification and cognition. One likely reason for the absence of rhetorical research regarding the body in motion is the challenge of developing a sophisticated vocabulary for talking and thinking about embodied movement, especially the body's movement in time. Nonetheless, our concern here is with the material interlacing of "moving bodies" and "moved bodies," that is, bodies that are affectively energized by rhetorical spaces. We enrich our discussions of embodied movement by drawing on the fields of architecture and musicology. Taken together, we think these fields aid us in better understanding and assessing the rhetorical consequentiality of movement.

On first blush, the marriage of architecture and music may seem strange. Architecture, after all, is concrete, enduring, and practical; a successful building needs to fend off the elements. Music is, on the other hand, ephemeral, ethereal, and effervescent. Though a musical score may survive for centuries, music only exists as music in the moment of its performance. Martin captures the distinction this way: "Architecture represents the art of design in space. Music represents the art of design in time."[11] Despite their differences, the two arts have long been linked.[12] One reason for this is that space and time are themselves always linked. "Without time and space," Martin writes, "matter is inconceivable; it is a dead thing, space gives form and proportion; time supplies it with life and measure."[13] Indeed, Doreen Massey teaches us that space and time are always knitted. "If time unfolds as change space unfolds as interaction," she writes.[14] A musical approach to architecture can help us think of architecture in time as well as in space, can urge us to investigate embodied movement through the built environment, and can help critics listen to the rhythms of architecture. It can attune us to the ways temporality as musical form can organize spatial and social interactions.

In fact, a musical approach to the built environment is well suited to our more general atmospheric approach to human surrounds. As Thomas Rickert suggests when writing about mood, atmosphere, and ambience, "the world reveals itself in a musical way, but it does so in such a fashion as to transform our experience of place itself."[15] Our embodied interaction with music is very much like our embodied interaction with place writ large. Most importantly, there is a deeply ontological relationship between the bodies and music. Bodies are necessary for the making of music, but the music made enters and remakes the bodies of the musicians, of the musicians' surrounds, and of the listeners. But, as Rickert indicates, we do not need to have actual music for music to help us disclose the ontological and rhetorical relationship between human bodies and place. Like formal music, places have rhythms, they have sounds, they have movement, they are always temporally changing. The atmosphere of a place is musical, even if there is no music playing.

Crucially, the Whitney draws on the musicality of space in its redesign, creating a more totalizing experience of the curated art. As we will show, the museum involves our bodies through rhythm and through dissonance and resolution. Following our theoretical predilections and the material facts of the museum, our criticism moves, like the redesigned gallery itself, away from the exploration of artists and their oeuvres, away from artistic styles and genres, and away from familiar museum codes and conventions. Instead, and homologous with the gallery itself, we turn toward a chorus of images, the visual and spatial arrangement of this hymn, the structured temporality of the space, and the rhythmic invitations to embodied affective suasion. To study the space's structured temporality is not simply to study its spatial juxtapositions of artworks (though that is one dimension of it), but rather to study the rhythms and harmonies experienced by the body moving through and with the museum's collected and displayed memory. Like music, the museum's rhetoric is punctuated by rhythm and harmony. These rhythms and harmonies are, of course, experienced visually and spatially rather than aurally, as the music is materialized by visitors' movements rather than the vibrations of musical instruments. Much as musician, score, and instrument intertwine to make music, the Whitney's hymn plays its visitors even as the gallery's visitors also play the music. Visitors are not simply resonating sounding boards but are both musician and instrument, as the gallery materializes structured opportunities for making music.

The Whitney's visual and spatial hymn is arranged as a series of stanzas; alternatively, we may think of it as comprising a series of movements. These stanzas come in the form of the museum's five major themes: wildlife, western landscapes, Native Americans, western heroes and legends, and historic events. These sections—which correspond to visitors' movements—are, in turn, built upon structured rhythms and harmonies. There are, we contend, rhetorically significant rhythms both within and across the individual movements/themes. By rhythm we mean patterns of intensity and release that repeat in time. For our purposes, this translates into visual and spatial patterns that recur as visitors move through the gallery. These rhythms work directly on visitors' bodies, producing a unique symbolic and material experience of the museum—one that, ultimately, harmonizes discordant images of the West into a unified vision, or as stated in the branding language of the BBCW, "The Spirit of the American West."

THE MATTER OF RHYTHM: WALTZING TO THE WINDOW

We begin our analysis of the Whitney's visual and spatial rhythms with a description of its overall layout. When viewed from the gallery's entrance, the space appears to be divided into three sections (or aisles)—left, middle, and right. This appearance is created by the presence of four slender walls that have been staggered—two on the left and two on the right—to form two parallel lines. Each of the walls is approximately twelve feet in length. As one walks down the center of the gallery toward the large windows at the far end, the first of the four staggered walls is on the left. It is followed by a short break, and then a second parallel wall on the right. After the second wall, there is a longer break in the middle of the gallery. This large open space is followed by two additional walls, which repeat the same spatial pattern as the first two walls—a wall on the left, short break, and a final wall on the right. Beyond the second set of walls, there is another large open space.

The latter half of this open space is elevated roughly a foot above the rest of the gallery and has a high cathedral ceiling that leads to a wall of natural light created by two rows of enormous glass panes. The cathedral-like windows located at the gallery's far end look out onto *Buffalo Bill—The Scout*, with the Rocky Mountains rising in the distance. The bright natural light spilling through the windows and the dramatic human sculpture and natural landscape visible draw visitors from the entrance to the conclusion of the museum/hymn.

The four staggered walls that direct visitors from the gallery's entrance to its spatial and visual apex produce a rhythmic movement through the gallery. As visitors' bodies follow the walls to the exciting and imposing picture window, they begin with the museum's entrance as the first, strong beat. The gallery then proceeds in this way: strong quarter beat, two weak beats; strong beat, two weak beats; pause, and a final, emphasized full beat. Expressed musically, the gallery would be composed in 3/4 time, much like a country western waltz. This governing rhythm invites very specific and felt movement through the space, with the visitors as musicians, dancers, and instruments; the gallery as spatialized score; and Bill Cody as conductor. Another way of thinking about how the rhythm of the gallery works is in terms of the appeal of form, which Burke defines as "the creation of an appetite . . . and the adequate satisfaction of that appetite."[16] The formal symmetry of the first two walls leads visitors to anticipate that symmetry again, just as the first open space (or pause) prepares visitors for the more dramatic open space (or pause) that concludes the hymn.

The rhythmic structure of the space, then, fulfills the formal appetites that it creates by the movement of visitors through it. The hymn captures well the result of the somatic experience generated by the museum's spatial rhythm: a visitor is momentarily seized by the grandeur of the museum's final artwork, which combines Whitney's sculpture with the sublime western landscape. And just as the final chords of a hymn are made meaningful by the rhythmic and harmonic movements that preceded it, the final space of the museum is made meaningful by the spatial movements that preceded it.

The cathedral-like windows that emphasize the sacredness of this hymn and the subsequent view of *Buffalo Bill—The Scout* and the Rocky Mountains are not a new feature of the museum. However, in the Whitney's previous layout, a series of walls ran perpendicular to the side walls of the museum, obstructing guests not only from seeing Buffalo Bill but also from seeing—and, thus, anticipating—what came next in the gallery. But in the redesigned gallery, the obstructing walls have been removed, opening a central sight line that extends the entire length of the museum to the windows at the far end. The new spatial layout centrally situates Buffalo Bill, allowing him to direct visitors' movement through the gallery from the moment they first step inside. The rhythmic movement from the entrance to Buffalo Bill also works to unify the gallery, providing a governing structure for the minor movements—the five thematic installations—that rise and fall along the way.

104 Chapter 5

The five thematic installations (that is, the five stanzas that comprise the gallery's hymn) encompass both the spaces created by the staggered display walls and a series of enclaves to the left and right of the center aisle-like space. The paintings and sculptures in these installations are, as previously noted, no longer arranged by time period, artist, or genre. Instead, the gallery stages a series of thematically unified displays. Each theme is introduced by a placard that provides an overview to guide visitors' understandings not of the individual artworks but of the theme as a whole. For example, the first theme that visitors encounter is "Inspirational Landscapes." "Is the West always picturesque and idyllic?" the text on the placard asks just below the thematic title and a small, nineteenth-century oil painting. In a few brief sentences, the placard explains that the western landscape paintings of the nineteenth and twentieth century left out Indigenous people while depicting the land as empty, pristine, and fertile. True to the placard's promise, the installation is populated by paintings of western landscapes that show the land as more or less empty and untrammeled. Though largely unified in their perspective of the West as picturesque and idyllic, the paintings span one hundred years of painting history and are composed in diverse artistic styles.

Similarly, the gallery's other installations—wildlife, Native Americans, heroes and legends, and historic events—subsume historically and aesthetically diverse paintings and sculptures into unifying themes, which preserves the rhythm of the structuring song. Combining dissimilar artworks produced over the last 150 years by diverse artists, each of the thematic installations brings the artworks into visual and spatial conversations that enliven the art and make the gallery's vision of the West and its art more complex. At the same time, the rhythm of the gallery reunifies the art under the watchful gaze of Buffalo Bill. Likewise, the visitors' own rhythmic movement through the gallery—the ways they stop and start, slow down, and speed up as they engage the thematic hangings—urge them to see the various thematic installations as unified by the museum's structure.

Even as the overall structure of the gallery suggests that the space unifies the art, the individual themes clearly strive to embody and engage diversity, mark conflict, and represent controversy. In fact, the new design creates instructive visual and conceptual tensions. These offer affectively powerful modes by which to think about and view the difficulties of the West. Turning again to musical modalities, the thematic hangings harmonize art through dissonance and resolution, and through balance. By using these two modes, the gallery presents the conflicts characteristic of white settling and exploitation of the West in a manner that not only resolves the tensions raised but also makes the resolution pleasurable. In fact, these resolutions further prepare visitors to see the Whitney, the western art it displays, and the West it represents as sublime. We turn to these affective engagements next.

THE MATTER OF AFFECT: DISSONANCE AND RESOLUTION

As with movement, affect is centrally concerned with bodies. We have already suggested that affect is a nonconscious, nonsignifying, unqualified intensity registered directly by the body, or seen from another angle, the body's immediate (autonomic) response to an encounter with any other "whole composed of parts."[17] This "whole" could be another body, an object, a work of art, or an environment, for instance. In the previous section, we described a visitor who was momentarily suspended in awe by the sculpture of Buffalo Bill; this was likely not a conscious response to the sculpture's symbolic meaning but an embodied or affective response to it. In this section, we are interested in a particular embodied response that recurs as visitors move through the gallery. We call this response affective dissonance, by which we mean the museum invites the body into a transitory state of dissension. This affective dissonance arises, we contend, from repeated encounters with discordant styles and perspectives.

Within each of the thematic installations, artworks reflecting different aesthetic styles and ideological views are placed in visual, spatial, and symbolic conversation with one another. Often, the first image in a themed installation will utilize a traditional, realist style and convey a celebratory or romanticized view of its western subject. But subsequent images frequently adopt a more playful or a more critical sensibility that comments on their subject matter. The visual and spatial juxtaposition of starkly different aesthetic styles, along with artworks' competing visions of the West, can be disruptive and unsettling, inviting affective dissonance. In the *Heroes and Legends* installation, for example, Audrey Roll-Preissler's seven-foot tall sculpture *Western Man with Beer and Dog* ridicules the traditional image of the cowboy as a hypermasculine hero who tamed the West.[18] Roll-Preissler's sculpture presents a pudgy, Budweiser-swilling cowboy with a scruffy dog curled unceremoniously at his feet. The sculpture startles, striking an affective (dis)c(h)ord with visitors expecting to encounter only Remington sculptures of rugged cowboys and bucking broncos.

Likewise, just inside this installation, visitors observe two distinctly different renderings of General George Custer. A painting by Fritz Scholder (Luiseño), *Custer and 20,000 Indians*, is deeply satirical. Based on a newspaper photograph of Custer, Scholder's work mocks Custer's heroism or, more to the point, mocks mass-mediated representations of his heroism. In the painting, the twenty thousand Indians are little more than black background images against a blood-red sky. Custer, who dominates the frame, brandishes a sword and a pistol and stares directly at the viewer like a demented cartoon character. The unsettling nature of this image is quickly offset by the painting to its left, Earl Biss's *Gen. Custer in Blue and Green*, which offers a more heroic viewpoint. Biss's painting imagines Custer as heroic but fatally flawed, unable to see beyond his own personal needs.

106   Chapter 5

If Scholder's image is a deranged cartoon character, Biss's Custer is a Shakespearean tragic hero.

In combination, these two paintings generate dissonance and its resolution. Scholder's piece confronts the viewer with its bright, electrifying colors and portrayal of Custer as a wild-eyed buffoon while Biss's painting soothes with its cool, blue tones and measured portrayal of Custer as a flawed, but heroic man. Like all great resolutions, the final note (Biss's complex treatment) contains traces of the dissonance produced by Scholder's piece. Placed side by side, the paintings invite visitors to toggle between dissonance and resolution, studying one and then the other. Moving between these two paintings allows for a continuous—and potentially pleasurable—repetition of dissonance/resolution/dissonance/resolution. This toggling is not only a cognitive move or one that is exclusively visual. Instead—and importantly—our bodies move in a syncopated manner, turning back and forth, walking from this side of the display to another. Our experience of dissonance and resolution fully engages our bodies. The paintings and their relationship to each other virtually demanded a sensuous *being through there.*

The gallery is not neutral about the relationship of these two images, for these paintings are not experienced in isolation. They are preceded by a cluster of traditional cowboy-on-horse sculptures, whose familiar images and style afford the comfort of tradition just before the clash to come. And the paintings are followed soon after by W. H. D. Koener's moving oil *Madonna of the Prairie*, in which the folds of a prairie schooner's canvas roof form a halo around a beautiful young white woman moving onto the Great Plains. Negative appraisals of western heroes and legends are resolved, then, both internally and by the surrounding landscape of sculptures and paintings. The general affective development of the thematic installations moves visitors from colloquial and comforting images, through dissonant critical appraisals, and toward resolution with a reassuring restatement of the theme. This repeated staging of tension and release, of dissonance and its resolution, is what makes movement through the gallery so pleasurable and compelling.

As compelling and important as dissonance and resolution is to understand the aesthetic conversation among images in the *Heroes and Legends* theme, these relations are most powerfully at work in the *First Peoples of the West* installation. In this space, the theme is announced by a placard that includes a small painting by William de la Montagne Cary titled *Indian Mother and Child.* The painting depicts a domestic scene with a Plains Indian teepee on the right, a mother wearing a colorfully decorated buffalo hide and holding her baby in the center, and a pastoral landscape on the left. This image of Native American life emphasizes tranquility, peacefulness, family, and a rootedness in the land (themes that are repeated in the PIM) both in its subject matter and aesthetic style, which carefully balances brown, green, and yellow earth tones.

Immediately to the left of the thematic placard containing Cary's small, serene painting is Albert Bierstadt's imposing *The Last of the Buffalo*, which charges the space with a discordant sense of loss. Visitors will have likely already viewed Bierstadt's well-known landscape paintings in the preceding installation emphasizing the western landscape; the colors, composition, and subject matter will be familiar. But rather than portraying a simple, romantic vision of the West, Bierstadt's landscape is littered with the sun-bleached skulls of buffalo, while a lone Native American horseman prepares to spear one of the few remaining animals. As we discussed in previous chapters, by 1888 when the painting was completed, the plains bison had been all but eradicated. In the 1870s white settlers killed buffalo en masse, sending their hides back east. Buffalo Bill Cody, the most renowned buffalo hunter, killed more the four thousand buffalo in just two years. While Bierstadt's painting poignantly laments the loss of the buffalo and, with them, a whole way of life, it does so without directly signaling the role of colonization in that loss. Through the elision of the subjects who produced the destruction—subjects with whom the viewer may easily identify—this historical absence opens the space for resolution of the affective dissonance it elicits.

While resolution will quickly follow as visitors move through this portion of the gallery, the nostalgic mourning embedded in Bierstadt's painting is reiterated in James Earle Fraser's sculpture *End of the Trail* (fig. 14). Even as Fraser's piece appropriates the defining trope of western sculpture—the powerful male body astride a well-proportioned horse—it generates dissonance by turning that trope on its head. In place of the furious action and heroic poses reflected in most western sculptures, both horse and Native American rider are hanging their heads, apparently sensing the end of Indian lifeways. Fraser's *End of the Trail*, which portrays "the theme of the passing away of the Indian race," is—like Bierstadt's *The Last of the Buffalo*—a deeply expressive piece whose sense of loss is shared by the visitor.[19]

But this loss is not as discordant is it might appear. In fact, these representations clearly express the settler colonial belief that Plain Indians ways of life and the Plains peoples themselves ought to be left in the past, destroyed to make way of modern civilization. As Emma Hansen argues, Euro American scholars, collectors, and museum curators collected stories, art, and artifacts and retold the stories and displayed the material culture as though these were "representative remnants of those 'dying' and 'disappearing' cultures."[20] This is a painting that powerfully captures this turn-of-the-century expectation about Native Americans. "In that moment," Philip J. Deloria (Dakota Sioux) writes, "according to most American narratives, Indian people, corralled on isolated and impoverished reservations, missed out on modernity—indeed almost dropped out of history itself."[21] In both of these artworks, the visitor is invited to mourn the loss of a culture, to witness Native Peoples almost dropping "out of history itself."

Figure 14. James Earl Fraser's sculpture *End of the Trail*. Photograph by Brian L. Ott.

But in neither case are those responsible for this loss (Euro American colonizers) named, imaged, or imagined. This absence is vital not only for the success of these individual artworks but also for the subsequent resolution offered by the installation.[22] The affective dissonance associated with imperialist nostalgia, while sad, does not invite reflection and, therefore, covers over wounds (painful memories) that might be truly disruptive to the unified "spirit" of the West.

This is also the case in the *First Peoples* installation. Immediately behind *End of the Trail* is Paul Manship's *Indian and Pronghorn Antelope*. This two-part sculpture—an Indian aiming his arrow and a fleeing pronghorn antelope—draws on classical forms to render the Native American subject of the painting as mythological rather than historical and creates a figure of great hunting prowess, rather than an individual struggling for survival.[23] Visually and spatially, *End of the Trail* and the loss it evokes is contained and recoded by this sculpture, which "harks back to both earlier American sculptures and to archaic European—especially Greek—models," thereby aesthetically evoking a unifying sense of Humanness.[24]

Similarly, to the immediate left of *The Last of the Buffalo* and just a few steps from *End of the Trail* is a 1972 sculpture by Doug Hyde (Ojibwa/Nez Perce/Assinboin), *Coyote Legend* (fig. 15). Completed nearly seventy years after Manship's sculpture, Hyde's mythological representation privileges a Native American rather than a European narrative. Nonetheless, Hyde's sculpture offers viewers the comforts of a universal and universalizing story. As in the PIM, which is partially guided by the narrative that Indians have always been here and so their future presence is also assured, *Coyote Legend* sutures Native American experience into an historical arc that, even as it alludes to colonization, transcends and ignores it.

Figure 15. Doug Hyde's *Coyote Legend* sculpture. Photograph by Brian L. Ott.

Figure 16. Allan Mardon's *The Battle of Greasy Grass*. Photograph by Brian L. Ott.

As should already be clear, as the visitor moves through and among the art in the Whitney, we experience a recurring pattern of tension and release. In the *First Peoples of the West*, the theme is tranquilly established with *Indian Mother and Child*, dissonance is produced by artworks like *The Last of the Buffalo* and *End of the Trail*, and resolution is afforded by Manship's *Indian and Pronghorn Antelope* and Hyde's *Coyote Legend*. While each of these artworks is compelling on its own terms, it is the rhythmic experience of affective dissonance and resolution created by the structured movement among them that lends the gallery its rhetorical force. The narrative, visual, and stylistic discord among the artworks in each installation is consistently subsumed by the unity of the governing theme and the melodic (or structured) movement through the space, which always leads to resolution.

This repeating structure builds toward climax, which comes near the end of the gallery. As visitors move through the *First Peoples of the West* installation and into an expansive space immediately preceding the cathedral-like windows that punctuate the finale, they encounter two final themes. To the left is a section devoted to the cowboy and to Buffalo Bill in particular, and to the right is the culmination of the *Heroes and Legends* installation. The constant vision of *Buffalo Bill—The Scout* throughout the gallery's space and the rhythm of the staggered walls has led visitors inescapably to this moment/space. Surrounded by images and sculptures of the heroic cowboy, visitors confront one final pair of discordant images. Highlighted by red walls, two enormous paintings engage the same scene: the Battle of Little Bighorn. The first painting in the pair is Allan Mardon's *The Battle of Greasy Grass* (fig. 16). Mardon depicts the battle not from a singular perspective as one moment in time but from a complex spatial and temporal perspectives that unfolds over several days; in so doing, he draws not only European aesthetics but also on the aesthetics of buffalo hide paintings (which are better represented in the PIM). Mardon's painting focuses attention on Native American warriors and, more particularly, the exploits of Crazy Horse. In short, this painting tells a revised, which is to say, dissonant, version of this famous battle, one that focuses not on General Custer's defeat but on Native Americans' resistance to colonization.

But the gallery cannot allow this remarkable work to be the only or even the last imagining of the battle. Opposite from Mardon's painting hangs Edgar Paxson's well-known *Custer's Last Stand*. This image wants us to see Custer standing amid his fallen soldiers, bravely fighting off the red hordes until his dying breath. Capturing the battle in a single moment, presumably just before Custer is killed, Paxson draws on a long lineage of European aesthetics to represent Custer as the hero. This painting was reproduced in multiple formats and, along with a series of similar paintings, became a definitive visual aid for many Americans to imagine this battle, while shaping the American mythos about how the West was won. As Dippie writes of the myth of Custer's Last Stand, the image of the battle is one that depends not on history but on repetition of "the image of a man standing tall on a western hill, oblivious to personal danger, facing a swarm of Indians who will in a matter of seconds annihilate his whole command. The setting, the Indians and the other soldiers in this mental picture are indistinct . . . All that matters is that defiant stance with which he confronts his destiny."[25] The mythical image of Custer is produced, in part, by Paxson's painting; but it is also produced by Buffalo Bill in his *Wild West* performances, which frequently recreated Custer's Last Stand.

While we certainly could analyze the content of these two paintings further, we want to concentrate on how the paintings are hung within the gallery. Situated side by side, the artworks visually balance one another. At the same time, hanging *Custer's Last Stand* temporally and spatially after *The Battle of Greasy Grass* suggests a progression, a rhetorical movement from dissonance to resolution. The movement from painting to painting strives to close the moral and political ambiguities the juxtaposition of these two visions of the battle—and of the West—seem to proffer. By the time visitors reach these two paintings, they have internalized the gallery's structured movement, which constructs this as another, though perhaps more dramatic, instance of tension and release and so we know in our bodies how this final movement is likely to end. In moving from Mardon to Paxson, from dissonance to its resolution, visitors sonically and rhythmically move one step closer to Buffalo Bill and his vision of the West.

Having finally arrived at the cathedral-like windows, visitors look out across the western landscape, where *Buffalo Bill—The Scout*, rifle in hand, is reading the trail and leading the way (fig. 17). But what precisely is the way of the West? What, visitors might ask, is the "spirit of the West?" The Whitney suggests the West is a diverse and often discordant set of ideas and images. But it also suggests the West is a place where these dissonances can be resolved and harmonized. Just as the tension-filled transformations in the final movement of Beethoven's Fifth Symphony are resolved through a series of powerful C-major chords, so too the affective dissonances of Whitney are brought to a compelling conclusion by Buffalo Bill. This final resolution is all the more potent for the manner it invokes the sublime—the subject to which we now turn.

Figure 17. View of *Buffalo Bill—The Scout* as seen through the window of the Whitney Western Art Museum. Photograph by Brian L. Ott.

THE MATTER OF SUBLIMITY: BUFFALO BILL AND THE SPIRIT OF THE WEST

In the previous two sections, we examined the Whitney's hymn to and about the West, attending, first, to its unique rhythmic movement of visitors through the space and, second, to its harmonizing of discordant images and views of the West through the repeated creation and resolution of affective dissonance. Here, we inquire into the consequentiality of those two rhetorical mechanisms, asking, in effect, what purpose do they serve? The chief rhetorical function of the gallery's visual and spatial rhythms and its recurring pattern of tension and release is, we posit, to prime visitors psychologically, viscerally, and affectively for an experience of sublimity. Sublimity is, according to Stormer, "any aesthetic that presents the possibility of the unrepresentable through a paradoxical attempt to express that which exceeds discourse."[26] In the case of the Whitney, the "unrepresentable" that the gallery tries to express or capture aesthetically is the spirit of the American West. Since the spirit or essence of a thing, properly speaking, lies outside of discourse, it can only be felt, not represented. The experience of sublimity is, as Stormer observes, "an affective response of solitary character that escapes accepted discursive forms."[27]

This response is precisely what the redesigned Whitney aims to do—to create an affective sense of the spirit of the American West. But coaxing visitors to experience sublimity, and specifically the western sublime, is far from a politically neutral endeavor. The western sublime, after all, operates much like "the American sublime," whose political function, according to O'Gorman, is to promote a unified sense of national identity by deflecting attention away from "the injustices, disparities, inconsistencies, and crimes of the nation."[28] Similarly, the western sublime constructs a holistic vision and understanding of the West, as well as a unified western subject, precisely by redirecting attention from the material realities of colonization—the violent devastation of the American bison and the forced removal of Native American peoples from their lands—toward an idealized vision of the West.

At the Whitney, the ideal of the West is embodied and em-bronzed in Buffalo Bill Cody, whose commemorative sculpture marks the precise place where visitors are invited to experience the western sublime. As O'Gorman notes, the sublime always converts upward, elevating "spirit above matter," ideal above reality.[29] But merely identifying what the Whitney is doing—fostering an embodied sense of the spirit of the West—does not explain how it is doing it.

The Whitney prepares visitors for the experience of sublimity upon reaching the gallery's conclusion. The hymn's finale, then, is hinted at from the very outset. The first of the five thematic installations that visitors encounter in the gallery is *Inspirational Landscapes*, which features stunning paintings such as Thomas Moran's *Zoroaster Peak (Grand Canyon Arizona)* and *Golden Gate, Yellowstone National Park* or Albert Bierstadt's *Island Lake, Wind River Range* or *Yellowstone Falls*. The landscapes depicted in these and many other paintings in the installation were, as Boehme explains, "a symbol of the uniqueness of America, its sublime wilderness which was America's history and its spiritual fountainhead."[30] While we would not argue that these paintings are themselves sublime, they do nonetheless equip visitors with specific ways of looking—namely a modern western gaze already attuned to the wonders of both the natural world and of art imbued with the artist's genius.[31] As the placard accompanying this installation highlights, "because we often view the landscape through the artist's eye, we are influenced by his or her point of view." The soft halo of yellowish light surrounding the key visual element in each of the paintings mentioned here inspires a sense of awe and reverence and associates the image with the spiritual and divine. In short, these paintings rehearse, in Stormer's words, "the act of looking into the sublime."[32]

As visitors continue to move through the gallery, the visual codes of awe and reverence associated with "the act of looking into the sublime" are repeated. This occurs not just in the images of the western landscape but also in the bronze sculptures of Native Americans and cowboys that adopt classical techniques rooted in Greek and Roman ideals of perfection. The consistent presence of visual codes oriented toward sublimity in the gallery is, of course, made more powerful by the invocation of those same codes in relation to the surrounding landscape. As we have argued throughout the book, the real and imagined landscape of the Yellowstone region positions visitors to look at the West with awe, wonder, and veneration. Thus, by the time visitors have reached the gallery's end, they are practiced in a manner of looking that actively anticipates an experience of sublimity. The carefully orchestrated rhythmic movement through the gallery and the continuous creation and cessation of affective dissonance has played a crucial role in priming visitors for an intense and awe-inspiring conclusion.

This priming has involved, as we have already noted, some strong moments of discord or dissonance. Scholder's *Custer and 20,000 Indians*, which is explicitly critical of the heroic myth surrounding Custer, for instance, may displease some visitors. But such frustrations are themselves just one more step in the general movement toward an overwhelming sense of satisfaction. Consider, once more, Burke's view of form as the satisfaction of appetites or desires: "This satisfaction—so complicated is the human mechanism—at times involves a temporary set of frustrations, but in the end these frustrations prove to be simply a more involved kind of satisfaction, and furthermore serve to make the satisfaction of fulfillment more intense."[33] The Whitney works in this way. While the thematic installations produce a series of stylistic and historical tensions, the gallery as a whole manages to restore balance and harmonize the artworks under a transcendent, unified ideal: the spirit of the American West. This is only possible, however, because the ideal is never exposed as an ideal. The redesigned gallery carefully structures the artworks to create rhythm rather than rupture, dissonance rather than deconstruction, and conversation rather than critical reflection. This delicate balance requires more than just thoughtful display practices, however. It also entails careful practices of selection. And sometimes what does not get displayed is just as important as what does.

When we visited the Whitney after its redesign, we noticed the absence of one artwork that had been on display in the gallery's previous design: Charles

M. Russell's *Making the Chinaman Dance*.[34] In this painting, Russell portrays a white cowboy firing his pistol at the feet of an Asian man, as the saloon's patrons look on in amusement. The artwork does not comment on its subject matter or pose a counterpoint to some other perspective on the West. Instead, it seems to express genuinely held prejudicial attitudes about Chinese workers in the West. It is not an artistic reflection on racism but a frank enactment of the latter. Had this painting been included in the gallery's redesign, it is difficult to imagine how the explicit racism it manifests would have been tempered or resolved. The movement in the museum has been between a critical and usually progressive vision to a reverential traditional vision. But Russell's work does not critique western representation from the left; instead, it clarifies the racism that is already embedded in the traditional art offered to the visitors as resolution. The edifice of the museum's celebratory and sublime hymn relies on hiding racism and resolving colonialism. In contrast, this now absent painting materially reveals the spirit of the American West at its racist worst. This is the image and the imagination that haunts the Whitney and the BBCW.

Greenblatt argues that the wonder encoded in art may be undercut by an overly scrupulous attention to the artwork's resonance. In his view, wonder is the "power of the object displayed to stop a viewer in his tracks, to convey an arresting sense of uniqueness, to evoke an exalted attention."[35] He contrasts wonder with resonance, which is the "power of an object displayed to reach out beyond its formal boundaries to a larger world, to evoke in the viewer the complex, dynamic cultural forces from which it has emerged and for which . . . it may be taken by a viewer to stand."[36] Art's ability to create wonder—to arrest motion, to stop the heart, to focus the attention, to at least point to the sublime—is, for Greenblatt, one of the greatest aesthetic pleasures offered in the Occidental world. In the Whitney, this pleasure does not attend, however, primarily to a single work of art but rather to the orchestration of the gallery, its proscribed rhythms, its powerfully affective production of dissonance and resolution. Where some contemporary art museums strive to historicize the art they house (Greenblatt points to the Musée d'Orsay as a prime example), making masterwork and everyday objects alike resonant, the Whitney strives to make even the most mundane of western art wonderful.

Here the effect of wonder has begun to shift from the artwork and the artist's genius to the space itself. This shift should not be a complete surprise. Built into a wonderful western landscape that both competes with the gallery and trains its visitors to be attentive to awe-inspiring western landscapes more generally, the revised Whitney reinstalls a modern museal gaze: that of wonder and the western sublime. Museum change and the gallery's rhetorical efforts coalesce. Built into the immediate aftermath of the culture wars and constructed in the heart of a deeply conservative state and region, the Whitney's and the BBCW's effort

116   Chapter 5

to make wonderful again the spirit of the American West—and to reconstitute a way of seeing—makes imminent sense.

While the redesigned Whitney displays a plentitude of artworks that vary in artistic style and historical perspective, it excludes those that would fundamentally disrupt its vision of an idealized West—a vision that is authorized by Buffalo Bill. Visitors move through the gallery drawn to and guided by its central artwork, *Buffalo Bill—The Scout*. In the gallery's final space/time, Buffalo Bill's vision frames our vision, his West becomes our West. Staring out at Buffalo Bill, the majestic Rocky Mountains rising in the distance behind him, the material reality of the gallery dissolves, if only for an instance, into a flash of awe. The Whitney—recalling memories of the sublime beyond its walls, displaying images of the sublime on its walls, and creating a rhythmic movement that anticipates the sublime within its walls—performs its hymn to the Spirit of the American West and makes possible the experience of sublimity.

This sublimity—or at least the representation of the possibility of sublimity—works in support of the BBCW spirit, or its haunt. Over and over the disturbing ghosts of the West are represented in this space. Images focus us on the deaths of American bison, pictures and sculptures puncture the heroism of the cowboy and remind us of the colonization of Plains Indians. These dead bodies and lingering spirits roam between the rhythmically placed walls, these specters are present, and their presence is felt. This is the affective discord produced by many of the artworks and their relationships to surrounding images. But this haunting is not the spirit that the redesigned museum of the rebranded center wants visitors to leave with. Covering these disturbing shades is the possibility of sublimity. In fact, this possibility is even more powerfully felt because of the presence of ghosts. The risk and danger produced as the potential of the sublime mounts up depends in part on the possibility of falling into the grasp of repressed memory. The statue *Buffalo Bill—The Scout* sees and reveals to us our barely seen ghosts and then leads us toward the (Euro American imagination of) sublimity of the West.

Earlier in this chapter we noted that museal change is motivated by a host of reasons, not the least of which is changing audience needs and changing social and cultural conditions. At least some in the United States bring with them the hauntings of settler colonialism, as well as the hope for a new and different haunt, a new and different home. The new design clearly addresses a series of contemporary concerns about representation. The museum's display of a greater diversity of artwork—diversity in form, in identities of the artists, of subject matter—broadens the museum's perspective on the West, enlarges the haunt's possibilities. In so doing, it invites more diverse audiences, audiences who are less committed to a singular vision of the West and its people. It also partially remakes our understanding of art itself. Placing paintings and sculptures in conversation across time, subject, style, and values suggests that art is an active participant in ongoing discussions about our individual and collective identity. This can make the art more vital, as it may feel like it connects with our everyday lives. And, at the same time, it can reduce the distance between the audience and the art, inviting audiences to be more critical of and engaged with the representations. Art and artists are (partially) removed from their pedestals. As such, the Whitney participates in a critical reevaluation of representations of the West and of the art museum itself. We can sense in this space western ghosts' ethical call for more complex ways of seeing and feeling the West. In tracking the changes to the museum over decades, we are well positioned to note the Whitney's deeper engagement with arguments about the West and its representation and to acknowledge the museum's participation in changing modes of museal display.

These changes became more pronounced in 2020 and 2021. Writing in the BBCW member magazine, *Points West*, the Whitney's curator Karen B. McWhorter outlines important revisions in the museum responsive to the "dual crises" of COVID-19 and "growing international dialogue about social justice."[37] During the pandemic-enforced lull in visitors to both the BBCW and the Whitney, the Whitney staff redesigned the introduction to the museum. The walls leading into the space are now painted a strong red. On the left, the museum briefly narrates its own history and urges us as visitors to reflect on how the displayed art might influence our perception of the West. The right wall offers ways for "Connecting with the Art in the Whitney." This section acknowledges that most of the artwork in the collection and displayed was produced by white men: "Though women artists are represented in the gallery, most artwork on view was created by men. And while some work of Native artists and artists of color is exhibited, most was created by artists of European descent." The text continues, "The museum staff is actively working to broaden the range of stories and points of view in the Whitney." Finally, "the museum staff seeks to acknowledge and address difficult subjects more clearly," inviting us to contact the curators with questions and ideas.

Pressed by calls for racial justice, given space by the absence of visitors during the pandemic to make changes to the museum, the Whitney continues to evolve. The museum has added work by white women (including *Naomi* by June Glasson) and Native women (*White Buffalo Reborn* by Julie Buffalohead [Ponca Tribe, Oklahoma]). The Whitney currently highlights the work of contemporary artists in the upstairs Grainger Gallery—though of course we notice that the contemporary and often critical art requires a walk up the stairs away from the main body of the center. And the museum is more explicitly fostering critical conversations in the ways it displays the art with revised ordering, updated placards, and efforts to teach us to view art more critically.

Despite these changes—changes that in our judgement make the museum more interesting and compelling—the Whitney's fundamental commitment to a specific vision of the West remains firm. Indeed, the gallery's new complexity offers a more compelling, more affectively powerful argument for seeing and feeling the West as a site of Euro American heroism and strength. Sure, that heroism is dented. Scholder's jaundiced view of Custer, Mardon's reenvisioning of the Battle of Greasy Grass, Roll-Preissler's parodic takedown of the cowboy, and Hyde's veneration of Plains Indian relationship to nature all urge audiences to see the dissonance in white western culture. The museum uses this dissonance to create affective tension. The resolution of this tension can be deeply pleasurable, making the (represented) sublimity throughout the museum even more desirable, more affectively captivating.

Woven into the Whitney, as into the BBCW, then, are the two forms of haunt. We can approach the ghosts we know are part of this home; we can look at them askew; and we can take in the pleasure associated with viewing these shades. We can do all of this by briefly viewing the contents of our repressed memory. But then we turn to the sublime, which is all the more sublime in the context of a ghostly scare we may have felt in the face of Scholder's Custer or Roll-Preissler's *Western Man with Beer and Dog*. We push these ghosts back into the corners or we leave them behind as we move from the Whitney's entrance to its commanding conclusion. Representation of the sublime, along with Buffalo Bill's/the BBCW's (and by extension, white masculinity's) affectively powerful telling of the story of the West, resecures our reverential relationship to the western landscape. We do not just instinctively follow Buffalo Bill along the back trail in the BBM, nor do we adopt a reverential perspective in the PIM without prompting. Cody's authoring voice returns, again and again, to guide our understanding of the West. In sum, the Whitney urges a particular mode of looking, one that simultaneously fascinates and frightens, as it invokes the ghosts of the American West.

6

Constructing the Master Naturalist

THE FIFTY-MILE DESCENT from the east entrance of Yellowstone National Park into Cody, Wyoming, is, by the standards of the West, short. But the scenery is breathtaking. Deep canyons, a rushing river that has carved caves in the rocks over millennia, rising mountains, jutting cliffs, and soaring eagles vied for our attention as we guided our rental car around the sharp curves. In our four visits as researchers to Cody, and as it was named at the time, the Buffalo Bill Historical Center, we had never arrived at the BBHC from the east entrance of Yellowstone, but rather via our typical route from Fort Collins, Colorado. On one of our journeys, we took the extra time to drive from the BBHC to the east entrance of the park and back again. Journeying through rustic mountainsides, around blue-toned lakes, and past bighorn sheep grazing along the western roadside, we arrived back at the Draper Museum of Natural History—the most recent of the five museums of the BBHC—having traversed the ecological wonders of nature. We had experienced the gusting winds and voluminous skies—skies complete with moving clouds that rustled up like cowboy dust upon the rugged land.

We were quiet during our drive back to the Draper, for there were vast landscapes, wild animals, and the hypnotic intrigue of nature to attend to, seen mostly from behind the protective glass of our car. This trip down the mountain to the museum functioned like a transformative channel that moved us from a shared atmospheric awe of nature in the great outdoors to the wonderment of a haunting nature (re)created in the great indoors.[1] Perhaps, as we have been discussing throughout this book, this trip was a transformation of the haunt and haunting spirit of the American West materialized across time and space. As we experienced the humility of having immersed ourselves in the sublimity of nature, a basic question became central to our journey at the Draper, both outdoors and indoors: What is our connection with nature?[2] This question is at the heart of the museum's mission. The Draper is designed "to encourage responsible natural resource stewardship by promoting increased understanding of and appreciation for the relationships binding humans and nature in the Greater Yellowstone Region."[3] Its rhetoric emphasizes "stewardship" of the earth's resources, urging us to see the earth as ours to control and use (fig. 18).

Figure 18. Exterior view of the Draper Museum of Natural History. Photograph by Brian L. Ott.

More specifically, the Draper is an epistemological and ontological machine working to produce what we term *master naturalists* through the rhetorical modes of directed movement and simulated environments. Crucially, the museum's rhetorical modes emphasize place over time, producing the master naturalist as an ahistorical (yet haunted) subject position and, in so doing, derailing critical engagement with the institution.

As we detail throughout this chapter, the master naturalists' subject position activates an ahistorical stance for the everyday visitor, yet allows for a performed mastery into the haunts of the wonders of (re)created nature, including safe glances into the dwellings of nonhuman animals or the otherwise often unexperienced haunts of nature. By engaging the (re)created haunt of the Draper through the master naturalist position, we, the visitors, are called to get closer to the land, closer to nature and all it symbolically offers, and ultimately, closer to the haunting spirit of the American West.

As we attempt to understand our connection to nature, the master naturalist position allows for insight into the character and ethos (or *éthea*) of our relationship to the land and animals, "since the word originally designates 'the places where animals are usually found.'"[4] In using the "Iliadic simile of the horse" along with "the power of habituation," Charles Chamberlain reminds us that "the horse longs to be in his éthea, feels pain at being locked at the manger and joy upon breaking free" while demonstrating the evolving path of "the development from 'animals' haunts' to 'character.'"[5] "As the adjective étheios shows, one's éthea form an arena or range in which the animal naturally belongs," or as Chamberlain further emphasizes in the development of the word by referring to the poems of Hesiod, "the places where human beings are found."[6] Perhaps somewhere between the places of animals (and land or the larger environment) and humans is the understanding of our connection to nature. Additionally, in looking at the poems of Theognis, Chamberlain assesses that "éthos refers to the range or arena where someone is most truly at home and which underlies all the fine appearances that people adopt."[7] As we will demonstrate, the Draper, in its (re)creation of nature and its animal and climatic habitats, positions the visitor into the role of the master naturalist, all the while (re)evoking an (un)natural atmosphere of awe and wonder, so that the stewardship of the western haunt and its haunting can be with us both during our visit to the Draper and in spirit thereafter.

The phrase "master naturalist" invokes quite precisely a way of seeing the world that constantly reminds us that not only is the world ours to use but nature is also defined by the master naturalist.[8] Understanding the Draper depends on recognizing that nature and culture are dialectically related, depending on each other for their meaning. The Draper positions visitors as the fulcrum of this dialectical relation even as the museum itself embodies the struggle it implies. This positioning resonates with the anthropological framework produced by the PIM's anthropologist we analyzed in chapter 4. In fact, we continue to trace the ways the Draper and the PIM intersect formally and stylistically. This intersecting should not surprise us since the dialectic between nature and culture is very much alive in the PIM, just as it is in the Draper.

In the Draper Museum of Natural History, the material resolution of this struggle depends on the museum's placeness. It is not simply that the museum arranges place—it clearly does that—but that the museum privileges place over time: the museum is a site about place. That the museum would engage us in a pedagogy of place should not be surprising. As a natural history museum dedicated to explaining a particular region's nature, the Draper emphasizes the place of nature. More, however, it privileges place over time (history or change) and sutures the master naturalist into an unchanging relation to space. Indeed, the Draper not only engages in questions of space but privileges space over time to the degree that time is erased.

Erasing time is odd in a museum in which history (or the understanding of change over time) is a part of its title. The museum refuses to think hard about change over time in two ways. The first is that, unlike nearly every other natural history museum in the United States or Europe, this museum is nearly silent on evolution. In fact, as Stephen T. Asma notes, since the rise of Darwinian evolutionary science, natural history museums have taken studying and representing evolutionary change as a core mission.[9] Yet, evolutionary change does not enter the Draper in any significant way. Here the place of Yellowstone takes precedence, even though—clearly—the place and its living things evolved just as did all the other parts of the globe. Since our focus in this book is on the rhetorical invitations to cultural identity, we do not linger on this science pedagogy oddity even as we acknowledge that digging more deeply into the ways science is presented in the museum is a worthy and important endeavor.[10]

The museum also refuses to think carefully or hard about the changes to the nonhuman world wrought by the invasion of Euro Americans in the Great Plains and Rocky Mountains over the past two hundred years and the political, ethical, or environmental consequences of these changes. This disjuncture between the "history" of the title and the "timelessness" of the museum serves as the point of entrance into the museum's rhetoric, the role of memory in the latter, and, more broadly, the rhetorical consequentiality of this spatial privileging. As we maintain, privileging place over time can have the function of derailing critical engagement with the topics at hand by dehistoricizing, naturalizing and, thus, depoliticizing the concerns raised within the space. In privileging place over time, the Draper captures, slows, even stops, time; in so doing the museum hides or covers the ways human agency is always remaking the "natural" world.

This effacing of time is central to Michel de Certeau's distinction between "place" and "space." For de Certeau, place halts change, setting ideas and concepts along with stones, trees, animals, and people into an "instantaneous configuration of positions."[11] As compared to place, "a space exists when one takes into consideration vectors of direction, velocities, and time variables. . . . Space occurs as the effect produced by the operations that orient it, situate it, temporalize it, and make it function in a polyvalent unity of conflictual programs or contractual proximities. . . . In contradistinction to the place, it has thus none of the univocity or stability of a 'proper.'"[12] Where place is settled and stabilized, space—as "practiced place"—emphasizes time. Instead of instantaneous positions, space is the performance of trajectories and movements.[13] We can think of place as offering a set of resources or a grammar out of which users produce their own meanings or produce space.[14] The function of place is to solidify time and history and, in so doing, to solidify subjectivity, or, put differently, to suture the subject into carefully constructed material narratives that limit agency. As we argue in the rest of this chapter, the Draper is a place that limits our agency with regard to itself and its rhetoric, while offering the position of the master naturalist as a subject position with nearly unfettered agency in regard to the natural world. This agency of the master naturalists, within the museum, situates an ahistorical resting place, a highly symbolic haunt, imbued with the deeply haunting spirit of the American West.

As the foregoing discussion suggests, the relations between place and time are intertwined. One may move through a place and consistently and constantly resist the demands for "proper" action (just as one can speak in ways that consistently break grammatical rules, whether due to not being aware of the rules, out of resistance to the rules, or because different rules apply). On the other hand, one can move through a place in much the way the place's structures enable. In so doing, the actions (in time) work to restabilize the place itself. Some places work more assiduously to contain and restrain such action while others are more "open" to spatializing and temporalizing action. Those places determined to fully structure movement offer a materialized narrative that, to paraphrase de Certeau, turns animals into taxidermized objects of study and humans into cadavers.[15]

In precisely this way—of narrating places in and through "death"—we can begin to imagine that we can "possess" the natural, Western world. At least since the Renaissance, European epistemologies have been deeply connected with the desire to possess.[16] This desire for possession often is expressed in an aesthetic that destroys the subjectivity of an "other," turning others into objects.[17] While representational strategies that turn others into objects serve numerous crucial rhetorical functions, for us the most important are the ways objectification allows viewers to imagine "possessing" those represented. As we have already argued, especially in our discussion of the BBM and the PIM, possessing others can take a serious emotional toll, especially if the violence central to the possession is repressed, not recognized. And, so, the act of possession must somehow be hidden.

Stephen Greenblatt, in his reading of early modern travel narratives—and in particular his reading of Columbus's journals and letters—argues that discourse of the marvelous and of wonder serves the function of hiding the violence of possession.[18] While a recognition of wonder and marvel could serve as a way for medieval and early modern European travelers and commentators to recognize in themselves the differences confronted in the new world, wonder more often was a way of creating a profound break or boundary between Europeans and the people, lands, and animals encountered in the Americas.[19] This "wonderful" break makes the Other fantastic—meaning both astonishing and a fantasy that is somehow unreal—and in so doing makes it available for possession and control.

This early modern representational mode corresponds directly to modern and early modern thinking about space and spatiality. As feminist geographer

Doreen Massey argues, one of modernity's characteristics is to turn space into a surface of representation that sutures static relationships into seemingly unchanging interconnections.[20] Modernity's transformation of space into surface underlies the particularly pernicious form of settler colonialism in the United States. Roxanne Dunbar-Ortiz argues that settler colonialism was wedded to a strong form of private property that relied on and made possible land ordinances produced in the late eighteenth century. These land ordinance maps and practices abstracted the land—including the people, animals, plants, and minerals in and on the land—into modernist, apparently rational grids. Thus, nature became little more than empty space, carved into rectangles, and given away to white settlers.[21] In this way, modernity turned others—human and nonhuman alike—into representational objects. Sometimes they were objects of wonder and curiosity, other times of fear and loathing. In all cases, this objectifying perspective undergirded the European and then Euro American involvement in settler colonialism, chattel slavery, and the destruction of nature.

The marvelous possession Greenblatt identifies in Columbus's journals can be read as a historical grounding for nineteenth- and twentieth-century spectacular imaginations of nature.[22] In the zoos of the nineteenth-century capitals of Europe and the United States and in institutions like the American Museum of Natural History in New York City, we see the appearance of captured (in zoos) and dead (in natural history museums) animals.[23] Donna Haraway, writing about the interaction between the taxidermized animals and the viewer in the American Museum of Natural History's Great Hall of Africa, notes, "The animals in the dioramas have transcended mortal life, and hold their pose forever, with muscles tensed, noses aquiver, veins in the face and delicate ankles and folds in the supple skin all prominent."[24] Crucially, the transcending of mortal life is also a "transcendence" of time. It is the forever-ness of the animal's pose— or, differently, the arresting of change—that allows the taxidermized animal to transcend life and, at the same time, to become wonderfully spectacular.[25]

In the European desire to possess lands, people, and animals outside of Europe, a vision of wonder covered over the violence of colonization in part by placing the Other in a timeless, deep past. In colonizing time, museums can visually and materially represent the colonization of peoples and lands even as they claim to understand and explain them. It is in this sense that museums can be place and memory machines that teach audiences not only particular details about the museum's apparent subject but also about time and space, agency and power. In our analysis of both the PIM and the Whitney, we explored the powerful ways museums can stabilize time while offering deep cultural histories for the nation. The Draper remembers nature as a mode for securing white identity in both the natural and cultural worlds. As we highlight in the coming analysis, by turning nature into an ahistorical object and paving constructed engagements of the master naturalist (the visitor) in an emic wandering within a reconstituted space of atmospheres of wonder and awe, the Draper inscribes nature in terms of exchange value. The narrative flow of the museum leads the audience from untouched nature to nature as a resource for wealth production. Throughout, nature remains timeless and unchanging as well as ripe for interpellating us into master naturalists who become the stewards of the essential haunt and its lingering hauntings.

INTO AND THROUGH THE MUSEUM

Though we had visited Cody and the BBHC (now BBCW) in years past and had often considered the location of the museum within the striking landscape of the West, we had never approached the museum from Yellowstone National Park to the west. Our travels had consistently brought us into the town through the wide-open spaces of central Wyoming. But, during our third trip, we realized we could not adequately understand how one might see the Draper without also experiencing the route to and from Yellowstone. And, so, we headed up the canyon into the high Rocky Mountains. This trip, of course, was structured by our past visits to Cody but also by our childhood memories of coming to Yellowstone, seeing grizzlies, bison, and Old Faithful.

Our journey was also influenced by our knowledge that this park was the first—and remains one of the grandest—national parks. On March 1, 1872, President Ulysses S. Grant signed the bill setting aside more than two million acres under the protection and control of the secretary of the interior, who was charged with protecting the land against destruction and maintaining it for the benefit of "all people."[26] While the explicit goal of the bill and the subsequent founding of the National Parks Service in 1916 was the preservation of wilderness, one of the major proponents of the Yellowstone National Park was the Northern Pacific Railway. In the late nineteenth century the Northern Pacific was completing its tracks across Montana to the West Coast. The railroad's owners immediately recognized the advantage a major tourist destination like Yellowstone would give to train travel. Yellowstone, even as it was protected from logging, mining, and other extractive uses of the land, soon came to serve as a key tourist site.

The park remains so to this day. Attracting over three million visitors a year, Yellowstone is one of the most heavily visited national parks and one of the most significant tourist destinations in the United States.[27] Visits to Yellowstone inform nearly all tourist visits to northwestern Wyoming and southwestern Montana. Indeed, the park is one of the main reasons why tourists visit Cody, the BBCW, and, by extension, the Draper. As much as the visits to the BBCW are influenced by vast plains and the rising foothills of central Wyoming, the BBCW and perhaps in particular the Draper need to be understood within an experiential landscape of Yellowstone.

Not only does Yellowstone draw people to Cody but Yellowstone and the national parks as a whole form the discursive, visual, and material context of the museum. As Richard Grusin argues in his book about Yosemite, Yellowstone, the Grand Canyon, and US national parks in general, national parks work to produce nature as a purified essence, distinct or separate from culture or society or technology, while simultaneously reproducing it as part of a complex and heterogeneous network of scientific, cultural, social, technological practices. From this perspective, Yellowstone comprises not just the natural objects and artifacts that one finds within the boundaries of the park but also their representation and reproduction in the photographs, stereographs, paintings, prints, maps, illustrations, guidebooks, laws, and scientific accounts that help to perpetuate the park and enable it to circulate within the heterogeneous social, cultural, scientific, and political networks that make up America at any particular given moment.[28]

To this list of "artifacts" that make up Yellowstone, we would include the Draper. In this sense, the boundary between the Draper and Yellowstone is hazy.[29] The blurring of boundaries is a clue to the museum's technology, for the museum consistently questions the relationships between inside and outside, the real and the simulated, nature and culture.

Out of the Park, into the Museum

From the grand entryway of the BBCW, we took an acute left down a long passageway into the Draper. Upon entering the Draper from the main floor entrance of the BBCW, we began to negotiate our expectations of what we believed the museum might be like with our actual experience of walking into the museum—perhaps in the process, we mistakenly privileged an emphasis on the term natural over the term museum found on the entrance sign. One of us commented on the dark aesthetic of the entrance hallway, which did not have much natural light thereby revealing an expectation that the museum might have had an airier, open-light aesthetic than it did. Another of us commented on how the colors of the entrance sign suggest early on in the journey the color scheme such as one might expect to experience throughout a natural history museum (i.e., varying shades of rich and/or deep blues, greens, browns, and reds). The entrance hallway's brown-hued, tiled floor mimics the rugged layout of a rocky terrain; the tiles are of varying sizes and shapes, and they have been left a little rough to mimic the roughness of a nature trail. Some of the tiled pieces flow in grayish blues, (re)creating the appearance of walking near a winding stream, an experience constituted in the visit to Yellowstone as we took a break from our rental vehicle and stood along a rushing river in nature's wind.

The trail leads us to two room-sized, side-by-side cabins on the right and a taxidermized tableau of pack horses on the left. The second cabin serves as a classroom for arranged tours, and seldom engages other visitors to the museum. The first cabin, however, located near the very beginning of the trail, situates the interpretive framework for understanding and imagining the role of master naturalist. In this cabin, we are informed that resident naturalist B. A. Ware is out in the field (fig. 19). In his absence, we are encouraged to explore the tools of the trade housed in the cabin. Immediately, one begins the educational journey by attending to the described role of the naturalists—to learn scientific names and identifications of plants, minerals, animals, and fossils as well as why these elements exist and what they mean to humans. This foundational rhetoric also appears at the museum's entrance: "The Draper Natural History Museum promotes increased understanding of and appreciation for the relationships binding humans and nature in the American West. With the primary emphasis on the greater Yellowstone area, the museum explores and interprets the ways nature and human cultures influence one another."[30] In front of the cabin is the first of several stamp machines that allow us to impress a passport-style stamp into a guidebook. The "Yellowstone Adventure" has officially begun, and it is an adventure that is legitimated by constant educational content and motivated by a central question asked in a cabin placard: "Why do we explore nature?"

Figure 19. B. A. Ware's cabin with trail sign. Photograph by Eric Aoki.

128 Chapter 6

To this question the cabin offers five answers and thus encodes five ways of understanding nature: (1) as a way of knowing; (2) for finding new riches; (3) for expanding our world; (4) for living; and (5) for inspiration. Oddly, we are differently invited to join in these five projects. The placards offering nature up for scientific exploration and artistic inspiration are written in the third person, removing the reader from direct address. Apparently, visiting the museum may teach us about but not involve us in science and inspiration. However, we are actively invited to join in the three projects of wealth extraction, curiosity fulfillment (a project that is related to, but different from that of science), and consumer exploitation of the land. While the scientist seeks knowledge and the artist seeks inspiration, we are invited to imagine the natural world for very direct exchange value. These five motives structure our ways of looking and knowing. The museum rhetorically encodes these ways of knowing through directed movement and the celebration of simulated environments working to produce the master naturalist.

Directed Movement

Throughout this book we have been interested in embodied movement, and it remains a focus in this chapter. That being said, movement works differently in the Draper than in the other museums of the BBCW. As the three of us debriefed after our visit, we each commented on the centrality of directed movement in this museum compared to the other four. One of us noted how, unlike the BBM, there is not as much freedom to "zigzag" from exhibit to exhibit. Indeed, the Draper is even more insistent than the Whitney, which fosters a particular *rhythm* of movement, on directing our movement and determining the order and pace for experiencing the museum. This kind of difference almost always piques the interest of rhetorical and communication critics. Why is this museum different from that one? What are the differing rhetorical invitations, differing spatial experiences, differing ethical considerations this difference makes? We pause on this difference not only because we are trained to but because difference is nearly always (intentionally or not) meaning-making. We seek patterns and we pause on the changes in patterns. Since visitors move among the museums, their differences matter. Just as we will return in the conclusion to wondering why the PIM and the Draper are the darkest of the museums at the BBCW, here we reflect on how and why the Draper directs our movement so carefully.

The Draper directs us through a spatial experience of descending elevation habitats, a top to bottom orientation, or alpine to the plains/basins movement. The directedness of the movement through the space is first introduced at B. A. Ware's cabin. In front of it is a trail sign, much like a sign that we would see in any national forest. The sign points museumgoers in the right direction, names the trail ("Expedition Trailhead"), and notes the type of movement to be expected (alpine-to-plains). B. A. Ware's cabin teaches us that we are in nature for a purpose; it "directs" our gaze, as the trail sign indicates that our embodied movement through the space will be similarly directed. It is this careful orchestration of movement through the museum that most thoroughly privileges space over time and that most carefully sutures the subject into a preferred spectoral relation to nature.

Following the alpine to plains/basins orientation, movement is directed so that we circle down through the museum's environments while "hiking" on a spiraling ramp.[31] The circular movement not only provides one with a sense of journeying along a mountain trail but also employs movement that mimics the roundness, and hence completeness, of such natural elements as the planet, the sun, and the moon, or the cycles of the seasons, thus emphasizing the natural in a culturally constructed space. In this sense, the space-time in the Draper may seem similar to the cycles of the seasons in the PIM. In chapter 4, we discussed how this cyclical approach to time can be felt as a mode of survivance, offering a temporality that actively resists Western progressive time. We also argued that the narrative of that exhibit and the museum as a whole offers this resistive temporality and then undercuts the resistance by demonstrating that Western time destroys Native time.

Here, however, circularity might be better understood as a spiral or a drill. Rather than experiencing a circularity that moves us from one spring to the next, we are following a drill that slowly but surely reveals powerful truths about our natural world—that the world is ours to study, understand, control, and use. This is more like the motion needed to drill water and oil wells than a temporality aligned with the rhythms of the more-than-human world around us. Thus, the spiral movement provides the museum with a narrative telos.[32] The museum, we contend, moves us from the deep past of the alpine meadows figured as a space outside of human intervention to the final exhibits emphasizing resource and wealth extraction. The epistemology of the master naturalist is produced through the movement from scientific observation of and curiosity fulfillment about the natural world to the use of the land for consumption and accumulation.

As we move past the cabin, out of the hallway, and into the top level of the museum, we are confronted with a complex, fascinating set of displays. Immediately in front of us is a set of scrims (to which we will return later in this chapter) that introduce us to the alpine environment with printed images of mountains and wildlife.[33] But, because we can see through and beyond the scrims, we also get our first vision of the whole museum. With a little movement around this mountaintop, we can get a bird's eye view of the complex. Just to make this masterful positioning as clear as possible, a few steps from the entrance we can look over a railing down into the center of the museum where, several stories below, we see a map of the greater Yellowstone region rendered in tile. This view from above offers a panoramic vision of the museum and, with the map standing in for the region (just as the museum does), offers us a classically modernist perspective of the world, all the while eliciting for the master naturalist atmospheric evocations of wonder and awe as well as continued movement and journey. Like de Certeau's visit to the top of the (now destroyed) World Trade Center and homologous with the eighteenth-century partitioning of land into abstract rectangles discussed by Dunbar-Ortiz, we are invited to see the world as a mappable space, an abstract vision of the natural world in which the natural world is made into a visible object designed for human uses.[34] Crucially, the subject position offered by the World Trade Center is that of the urban planner, one who creates the city as a place, structuring the inhabitants into roles useful for capitalism. Here, the urban planner is replaced by the master naturalist and a mapper of the nation. Where one role gazes on and structures the city, the other gazes on and structures nature, but both share the basic motivation of creating a place that determines agency and stops time. While we are not directly invited to share in the scientists' project, the museum possesses, embodies, and literalizes "objectivity."

After exploring this mountaintop scene, we necessarily move to our right to follow the descending, winding path from the timberline environment of small rodents and hardy birds into the more heavily forested lower elevations. Slowly, we are led downward, from the inhospitable mountain heights into increasingly comfortable parts of the wilderness. This downward descent also moves us from parts of the wilderness relatively untouched by humans (and not particularly useful economically) into images of interactions between humans and the wilderness. The theme of the journey shifts from scientific understanding of animals and plants to discussions about the controversial resurgence of wolves in the West and their conflict with ranchers, to the place of forest fires in the "natural" evolution of the forest and the human responses to fires, and finally, by the time we reach the plains, to images of barbed wire and oil derricks. The directed and embodied movement not only shifts us from high to low, from alpine to plains, but transports us from wilderness to civilization. In other words, the journey begins with civilization's understanding of wilderness in B. A. Ware's cabin, moves to the scientifically knowable, panoptic, but untamable mountaintop, through the forests down to the plain, and so back to civilization. As we move down the pathway, we move through the ways of seeing the natural world, shifting from nature observer to manager and tourist to user and extractor of natural resources.

Movement is also directed toward a stop that appears midway through the exhibition at the back of the complex, which invites individuals to explore the Seasons of Discovery Gallery. In this gallery, we are encouraged to literally see the light (as this area is one of two areas where natural light from outdoors filters into the museum) and to become better educated about animal migration patterns in the fall and hibernation and food storing practices in the winter. As noted in the Draper's "Explorer's Guide for Families," "spring is the time of the year that many naturalists and scientists go out into the field to observe, explore, and document spring activities," while "summer is the time of the year many people go out and play in nature. Hiking, camping, fishing, and swimming are all activities that people participate in during the summer."[35] This seasonal information adheres to the Draper's foundational mottos that "Exploration is a way of knowing!" and "Exploration is a way of living!" Just as importantly, it continues to divide the natural world into the cyclical experiences of the seasons as well as to segment the audience by both time and function—with scientists working in the frigid spring weather and tourists playing in the warmth of the summer.

In addition to the focus on animal and human engagement of the land and its resources through the seasons, a laboratory area, reading area, tent area, and cabin area remind us that to know about and to survive the seasons, we must understand nature. Additionally, this marked educational space makes clear the role of the scientist to help advance our understanding of nature, and hence, our relationship to it. The directed movement into this educational space works to imagine further the role of master naturalist, allowing us to mark our skills and learned knowledge more overtly in this designated space for learning. Finally, the "Please Touch" symbol (like in B. A. Ware's naturalist cabin) reminds us that to be curious and to engage the designated objects is a sanctioned and encouraged practice.

Simulated as Natural

The directed movement explored here moves visitors through simulated environments constructed of taxidermized animals, plasticized plants, and carefully rendered scenes of nature. It is a major rhetorical/material mode that privileges place over time. The simulated natural environment—wonderful in its technologies and the beauty of its renderings—performs the wonder that helps justify the possession of the land offered by the museum.

The Draper is a place where simulated and real becomes indistinguishable. What was once alive is now preserved in a state of taxidermy; what was once an authentic animal sound heard in nature has now been perfectly recorded and released into the new museum wild.[36] The scent of smoke indicates that something, perhaps the forest, is on fire while the burning orange neon lights help complete the visual experience of a fire off in the distance. Within a single visit to the museum, we can experience and become better educated on a vast array of nature's habitats and inhabitants. By the end of the Draper expedition, we will have journeyed through the alpine, mountain forest, and mountain meadow

132   Chapter 6

and aquatic environments, and down to the plains/basins environment. In each of these, the simulated and real cooperate to teach and (re)create a space where one is able to journey into many habitats in a brief amount of time.

These simulated environments participate in a double representational strategy. Writing about the representational technologies that first introduced mass audiences to Yellowstone in the nineteenth century, Richard Grusin argues that stereographic photographs were especially important. "These stereos operate according to a twofold logic of fidelity to nature, providing an accurate record or representation of the object photographed as well as an accurate reproduction of the experience or feeling of scientific experience."[37] If black-and-white images viewed through a stereographic viewer can hope to capture the experience of scientific discovery, the fully immersive (if simulated) environments of the museum can reproduce this experience even more compellingly. The simulated environments powerfully efface the real and the simulated and, in so doing, efface the distinction between the museum and nonmuseum experience. The museum's simulated displays serve as persuasive technologies in producing master naturalists.

As we journey the long, winding entrance hallway and hike past the two introductory cabins, we move toward an open rotunda area and somewhat circular museum space. This centralized area descends from the high alpine to the plains/basins environment. Prior to even reaching this central area of the (re) created environments, we can hear recorded animal sounds that appear to be coming from nature's animals that are now preserved in a state of taxidermy; the sounds, we soon learn, are controlled through several "explorer's listening posts of forest sounds." As we press buttons corresponding to animals in various environments, we hear the sounds of animals (perhaps even more distinctly than one might be able to hear within the rustlings of nature) as they walk from museal environment to environment, leaving us ripe for a dreamlike experiential blurring of bringing the outside, inside. For example, at the beaver pond one can hear the sounds of the boreal toad, red wing blackbird, and a beaver. The sounds of the animals are layered into the environments so that the imagined master naturalist becomes more competent in identifying and learning about what various animals sound like in nature.

Scrims, or digitally produced hanging photos, provide landscape and skyscape to the open and airy space of the Draper. While providing visual context for each of the natural environments, the scrims are sheer, allowing us to both imagine the depicted landscape and see through them to more distant exhibits within the museum. The scrims also help to distract one's attention away from the ramp railings and the more obvious "human-made" spiraling ramp used to descend into the various environments, as we focus on these digitized photos.

It is a mistake to think these simulated environments as "virtual" or as directly opposed to reality or real experience. As is most obviously the case in the forest fire display, they offer fully embodied experiences and, in this sense, real fragments of the natural world. From the moment we enter the alpine display at the top of the museum, the burnt umber of the forest fire displayed several yards away is faintly visible. The color is not strong enough to capture our full attention, serving instead as a background to the nature scenes immediately in front of us. But as we navigate down from the alpine heights, the ambient light lowers and the orange of the fires become more apparent and central. Approaching the display, the induced atmospheric sounds of a roaring fire begin to drown out the chirps of birds and squeaks of chipmunks. Most evocatively, however, as the fire's colors and sounds begin to predominate, we begin to smell the conflagration.

By the time we enter this display, we are surrounded by images of burning fires, crackling sounds, and the smell of smoke. Information boards detail how early firefighting was not as sophisticated as today's methods, how wildfires are a natural process, and how "Today Wildland Fires Are Fought Like Military Campaigns." In this smoke scented area, there is a black-and-white life-size photo of an old firefighter, placed next to a model of a contemporary firefighter outfit.[38] Several information boards declare that a big western fire is not a natural disaster but a normal event, that only individuals can prevent forest fires, and that there is one forest with many uses. As we walk out of the fire section, there is an information board that says, "A new forest is born." There are three billboards in this area, which inform us that the forest grows, the forest enters middle-age, and a new forest is born. As the "Explorer's Guide for Families" further details, "eighty percent of the trees within Yellowstone National Park are lodgepole pine trees. Lodgepole pine trees have cones that depend on fire to open and release their seeds."[39] In the presence of a simulated fire, which poses no material threat, it becomes easier to understand how fires can be controlled for safety and yet comprehend that wildfires are also a natural process. Moreover, visitors have in some small way experienced the fire's sound, smell, and color. With this "experience" in place, visitors can become competent participants in a conversation about the role of fire in managing forests: in short, they can engage in the position of the master naturalist.

Simulated Tensions

The fire display—with its sounds, colors, images, and smells—points to a larger set of tensions within the museum between the real and the fake. Reflecting the contemporary moment of aesthetic, economic, and political consumptions of faux fur, faux Prada bags, faux Dolce & Gabbana sunglasses, and faux home countertop finishes, the Draper materializes simulated (re)presentations of nature in real time. Within the immediate borders of the museum, the journey does not function as the actual experience of engaging nature or the natural

134 Chapter 6

as one might do outside; rather, as we argued earlier, it involves "substituting signs of the real for the real itself; that is, an operation to deter every real process by its operational double, a metastable, programmatic, perfect descriptive machine which provides all the signs of the real and short-circuits all its vicissitudes."[40]

For example, the taxidermized animals central to the displays are frozen into a liminal state, where time itself stands still; they are not strictly real or fake but rather caught somewhere betwixt and between.[41] The taxidermized animals function in the museum like the stereographic photographs of Yellowstone in the nineteenth century. The stereographic image seems to have a real or analogical relation to the object photographed. Clearly, the stereograph is not the same as the object and yet there is some real relation that inheres between the stereograph and the object, and importantly, seems to place the viewer in the midst of the depicted nature. This strange relation is even more strongly felt with taxidermized animals. The beavers, bears, mountain lions, and birds that inhabit the museum once inhabited the natural world. The beaver building the dam in the museum may once have built dams on the rivers in Yellowstone. This dead, stuffed, but action-posed animal embodies the memories of nature, offering these memories of the real to us. It is very precisely this morbid mnemonic relation embedded in the dead animal that most completely realizes the museum's technological production of the master naturalist.

Significantly, however, we do not simply view the animals from afar but rather are walking among the creatures and within their environments. In this way, the Draper's exhibits are an advance over those described by Haraway in the American Museum of Natural History. In that museum, the audience and the dioramas are separated by glass. Between the visitor and the diorama, Haraway writes, "there is no impediment to this vision, no mediation. The glass front of the diorama forbids the body's entry, but the gaze invites his visual penetration. The animal is frozen in a moment of supreme life, the man is transfixed. No merely living organism could accomplish this act."[42] In the Draper, the "glass fronts" come down and we seem to walk in and among the animals, the birds, and their natural settings. Thus, the "communion" between the dead animal and the living human is even greater, even more wonderful, even closer to the atmosphere of the outside, allowing for the haunting spirit of this magnificent haunt, where place is privileged over time, to do its necessary work.

Although the sensory content of the Draper echoes real nature, we are never fully vulnerable to the powerful vicissitudes of nature itself. Perhaps the variability of experience is disrupted within the cultured space of the museum because "man" is in control of its contents.[43] As visitors, we are allowed to observe and interact safely within hyperreality while standing face-to-face with animals and elements of the taxidermized wild and their simulated habitats. Visitors to the museum are able to stave off the vulnerability inherent in actual experience where the primal instincts of animals to attack or protect and preserve their domain are suspended (at least as seen from our subjective stance); the animals are no longer life-threatening, except perhaps in the memory and imagination of the visitor.[44] Over the course of a visit, the veneer of a polished (re)presentation of nature's habitats may lose a bit of its luster as interpretive tensions between real and simulated become more pronounced and more apparent. Regardless, the museum experience sustains force by impressively (re)presenting that which we know exists outside of the museum's walls.

Crucial as well is the interaction between the wonder of the simulated environments and the spatiality of directed movements. The simulated environments—and the simulated tensions between danger and safety—depend on already dead animals and plants. But because their journey is so sharply constricted, the people traveling through these environments are not all that different from the animals. What we have, then, are people and simulated natural environments arranged into place where neither the animals nor the people are agents of change or subjects of history.

Thus, the simulated as we use it here is not an opposite of the real thing in real time. In fact, the simulated may engage or disengage from the materiality of visual consumption and experience. As Baudrillard asserts, "To dissimulate is too pretend not to have what one has. To simulate is to feign to have what one doesn't have. One implies a presence, the other an absence."[45] And, perhaps because the museum is caught somewhere in between these processes of interpretation, the implications and material consequences of the simulated become central to understanding the erasure of the real.

In the examples that follow, we illustrate how and where the simulated articulates simultaneously a tension of presence and absence. Following the Draper's prescribed path, we are visually invited to walk, literally, toward the light (i.e., the natural light, in one of its rare appearances, filtering in from the great outdoors) and toward the enormous sculpted bronze bison falling over a ledge. The indoor cliff, the interior museum wall, and the architectural dig in the pit below provide an authenticity and pedagogical force to simulate the fall, particularly as the trees sway and the sky changes color just outside the borders of the museum's windows. As the environmental elements outside give light and backdrop to the bronze bison exhibit inside the museum, we are asked to see the two spaces and the scene's contents as one and the same—a moment caught within simulation. In approaching this simultaneously real-simulated scene it becomes clear that the simulated gestures toward the real via the accoutrements of aesthetics and design and through its invitation into a moment of visual delight—a bronze bison defying gravity while frozen in the penultimate moment of the scene's resolution.

136   Chapter 6

An information placard placed near the sculpture (which is titled *Bison Jump*) reads, "Once nearly exterminated the bison has become a symbol of North America, especially the American West." Photos of the sculpture and educational information on how young Native American men imitated sounds of lost bison calves to draw the bison to the ledge only to scare the herd from behind to drive it over the cliffs actively invite us into the imagined position of the master naturalist or, in concert with the PIM, the anthropologist. Standing below the simulated fall of the bison/bronze sculpture and beside the informative placard telling of the symbolic importance of the bison of the American West, we are asked to reconcile their positionality in resolving the loss of or threat to bison. The more you look and learn, the more active the position of master naturalist is refined through the historical (re)telling of the bison jump practices. Despite the strengthening of this position, we continue to simultaneously access the safety that lies within the simulated—a similar type of simulated outcome that works to make faux furs, for example, pronounced in aesthetics yet simultaneously stripped of the vulnerable consequences of association with reality, in this case, the real danger in performing bison jump practices in real time.

At the same time, even as the placard acknowledges the near extinction of the bison, the visually imposing image of the bison falling off the cliff is embedded in the narrative of Native American hunting and uses of the bison. The dramatic fall of the bison paired with the abstracted narrative of "near extinction" leads us to imagine that Native American practices were at least part of the reason for the bison's near-death experience. In this way, the changes wrought by Euro American colonizers are held at a double remove from us. First, the rapacious hunting of the bison by whites is hidden behind the scrim of a "once upon a time" narrative. Second, the visual and material wondrousness of the sculpture and of the animal it memorializes overwhelms the plainly stated, verbal message of loss. The bison, their near extinction, and the social relations that motivated and justified the mass killings are hidden behind a fairytale story and a powerfully moving image.

Further accentuating the tension between real and simulated is the exhibit addressing the wolves in the greater Yellowstone region. As an informative placard asks, "Is there room for wolves? Wolves are large predators that impact their environment and are impacted by it. People often portray wolves as 'good' or 'bad' animals. Nature, however, does not place value judgments on wolves or other creatures. Scientists work to understand how wolves interact with their environment, but policy makers determine if and how we will share that environment with wolves. Please share your opinions about wolves or other wildlife issues with us. Is there room for wolves in the greater Yellowstone region? Is there room for wolves?" (fig. 20).

Figure 20. Wolf exhibit at the Draper museum. Photograph by Brian L. Ott.

Inside a glass display, about twenty or so selected notes respond to the question above, including the following responses: "Yes there is room for wolves. They are an important part of the ecosystem and must be preserved and protected." "No, they kill all the elk. They are evil." "No, we don't need wolves to kill our livestock." "I am a hunter who supports the reintroduction of all natural wildlife. The good Lord put them here for a reason." Despite the educational strength and variety of the responses, the (re)presentation of wolves through taxidermy and media images takes on its own simulation of nature, devoid of any immediate threat and perhaps even imbued with an enhanced fascination with the animals. Within this simulated habitat, and even outside of it, the wolves are controlled by humans. In the offered written responses and within the placard that structures the debate, visitors are inscribed into the imagined position of master naturalist who can help reconcile the debate: "Please share your opinions about wolves or other wildlife issues with us."

Although the imagined position accentuates a tenet of exploration as noted in B. A. Ware's cabin—"Exploration is a way of knowing!"—it does not fully capture an underlying narrative of exploration as a way of structuring the power relations between humans and animals. In this case, however, the debate, as centered within the simulated habitat and within the presence of simulated on-looking

138 Chapter 6

wolves, works to potentially move the master naturalist into a state of final resolution. Even though the Draper's curators acknowledge the ongoing nature of the debate, there is no suggestion of how to actually address the issue, which contributes to the perception that the master naturalist's work has been done.

Upon arriving at the simulated beaver dam exhibit, we are enticed into the technological marvel of a life-size dam habitat. With godlike presence, we are able to stand above and see down into the underground habitat through a clear floor that illuminates the world of the busy taxidermized beaver. As we step down into the beaver dam habitat, television monitors inform us that "beavers stay busy all year long." Beavers, one learns, not only raise young and fell trees eight inches thick (the exhibit includes sounds of falling trees) but they also are given privileged position within nature: "Native Americans were perhaps the first to understand the ecological importance of the beaver, referring to this animal as the 'sacred center' of the land." The simulated habitat of the beaver dam manifests as a shrinelike presence in which we can pay homage to these sacred animals and their sacred spaces. The beaver dam is perhaps the most physically interactive of the animal exhibits in the Draper. For example, during one visit, a young child went in and out of the dam habitat numerous times while laughing and engaging the technology and aesthetic design of the habitat, tapping into the master naturalist exploratory tenets of "Exploration is a way of expanding our world!" and "Exploration is a way of living!" As we watched the child engage the beaver dam exhibit/simulated habitat, the exploration outcomes of curiosity and fun were apparent in the child's experience within this simulated habitat of a (re)created haunt that will likely continue to haunt.

Where the beaver dam invites us to experience nature as a scene of curiosity and fun, the final exhibits in the museum urge us to think about nature as a scene of wealth production. The simulated and highly nostalgic gas pump and windmill exhibit opens the concerns and debates surrounding land use. As noted in the exhibit, "Windmills helped pave the way for Euro-American settlers." The exhibit celebrates the pumping of deep underground water for settlers and livestock. While noting that "collaboration is better than conflict" as it explains how coal has been used to light the West, the exhibit raises questions, such as: How would you reduce our dependence on foreign oil? It also nods to the fact that some people call for oil conservation and alternative energy sources to reduce dependence.

Most powerful in this display, however, are the nostalgically rendered technologies of resource extraction and wealth production. A large wood-framed windmill, "staged materiality" of nostalgic inducement, serves as the visual centerpiece of the display (fig. 21).[46] The windmill, like the bison that looms above and behind the display, serves as visual trope for the West. Unlike the bison's connection to the deep past of the prairie and its role as a sacred animal for

Native Americans, the windmill speaks of the nineteenth- and early twentieth-century effort to wrest more intensive agricultural gain from the arid land. Seen from afar, the windmill signifies the presence of a farm or ranch, the rationalization of the land into lines of individual ownership, and the production of cattle, sheep, and grains. Emphasizing this rationalization of the land, next to the windmill is a display of barbed wire, a technology that profoundly shaped the plains over the last one hundred and fifty years.[47] Surrounding the windmill is a vintage Husky Oil sign, joined by images of coal mining. It is no mistake that this exhibit serves as the last display in the museum.[48] For all of the circularity and emphasis on the cycles of life and of the seasons in the hike down to the plains, in this final display we are sutured into a linear narrative of progress. Technology, the display asserts, allows humans to extract wealth and riches from the earth and, in exchange, humans tame, civilize, and rationalize the world.

Figure 21. Windmill at the Draper museum. Photograph by Brian L. Ott.

140   Chapter 6

Casting the changes wrought in the landscape by ranching, farming, drilling, and mining in a nostalgically imagined past has the crucial rhetorical effect of distancing us from the practices of destructiveness. By placing wealth extraction in the past, the museum removes the practices from the present, removing them in turn from critical analysis. Rather than historicizing the decisions about and struggles over the western landscape, the museum places them into a space that stops time and asserts that nature has, in some sense, always has been and thus always should be at the service of human needs. In short, rather than historicizing nature as wealth extraction and thus offering this way of seeing to revision, the museum naturalizes nature as exchange value, removing it from critical engagement. Put differently, the Draper Museum of Natural History naturalizes history by creating a place that stops time.

REMEMBERING NATURE

Early in this chapter we suggested that the curvilinear form of the alpine-to-plains trail was not circular like the seasons but spiral like a drill. As we have seen, the museum has literalized the metaphor. As we drill down into the depths of the museum, we finish with our contemplation of the impact of drilling—for water and oil—on the Yellowstone region. In 2018 the Draper added a new exhibit on golden eagles called *Monarch of the Skies*. Installed near the windmill, oil derrick, and barbed wire, the exhibit weaves Native American cultural artifacts, contemporary Draper-sponsored research on golden eagles, and the effects of human-influenced landscape change on the birds. The accompanying video—drawing on stirring western scenes and images of researchers clambering down cliffs to tag the birds—raises the issue of eagle survival and human landscape change.[49]

Here, obliquely, in a voice-over by the former museum curator, the museum wonders about the survival of the majestic golden eagle amid ranching, farming, and housing developments. By the time we arrive at this exhibit, we have learned our lessons well: as master naturalists, we can drill into the land and nature, change its patterns for human benefit, and then research the consequences.

The rhetorics of directed movement and simulated environments together produce the master naturalist, who has four major characteristics. First, this figure is an observer and explorer who can decipher nature's signs; second, the master naturalist makes these observations at little risk, as the bears do not bite and the fires do not burn; third, these safely rendered observations provide the master naturalist with the necessary resources for making decisions about the natural world; and fourth, the master naturalist's decisions will favor human control over the world and focus on human use and extraction of natural resources. In fact, this final characteristic most fully embodies the master naturalist's position: the master naturalist's job is to master nature.

The mastery of nature as offered to and by the master naturalist depends on the museum's privileging of space over time. The master naturalist is trained to see the land for its exchange value. But in offering a place outside of time and thus outside of social production, the museum represses the social nature of this exchange value. One of the crucial ways this repression is managed is through the technological and aesthetic simulation of the natural. This simulation at once offers and performs the marvelous, which, as Stephen Greenblatt argues, can serve the Western dream of possession.[50] The museum offers visitors—the newly minted master naturalist—a vision of the natural world that they can fully possess, which they have always already possessed, the possession of which is "naturalized" and mythologized through a displacement of time and history.

Crucially we and the museum perform this possession through directed movement, which necessarily implies movement through both time and space. And yet, at each turn, the museum (re)places the master naturalist in some slightly removed past, a past that is at once removed from the present by some years and yet, in the marvelous performance in/of the museum this past is also the present (as we have argued, memory is at once about the past and the present). In placing us either in a cosmically ordered present/past in the alpine meadows or in some moment in the nineteenth and twentieth centuries (through images of early forest fighting gear, narratives of the huge Yellowstone forest fires of 1988, and nostalgically rendered ordering of natural resources), the museum imagines time as a moment already gone. This spatialized past/present of the museum, then, refuses to engage in critical examination of the present/future, thus allowing the Draper as (re)created haunt to evoke a stabilized, essentialist, and perhaps practiced positionality to nurture, as master naturalists, the haunting spirit of the American West.

It is in this sense that the Draper is a history museum. It does not narrate a story of change over time; rather, it is imbued with the more common-sense version of history encoded in the phrase "it is history," meaning it is finished, gone, over, done. This doneness of history undermines the possibilities of agency or critical engagement. It is a shift, to paraphrase Roland Barthes, from lower-case "history" in which humans are agents of history to upper-case History in which History is turned into Nature.[51] Thus, the relationship between the master naturalist and the natural world is History. This subject position is, in some ways, like the taxidermized animals and plasticized plants: dead, static, but marvelously beautiful for all that.

The Draper is an indoor, built place that stories and simulates an outdoor, natural space. In doing so, it not only teaches us about the animals, processes, and environments of the greater Yellowstone Region but also shapes how we remember them. Unlike history or heritage museums such as the adjoining BBM and PIM, which remember specific people, events, or cultures, the Draper (re) collects the history of man's (the gendered language is intentional given the masculine character of the master naturalist) involvement with nature in one particular geographic region. Its rhetoric is so naturalized, however, that we are largely unaware that history is being told and memory is being activated. The invisibility of memory is due, in large part, to the highly structured organization of the museum and the way it directs our movement. The preservation of an essentialist notion of the natural haunt, outdoors and (re)created within and experienced through the master naturalist's positionality and agency, allows for the preservation of a particular place (the privileged haunt). It also allows for an invested stake in how the Draper directs our movement into a stewardship of how we know and remember nature.

Beginning as it does in the alpine area where human involvement with the land is minimal, if not absent, the Draper fosters a sense of space outside of time and a view of nature as ahistorical. Thus, as we trek down the path (which has itself been disguised as natural rather than manufactured) and modernity comes closer and closer into focus, museumgoers have passed, rhetorically, through space but not time. This is the inverse operation of most history museums, which move us temporally—chronologically—through the past. By the time we reach the bottom (not the end!) and the plains environment (a place not an event!), we hardly notice that the sounds, sights, and smells of nature, along with its sensuous atmospheres evoking awe, wonder, and journey, have steadily been replaced by windmills and gas pumps—both symbols of man's ability to harness nature for productive use. There is, in fact, very little nature at the ground level of the museum. It has been supplanted by man and modernity and situated as the spatial (and atemporal) outcome of the museum. In place of the biological changes described by evolutionary science, we get the naturalized march into modernity. In place of a deep understanding of biodiversity and the ways humanity's fate is linked with that of the beaver and Miller moth, we get the inevitability of water wells and oil derricks. Indeed, the final thing we encounter in the Draper is the tiled map of Yellowstone (fig. 22). There could be no clearer representation of man's desire to master space, to determine what is remembered and what is forgotten.

So, while the Draper is ostensibly a natural history museum, it really stories the history of man's involvement with nature, celebrating him as explorer and protector. Because this history is remembered spatially rather than temporally, however, it suggests that nature did not exist (or did not matter) when there were no humans present to study, enjoy, or use it. Though the alpine region appears to be space untouched by man, we arrive here having already been equipped with the master naturalist perspective proffered in B. A. Ware's cabin. The sounds and sights we encounter in this region exist, then, only because they have to be studied, gathered, and preserved by naturalists. Even here, where it is

Figure 22. Tiled floor of "Western" region at the Draper museum. Photograph by Brian L. Ott.

challenging for the museum to construct a human history of the space, human exploration is encoded. The objects and artifacts collected in this space refer not simply to their real-life counterparts but to the experience of discovery. In this way, this first exhibit of Yellowstone's environment reminds us that nature qua nature does not exist (or is unimportant) outside of human intervention. Nature makes the master naturalist possible and, of course, the master naturalist makes nature possible.

The master naturalist is the hero remembered and reenacted in this story. The master naturalist is not simply a role produced in the museum to be enacted elsewhere, it is also a role that is produced and enacted within the walls of the museum itself. Certainly, the museum would urge us to embody the values of the master naturalist when we leave this space to visit Yellowstone National Park so that in effect the haunting of the haunt and our master naturalist subject position can continue forth in its stewardship. The Draper in situ affords us the possibility of practicing and performing the role even as we learn about it. In fact, this is one of the powerful rhetorical consequences of memory places; they do not simply point outside of themselves to some other action, in some other place, at some other time. Instead, the site becomes a site of enactment and performance of the memories and the values memory encodes.

We have argued that the enforced, directed movement of the Draper is the embodied experience of place over time, that it is the movement of the master naturalist. We noticed and noted this enforced movement because it was so different from the invitations to movement in the BBCW's other museums. We want to reflect, however, on another crucial formal relationship between the Draper and the other four institutions. Of the five museums, the Draper and the PIM are by far the darkest of the spaces. The darkness of the Draper is striking considering that we come into it from the bright, sunlight mountainscapes of the Rocky Mountains. We have pictures of ourselves exploring the canyon between Yellowstone and Cody. We are all wearing sunglasses or squinting as the high-mountain air refracts the sunlight off water and stone. But this brightness is gone in the Draper. Here we are plunged into a dusk-like environment. The darkness, of course, helps the museum feel more immersive, focuses our attention on what is right in front of us or is highlighted by the designers via slightly brighter light. And yet.

And yet, the Draper and the PIM are the two museums that most directly imagine and image white domination. As a museum about the Yellowstone region, the Draper is about Euro American domination of the natural world. The PIM—though far more complicated in its rhetorical invitations than the Draper—is about the dispossession of Native Peoples from this very same land. We wonder: are these museums dark because the spaces desire us to locate ourselves in a deep and nearly unknowable past, a past that is hidden by the veil of time, a past that is nearly impossible to bring into the present? It is not surprising that the Draper's lowest level, with the windmill and the oil derrick, is also the brightest. Or, differently, do the museums wish to create a dreamlike setting that, while engaging, does not invite us to fully see or feel the loss of humans and animals or the destruction of nature? It seems to us that the darkness urges our bodies to *feel* these museums as particularly haunted and urges us to ignore that which we know in our bodies and our souls is present.

Just as haunted house movies are visually and tonally dark, so, too, are these museums. If we are prepared by our past, our histories, our knowledges, by our experiential landscapes, then we are invited to see the shades of our deeds and the ghosts we have created as necessary detritus to white domination. We sense here that we live on hallowed ground, ground that is not ours, ground on which we are interlopers, ground from which we have disposed those who more properly belong here. Here we confront yet again the multiple meanings of haunt. The land represented in the Draper is the proper haunt of Native Peoples. This is the haunt of the eagles and bears and pine trees. Meanwhile, in an act of self-deception, Euro Americans have framed this land as *their* proper haunt and imagine it as riven into squares and rectangles, its resources ripe for extraction, and its deep past honored and then interred.

7

New Modes of "How (Not) to See Guns" at the Cody Firearms Museum

When I was about nine years old, our family grocery store was held up at gunpoint. It was the only time in twenty-five years of ownership that our family went through something like this. I remember vividly seeing the gun pointed at my mother, brother, and me. I have not handled a gun since my youth.

—ERIC AOKI

In my second year as a hunter, I shot my first deer. It was both frightening and exhilarating. I was at very close range when I shot it, but I recall vividly that it would not die. I had to shoot it at point blank range in the head several times before it stopped moving. That experience soured my interest in hunting, and as I got older I increasingly declined my father's invitation to go on hunting trips. I would say that because I grew up around firearms, they seemed perfectly natural to me. I don't ever recall being frightened of them. But hunting just turned out to be something that held no personal pleasure for me.

—BRIAN OTT

My first thoughts about guns and my childhood have to do with toys. My parents were very careful about the toys they would let my sister and me have. My sister was not allowed to have Barbie dolls (though she certainly had dolls) and I was not allowed to have toy guns. All my friends on my block had toy guns—usually cap guns, but later, BB guns as well. The exception (for whatever reason) was that I could have and did have water guns. But cap guns (which I desperately wanted) were not allowed. My parents, as

I recollect, told me that I couldn't have a cap gun because they were too violent (would they use that word for a six-year-old?). Killing people was wrong, they said. Playing like you are killing people is also wrong.

—GREG DICKINSON

WHEN WE FIRST wrote about the Cody Firearms Museum in 2011, we argued that the "CFM works to replace (or at the very least repress) visitors' individual understandings of guns in favor of a universal (and universalizing) interpretation of them as inert objects of visual pleasure":

> As grown men whose childhood experiences with and relation to guns varied widely, we each came to the Cody Firearms Museum (CFM) and its primary object of display, firearms, with distinct memories, backgrounds, and expectations. In our nine-hour car ride to the museum, we shared and reflected on what the West means to each of us and discussed (prior to and following our visit to the CFM) how we understand and regard firearms. Childhood experiences, potent though they may be, are not, of course, the only way individuals are socialized in relation to guns. Representations of handguns and rifles within and across media and popular culture also contribute to popular perceptions of firearms.[1]
>
> As cultural critics, we highly anticipated our foray into the CFM, the nation's premiere firearms museum, housed within the Buffalo Bill Historical Center in Cody, Wyoming. Inevitably, our experience of the museum, like those of other visitors, was shaped to some extent by our unique childhood experiences with guns as well as our mediated understandings of them.[2] But, as we will demonstrate through an analysis of its distinctive mode of rhetorical address, the CFM works to replace (or at the very least repress) visitors' individual understandings of guns in favor of a universal (and universalizing) interpretation of them as inert objects of visual pleasure. As much as the museum's ocularcentric focus, and its attendant creation of "visual space," functions aesthetically to domesticate and sterilize firearms, it cannot fully erase or eradicate the history of violence and colonial conquering in which guns have played a starring role.[3] Consequently, the museum's rhetorical effectivity/affectivity, we contend, is animated by a unique interplay between what is present (displayed, revealed) and what is absent (not displayed, concealed), as well as how what is present is displayed (through visual space) and how it is not displayed (through acoustic space).[4] What is absent from the museum (i.e., virtually any association of guns with violence or humans) is conspicuously absent. We argue that these conspicuous absences are made meaningful and felt powerfully, if only by tapping into unconscious desires. Any analysis of the

museum, therefore, ought to attend to both the (re)presentations of firearms in the CFM and its meaningful absences (i.e., the return of the repressed).[5]

But museums change. The museum we visited October 31 through November 1, 2020, is in many ways different from the previous CFM. In place of near total silence, we can hear martial music from the *Cost of War* exhibit in the front third of the museum and the quieter pop, pop, pop from a large video game that anchors the first set of displays. Where the previous version of the museum divorced guns from the bodies that carried them, used them, and were shot by them, the new version more regularly depicts humans as gun users. Throughout the museum, images of people standing behind guns, holding guns, and shooting guns often take center stage in the new displays. In the previous museum, designers used wars as titles of exhibits, displayed firearms as objects of antiquarian desire, and repeatedly raised and then turned away from firearms as active in human history and the history of violence in the West. In the new design, we read expanded placards explaining how firearm display changes responded to and drove cultural, manufacturing, and warmaking history. As if responding to our criticisms of the former version of the museum, the new design paints over the heightened sterility and contextualizes firearms, placing guns in people's hands and figuring firearms as central technologies of modernity.

Even as the museum shifts its focus from antiquarianism to contextualism, it also memorializes its past iteration. The CFM narrates its own history as a way of introducing visitors to the rest of the displays. Claiming a conceptual founding in the nineteenth century, the institutional development of the CFM spans multiple walls. That dramatic firearm fan that was the former museum's introductory display is noticeably absent, but a few steps into the new CFM the fan reappears in less dramatic form with an explanatory placard acknowledging the fan's movement from a compelling—even scary—three-dimensional display to the flattened version on a sidewall in the museum's interstices. Rather than completely covering over the museum's past as many (re)built spaces do (including the redesigns throughout the rest of the center), this museum brings its past into its present, inserting what could have been absent (but felt) into presence.

The changes in the CFM, then, are of two broad categories. First, there is the change in the way firearms are presented to visitors, as the museum offers more context, history, agency, and narrative within the displays. Second, the CFM reflects on its own changes, offering visitors consistent reminders of the way the museum once was. In this chapter, we address the rhetoricity of the new design by attending to both the new ways the museum performs its firearm collection and the ways the museum performs itself.

Offering more than a critical assessment of the new design, we follow the interpretive framework of the museum by weaving in our own critical performances of the CFM. Like the CFM returning to its earlier iterations, we return to our earlier work on the museum, weaving portions of that essay into this one. We believe that in so doing we can begin to unlock the CFM's sense-making (meaning and affect) process. Even as the museum is haunted by its past, so, too, are we as critics. As we noted in our initial essay, our individual and collective history with firearms informed our first visits to the museum. These experiences with firearms, but also with the CFM and the BBCW, are all constitutive parts of the experiential landscapes that shape our understanding of the CFM. And so, we began this chapter with the autoethnographic fragments that opened our earlier essay. But we also carry our experiences of that past museum with us into the museum of 2020, experiences accreted over the years of our visiting the center and CFM from 2002 through the present. We carry with us the critical work we performed with that former museum. We are seeing this new design with changed bodies and remade psyches, but we are also bringing fragments of the trio that created the previous analysis.

This chapter offers a complex knitting of arguments. We make claims about the museum's efforts to contextualize firearms within historical, cultural, economic, and museal frameworks. We also address our ongoing engagement with museal change as refracted through the museum's self-memorialization. The final intertwined arguments address who we are as rhetorical and cultural scholars. In the following pages, we argue that the CFM remains a haunted space that, using a rhetorical mode we call *dissociative contextualization*, acknowledges and makes present the force of firearms in historical change while dissociating from and making absent the horrors wrought by, undergirded, and partially produced by firearms.[6] The rhetorical consequences of this affective dialectic of presence and absence is the continued embodied adjustment of our bodies to the firearm and, more broadly, to the colonizing force of the gun. Meanwhile, our complex and complicated history as critics, westerners, and US citizens continues to inform our embodied engagement with the museum.

RETURNING TO THE CFM

In late October 2020, as COVID-19 cases were once again rising in Colorado, Wyoming, and across the nation, Eric and Greg (and Brian engaging virtually) set off to see the newly redesigned CFM. Indeed, the trip was necessitated by the museum's redesign. We had submitted an earlier version of this book to the publisher and reviewers had urged a full rewrite of this chapter and, indeed, by the time the reviewers read the manuscript the museum was redesigned and had reopened. We left the morning of Friday, October 31, and as we left, we reflected on the propitiousness or perhaps ill-fated choice of heading to Wyoming on Halloween only days before the most contentious and worrisome national election of our lifetimes.

Traveling to Cody had always raised excitement, concern, worry, and hope. Our first trip in 2002 was marked at every turn by a simple phrase from Codyites: "Y'all ain't from around here, are ya?" We were not, but we arrived in Cody in 2002 familiar with rural landscapes as each of us had been raised in rural United States. We were well acquainted with farming and ranching. Eric grew up in a small family-owned and operated store that served the raisin and agricultural farmers and workers of California's Central San Joaquin Valley, Brian's father was a county extension agent in rural Pennsylvania when he was young, and Greg's first jobs were on a produce farm and then at a large dairy with a hay and corn operation in eastern Washington.

Our travels were further influenced by our historical context. Considering the many events of 2020 (the rise of the global COVID-19 pandemic; demonstrations and protests following the police killings of George Floyd, Breonna Taylor, and others; and increasingly antidemocratic impulses by members of the Republican party in the national elections), it is not surprising our conversation was directed to thinking hard about our lives and our place in the world. In our hours of driving north and west, we talked about race and identity and more broadly about intersecting diversities and the times. Our conversation was laden with our thoughts about Black Lives Matter. It was interlaced with discussions about the racism and sexism and homophobia and anti-Semitism on our own campus and community. The conversation was shaped as well by our worries and fears about the growing white supremacy in the United States, a white supremacy fostered by Trumpism that was alive and vigorously on display for the four hundred miles between Fort Collins and Cody.

And we thought hard about traveling in the era of COVID-19. We had both completed saliva tests at the university before leaving and, when the tests returned negative, convinced ourselves we could travel comfortably together. We brought our masks with us and kept them at the ready whenever we jumped out of our Honda CR-V. We suspected—and we were right—that our rural companions along the route would not wear masks at gas stations and rest stops. In fact, after Eric, with mask on, entered the first gas station to use the restroom, he returned to the vehicle and reported to Greg that he had experienced what initially seemed like a polite engagement by a visibly white American male who approached him, but subtly uncomfortably so, now quite close in proxemics and without a mask on, to ask if he could help him with anything. We felt in our bodies the risks and cultural negotiations we were taking and performing to complete our research. We contemplated the risk of being Other in spaces that have regularly and forcefully expelled the Other (we remembered the murder of Matthew Shepard as we drove by the turnoff for Laramie, Wyoming).[7] We considered the risk of traveling both within the cultural stressors of the contemporary moment and in an era of airborne, political, and digital viruses. But, nonetheless, we traveled.

Cody Firearms Museum Redesign

The CFM was overdue for a renovation, as its design was the oldest of the center's five museums prior to the renovation. Built before the PIM and the Draper and designed long before the renovated BBM and Whitney, the CFM was long in the tooth and far out of date in the ways it displayed its objects and narrated the development and use of guns.

The narrative that the museum offers about itself starts the collection in the late nineteenth century, when Oliver Winchester began his own firearm collection. As we note in chapter 1, the earliest installment of what would become the CFM was in the basement of the BBM. In the late 1980s, after receiving the Olin collection of firearms as a gift, the BBCW designed and built a forty-thousand-square-foot museum and firearms archive, which opened to the public in 1991. It is this space that was completely redesigned between 2017 and 2019. The center hosted the redesigned museum's reopening on July 6, 2019, to positive reviews in firearms, architecture, and design magazines.[8] The *Wall Street Journal* published a laudatory review of the new space. Edward Rothstein—unlike the other reviewers who dehistoricized the museum—placed the redesigned museum into the context of mass shootings in El Paso, Texas, and Dayton, Ohio. How, Rothstein wondered, might a firearms museum escape the narrative of guns as "instruments of terror and mayhem?" In place of this narrative, the new museum "takes gun use seriously—without allowing it to be eclipsed by gun misuse. It treats guns as objects that will be handled, fired, admired, taken apart and put together—as well as objects that require caution and care."[9] Indeed, as Rothstein pointed out, the museum focuses our attention on gun use and firearm history, turning away from its previous instantiation as a "gunquarium," while also studiously avoiding the difficult violence encoded in the firearm.[10]

A studied neutrality regarding firearms and their role in society drove the museum's redesign, according to Ashley Hlebinsky, the curator in charge of the project. For Hlebinsky, offering an unbiased narrative of firearm development and firearms' multiple uses gives visitors the context needed to make decisions about the roles of firearms in society and culture. Appealing to a professionalized understanding of history as a dispassionate narration, Hlebinsky writes that "rather than using beliefs and perceptions of firearms today to inform my knowledge of the past, I rather use the historical past to inform why we feel the way we do about guns in the present and where in history those feelings developed."[11] She goes on to argue that "people often focus on weapons of violence, as that is the most common discourse heard today, and struggle to disassociate those objects from a large percentage of firearms that have never been used for such purposes. It's more the concept of place and the story associated with certain artifacts (not just guns) that hold power."[12] For Hlebinsky, the museal design should/can "dissociate these objects" that have been used for violence from the larger narrative of firearms and instead locate them in a "concept of place and story." Doing so contextualizes firearms but this contextualization is explicitly also a dissociation, walling off the relationship of gun and violence through narrative devices.

In a published interchange among museum professionals regarding the firearms museum, Hlebinsky is pressed on how the CFM manages the role of firearms in the colonization of the West. She notes that "down the hallway from the CFM is our Plains Indian Museum, which interprets both the historical and contemporary cultures of Plains Indians. The Cody Firearms Museum also has an extensive Native American firearms collection. Because we are part of a larger institution, many of our historical conversations are approached in a multidisciplinary fashion." Hlebinsky at once dissociates firearms from violence and justifies the dissociation by relocating the discussion of colonization from the CFM to the PIM (interestingly, however, not the BBM) and, to a lesser extent to the CFM's collection of Native American firearms (not on display). Hlebinsky's apparent acknowledgment that the CFM avoids the topics of violence and colonization corresponds with our own experience of the museum: more attuned to the context and history of firearms, the museum's use of contextualization is a rhetorical mode by which it maintains the dissociations we explored in the earlier version of this argument. Still haunted by the violence of settler colonialism and constructing a homely/homey/inviting/enticing haunt for its visitors, the CFM is riven by presence and absence, by explicit narrative and implicit affect.

We can know, then, from these interviews with and essays by Hlebinsky that her hope was to create a museum founded on a double move. First, the redesign needed to narrativize firearms, placing them into specific places and times, locating guns at the heart of crucial historical transformations. This recasting, as we have already noted, is a dramatic change from the previous museum's approach, which relentlessly decontextualized firearms. Second, the redesign needed to dissociate firearms from a representational centripetal force of violence. In place of a story linking violence and firearms, the new design narrates guns as sporting technology, hunting equipment, harbinger and producer of manufacturing and economic change, a force in military tactics revision, and a bystander in the costs of military service. Layered into these two dissociative contextualizing moves is the constant recollection of the museum's past selves, as the current museum consistently memorializes itself. As we explain, this self-memorialization articulates with dissociative contextualization we explore, which we now briefly outline.

DISSOCIATIVE CONTEXTUALIZATION

The two crucial rhetorical strands of contextualization and dissociation form the warp and woof of the museum's newly woven textures. We do not mean anything particularly fancy by our phrase *dissociative contextualization*. In many ways, we have simply reworked what we take to be curator Hlebinsky's own assertion about the CFM: that the museum uses stories of place and time to dissociate firearms from the violence they could enact and for which many of them are built. But it should not be a surprise that the professional talk of a curator contains within it a simple theoretical nugget that can help us engage our embodied responses to the space.

DISSOCIATION AS ARGUMENT AND AFFECT

By *dissociative* we note that a symbolic action or a material performance may work to untether two otherwise linked ideas, feelings, or places. As Agnes van Rees argues, argumentative dissociation creates a distinction in a notion that had previously been unitary. The dissociation creates two (or more) terms out of what had been a single idea, giving to one of the terms the positive attributes of reality and truth, and to the other term appearance and falsehood.[13] This form of dissociation, as Kenneth Burke points out, always serves to create new associations—where there is identification there is division, where there is division there is identification.[14] Dissociation—or what he calls a similar function in *Permanence and Change*, perspective by incongruity—can upend taken-for-granted pieties.[15] Again, as one grouping of pieties is undermined, a new set of pieties is being built.

Hlebinsky's notion of dissociation is at least partly of this argumentative form. She asserts that most firearms are not used for violence, that they only appear to be violent. In response to those who hold the unitary idea—guns are designed to inflict damage—the CFM tries to split that notion into many parts. As we will see, the museum offers an abundance of alternative realities for firearms, downplaying the bodily harm guns can and do produce. We use Hlebinsky's urging that we dissociate in an affective mode, for as, as Burke points out, "the symbolic act is the *dancing of an attitude*. . . . In this attitudinizing of the poem, the whole body may finally become involved."[16] Hlebinsky's urging to wander down the hallway to another museum to explore certain forms of violence and her choice of the affectively charged phrase "dissociation" primes us to think of dissociation affectively and as an embodied practice.

In fact, unreality-creating dissociative argumentation has a homology in what we call *affective dissociation*. In the affective sense, dissociation occurs when someone is overwhelmed by affect and takes mental or psychological leave of the present place or feeling. As the *American Psychological Association Dictionary* states, dissociation is "a defense mechanism in which conflicting impulses are kept apart or threatening ideas and feelings are separated from the rest of the psyche."[17] Likewise, the *DSM-5* defines dissociative disorders as "characterized by a disruption of and/or discontinuity in the normal integration of consciousness, memory, identity, emotion, perception, body representation, motor control, and behavior."[18] Dissociation is often understood to be a response to experienced trauma. In Western psychiatric understandings, dissociative disorders—like dissociative amnesia—nearly always arise out of traumas like abuse, experience of natural disasters, engagement in military combat, and the like. The mind and body dissociate around the traumatic event, undoing the relationship between the subject and themselves and between themselves and the world. Closely related to other ways the mind and body manage overwhelming trauma, like post-traumatic stress disorder and acute stress disorder, these trauma-influenced psychological states include characteristics of dissociation.[19]

Dissociation, however, is not only an experience or behavior of those with dissociative disorder. In fact, nearly all of us dissociate in some form or another regularly. Scholars studying dissociative behaviors and experiences often understand dissociation along a spectrum.[20] One end of the spectrum might be daydreaming as a short escape from the boredom of everyday life or in response to an unengaging lecture. Absorption in a hobby, book, movie, music or losing oneself in fantasy, thoughts, or activities like writing are all examples of this sort of dissociation. Often these forms are well-suited to everyday life and can even be productive.[21] On the other end is an ongoing and a nearly complete break with reality. This dissociation troubles the subject's relation to themselves and the external world. Regardless of the place on the spectrum, dissociation in this psychological sense is like the argumentative version in that it serves to separate otherwise unified events. When we daydream, we are at once in the lecture hall and lying on a beach in the Caribbean and for a moment, the Caribbean experience may feel just as or more real than the droning of an uninspired lecturer.

Unlike the argumentative form, affective dissociation is not primarily conceptual or symbolic. Instead, this dissociation is an embodied affect. Daydreaming or absorption in a basketball game can be deeply pleasurable and involve the whole body. The shift from presence in the classroom to presence in a daydream may be triggered by some symbolic act by the lecturer but is more likely to arise for other reasons—timing, memory, other emotive states.[22] Similarly, less adaptive modes of dissociation are not linear, symbolic, or in any sense argumentative.

Affect can serve as a capacious category that allows us to attend to our own embodied and emotive responses to the CFM and the BBCW and to explore the material modes by which the museum invites these engagements. "Experienced by the body as fluctuating intensities," Brian and Greg argue elsewhere, "affects are a mode of becoming and, hence, a way of knowing. They promote a visceral or carnal knowledge, one that escapes, but runs 'parallel to signification.'"[23] In the CFM, we will be exploring the affective as well as argumentative—that is signifying—dissociations the CFM is urging us to feel, become, and know.

Clearly, we have moved beyond affective dissociation as a behavior or experience of an individual subject. To use the term in rhetorical criticism requires us to use dissociation and dissociative heuristically and analogically. We are not, for instance, going to diagnose the museum as dissociative; that clearly makes little sense. Instead, we note how the design of the museum is homologous with or analogical to dissociative practices within subjects.[24] Just like memories are not located in museums—memories are located in audiences and the museum materials weave with the audience's memories to make meaning—so, too, the museum's design can knit with already existing concerns about firearms, violence, trauma, and identity. We are shifting the focus from individuals experiencing dissociation to a museal design and its production of a dissociative rhetoric.

In the coming pages, we draw upon these understandings of dissociation. Like Chandra Maldonado's critical efforts to engage "amnesiac state of memory," we weave what is present in a memory site with known absences, our own embodied movement through the spaces, and our observation of others' bodies to explore the identities left out, shunted aside, dissociated.[25] We attend to dissociation as an argumentative form that distinguishes conceptually and symbolically between reality and appearances. We also attend to dissociation as a powerfully affective response to painful memories, experiences, and behaviors. Thinking through the argumentative forms urges us to pay attention to the placards and other symbolic material. Feeling the affective form urges us to attend to how our attuned bodies are responding to the spaces of the museum and beyond.

CONTEXT AS RHETORICAL MODE

By *contextualization*, we mean here the mode by which the museum strives to dissociate firearms for/from a wide variety of violent actions. As with dissociation, there is a large literature both within rhetoric and outside of it on context. In rhetorical studies, context is often thought of as an explanatory approach for rhetorical critics rather than a mode of rhetorical action.[26] That rhetorical action occurs within a context is at least broadly noncontroversial. The field accepts that the historical, social, cultural, economic, interpersonal milieu of rhetorical actions shapes, frames, generates, and is generated by rhetoric. We may argue over the constitutive character or the epistemological or ontological statues of context, but those of us in the field seldom disagree that context matters. Our own conceptualization of experiential landscapes outlined in chapter 2 and utilized throughout this book is our spatialized way of explaining the deeply situated and contextual nature of the BBCW and of visitor experiences in the space.

However, we mean something different by "context" in this chapter. Rather than studying the *context of* the museum's rhetorical actions, we are studying *contextualization as* one of the museum's rhetorical actions. Here we are asserting that the museum uses contextualization as a rhetorical mode to create and foster dissociation. One element of this is the need for the design to meet current standards for museal experience. As the other museums in the BBCW demonstrate, contemporary museum design focuses on narrative, immersion, and audience engagement. However, conforming to these broad principles does not explain the specific choices regarding the stories told or the immersion invited by the redesigned CFM. Dissociative contextualization helps explain these contextualizing choices. The rhetorical impulse for the museum's turn to firearm's stories is (at the most innocuous) like that of the daydream—a diversion from reality that allows visitors to move on with their day. More pathologically, the contextual diversions are a form of dissociative amnesia whereby a subject's crucial memory is fully recorded but also unavailable to consciousness.[27] In remembering how guns are used in movies or games or as part of manufacturing—all important and real contexts for firearms—the site also urges us to lose sight of others, or in the language of the *DSM-5* to forget "important autobiographical information" that is in fact fully stored and would readily be remembered were it not for dissociation. We explore the ways the CFM consistently urges us to attend to firearm contexts that demonstrate that the culturally troubling memories of guns are fully available even as the memories offered constantly turn our mnemonic attention in other directions. Our job, then, is to build an interpretive context of the CFM, *and* to trace the ways the museum uses historical, cultural, and economic surrounds for firearms to give firearms location in place and time while also distracting us from the firearms' role in disconcerting violent actions like mass shootings and colonization.

We devote the next sections to our exploration of the museum's redesign and the ways it utilizes dissociative contextualization to create an affectively powerful museum. First, we focus on the ways new design weaves together the double maneuver of contextualization and dissociation. We then explore the ways the CFM's self-memorialization further dissociates firearms from violence and interpellates the returning audience of gun aficionados. In the final section we reflect on how our own positionalities as critics—and citizens—influence our understanding of this newly designed museum.

PLACE AND TIME IN THE CFM

The new museum is designed as a series of narrativized installations that embed guns with specific, meaningful, compelling, and contextualizing stories. As Hlebinsky suggests, these stories often work to embed firearms into a particular place and time. The images and narratives curated introduce us to people associated with firearms, the uses they make of the weapons, and the places where they employ the guns. These narratives weaving place, time, and use specify guns, locating them in particular symbolic and material contexts and, in so doing, shunt other less desirable meanings.

Contextualizing narratives begin early in the museum. Just past the CFM's story of its own founding, "A Matter or Record" (to which we will return), the first room carefully sets the rhetorical and embodied modes of the museum. The lighting is dimmer than in the passageway into the space. The carpet is a soft neutral. As we pass the walls leading us into the museum, we are told we are about to explore "Tools of Endeavors," different yet reminiscent of our time spent learning to become a "master naturalist," as discussed in chapter 6 on the Draper. We swivel to read the next panel explaining that the space we are entering provides an eight-hundred-year historical contextualization of firearms while the basement provides the chance to dig more deeply into individual firearms. And, on a large panel we read "101" set vertically, with "Keywords to Get You Started" as the header, not unlike an academic course numeration at education's most introductory level. These panels suggest that guns are important technological items whose purpose is not that different from other utensils like cooking vessels or clothing that mark humans as civilized. Like other sophisticated civilizing tools, firearms are complicated and arcane and so the earliest exhibits again serve as an introductory class (Firearms 101) that defines basic terms, overviews firearm functions, and introduces four rules of firearm safety.

There is a subtle, yet effective transitionary mode provided by these early exhibits. Appealing to both the aficionado and the novice marks one of the pivotal innovations of the new design. Designed for a firearm novice (like at least one of us), this part of the museum is a crucial introduction to museumgoers not already inscribed as firearm users or aficionados. As Hlebinsky points out, the CFM is designed to appeal to both the firearms enthusiast and a less experienced audience. The previous version's antiquarian impulse limited the interested audience, making little effort to reach those of us not already excited about guns. In previous visits, in fact, we regularly heard one member of a BBCW visiting party tell the rest of his (and it was always "his") group to leave him in the museum. His excitement was palpable, as we argued in the previous iteration of this essay—an affectively powerful response to the aesthetics of the gun and the extraordinary number of guns hanging on walls. The previous version's mission was simpler, for its audiences' attitudes were already well formed; there was little need to go beyond the iterative process of showing gun after gun.

To appeal to the rest of the center's audience, the new museum needs a more complex approach, one that does not assume an already built knowledge of firearm history and culture and does not rely on already installed positive associations with guns. This more nuanced approach is imperative to widening the museum's appeal since attitudes and understandings of guns varies widely in the United States and globally. A Pew Research Center report notes that gun owners are deeply committed to owning guns, see gun ownership and use as fundamental to their identity, and imagine gun ownership and use as a means of creating security.[28] Meanwhile, nonowners are more skeptical of guns, indicating that gun ownership is not a central part of their identity and suspicious of the claim that owning guns is a way of ensuring personal safety.[29] While many attitudes about guns, gun ownership, and gun use vary across the surveyed population, those surveyed agreed: gun violence is a significant problem. Eighty-nine percent of non–gun owners say that gun violence is a major or a somewhat major problem in the United States; 74 percent of gun owners agree.[30]

The museum—in a move familiar from its previous version—acknowledges this shared worry about gun-involved violence but only askance. Focusing our attention on gun safety and on the parts that make up each firearm acknowledges that the firearm is a dangerous technology. The initial displays are low, angled, made of light wood, and plexiglass. The displays are filled with firearms and firearm parts arranged on a simple white background. Introducing the novice to basic elements of firearms and to the rules of safety, these displays are in their own way aesthetically relaxing. The displays immediately address basic concerns about firearms. Suggesting that some fundamental and easily learned practices make gun ownership safe and pleasurable, the displays can reduce anxiety around guns. One early contextualization of firearms, then, is as civilizing tools that demand respect and require careful training. Approached with this respect and training, however, the firearm is much like other tools: useful, safe, and productive.

Likewise, disassembled firearms pose no risk to the viewer or the owner. Rather than a materialization of violent possibilities, the deconstructed guns of these early displays become less than their whole. Here we see inert bits of highly finished steel. We see how parts might fit together, much like a puzzle where the *doing* is placed with the skills and agency of the human. We are introduced to the fact that guns are designed, engineered, and manufactured, which is an important theme throughout the rest of the museum.

The dangers of guns, then, can be easily overcome with a few safety practices and an understanding of how guns work. For the uninitiated—who may well be more skeptical of guns—these early exhibits invite viewers to pivot away from their focus on violence toward firearms as tools that can be managed by well-trained humans. Combined with the discussion of firearm safety, the displays of dissembled guns also urge us to imagine that we have agency regarding guns. We can take the firearm apart and reassemble the instrument at will. We can make sure it is functioning correctly. We can deepen our understanding of the mechanical workings of the gun. In this way, guns become more like the saddles that the saddle-making interns are producing in the exhibit entrance hallway at the very start of the CFM than like instruments of death and destruction. Presented as more (or less) than the human-created objects of the western experience, these early exhibits condition viewers for their encounter with the remainder of the museum. Carefully dissociating guns from violence, turning them into manufactured and designed goods, and presenting guns as items over which the user has agency prepares the visitor to move into the next exhibits, which focus on guns and play.

Guns as Play

In the next set of displays, we are invited to explore firearms as sporting and playful objects, as parts of military efforts, as objects of manufacturing innovation, as agentic props in the entertainment industry, and as material objects with their own historical manifestations. As we will see, taken together, the contextualization of firearms allows us to envision the gun more fully in use than in the previous iteration of the museum while hiding the social and political violence behind said uses.

Though themes of manufacturing and war, hunting and commerce, history and entertainment make up the displays the visitor will see, it is not surprising that that the most easily accessible displays beyond the "101" exhibit are devoted to sport and play. From the end of the main entrance hallway looking ahead and right, we are invited to participate in two interactive exhibits. The first offers us the chance to learn the proper stance for accurately firing a gun. Foot-shaped appliqués on the floor urge us to hold our bodies in a slightly angled fashion. We raise the provided model gun to aim carefully at the wall. Over the days we visited, we observed visitors engage this exhibit, take up the gun, position their bodies, and imagine shooting. One of us watched from a distance as a man carefully instructed a woman on the proper way to hold the gun, adding his own embodied instructions to the material guides of the space. Adjacent to this tutorial is a large, interactive, first-person shooter game. The pop, pop, pop of the game as visiting contestants attempted to top the recorded best scores served as one of the museum's constant soundtracks, breaking through the more sterile soundscape of the previous version of the CFM. Indeed, these two exhibits—the shooting stance and the first-person shooter game—engage nearly all senses. We are encouraged through prompts of kinesics to move our bodies in specific ways and to touch and hold the model weapons; we listen to the game's sounds of gunfire. Embodied movement, touch, sound, sight, and the complex combinations that make up proprioception (balance, motion, direction) are all engaged.

Having learned how to dissemble, reassemble, and shoot a play gun, we are invited just beyond these exhibits to view displays about guns and sport. In the Woodruff Modern Shooting Sports Gallery, we are introduced to photographs of people famous for their sharpshooting skills (fig. 23). We read about and see images of the Fabulous Topperweins, a married couple whose shooting tricks included "upside down shotgun shooting, creating artwork with .22 caliber rifles, and redefining the boundaries of marital trust." This gallery makes a point of noting that sharpshooting can be both competitive and exhibition—and through the pronounced visible diversity used within the displays—that these shooting skills appeal to women and men and to white and nonwhite individuals alike. The exhibit focuses attention on Kirsten Joy Weiss, who has over three hundred medals for competitive shooting and a very popular YouTube channel, Julie Golob who is a professional shooting athlete who has won "more than 50 world and national titles" and authored a children's book on safety, and Chris Cheng, who "originally worked for Google" before leaving Silicon Valley to devote himself to shooting sports (fig. 24).

Figure 23. Robert W. Woodruff Modern Shooting Sports Gallery. Photograph by Greg Dickinson.

Figure 24. Exhibit featuring female sharpshooters. Photograph by Greg Dickinson.

The display's rhetorical force works in the interplay between specific details and the overall exhibit. Standing back at a distance, the details we just described resolve into an image of firearms as entertaining, fun, and playful. The action-filled photographs of Dave Miller shooting from between his legs weaves with the glamor shot of Weiss staring into the middle distance and Cheng smiling broadly in an unposed photograph that appears to be from a shooting competition; these collective photos meld into an argument that people can leverage guns for interesting careers, like professional athlete, YouTube star, and entertainer. The composite image is one of diverse peoples—men, women, white, Asian American—finding joy and pleasure in handling firearms. Perhaps just as importantly, the affective relationship between the museumgoer and the gun in this display is one of skilled, yet carefree play. Guns are—like footballs or skis—used for joyful diversion.

At this point in the walk-through of the CFM, we are positioned to experience guns as complex but nonthreatening technologies, even as engaging and entertaining games. What we know so far is that firearms are useful civilizing tools, machines with individual parts that can be studied and understood, material components enabling games and athletic endeavors, and technologies skillfully and playfully used by diversely represented and embodied individuals. These themes reappear throughout the rest of the museum, and these early exhibits prepare us well for a benign and perhaps soothing rendition of firearms.

The playfulness of firearms intersects well with other layers of dissociative contextualization. For example, near the middle of the museum a large exhibit explores early factory manufacturing of firearms, emphasizing the ways it drove and was driven by Fordist economic logics of the early twentieth century. Factories like the Colt factory represented in this exhibit offered lifelong employment to their workers while also expressing the drive to mass production. As with the early exhibits showing us dissembled guns, the reproduced factory focuses our attention on the design of the machine and offers a comforting image of work. Hlebinsky's place and time are powerfully resonant, urging visitors to identify with factory workers and with a form of capitalism from this historical moment.

Later in the museum, we can wander into a reproduction of a hunting lodge. Filled with taxidermized Rocky Mountain animals (elk, American bison, black bear), western art, a large fireplace, and, of course, guns, the lodge situates us in a very specific time and place. Set in a dim and warmly lit elegant glow and located at the far end from the pop-inflected gun sounds of the first-person shooting game, this quieter and more removed lodge space is primed for reverence and relaxation. The images, firearms, and placards all draw us into the turn of the twentieth century, harkening to the time of Teddy Roosevelt. This era, of course, makes good sense in terms of the museum's theme. Roosevelt was an important conservationist arguing for setting aside wide swaths of western land, preserving the land for recreation—in particular, for hunting. Founding the Boone and Crocket Club, which advocates for hunting and conservation of wild lands for the sport, Roosevelt and others pressed for the legislation that would eventually create Yellowstone National Park and many others.

One end of the lodge is anchored by a video presentation regarding the relations among hunting, national parks, and conservation. In another nod to diversity, the video rightly notes that setting aside spaces like Yellowstone with restrictive hunting guidelines made hunting possible for visitors and sportspeople. At the same time, it undermined the ability of Indigenous people and local hunters to hunt for sustenance. Nonetheless, the video argues, supporting hunting and the fees that are associated with hunting licenses is the best way of supporting conservation of open space. The lodge reminds us, then, that guns have been used for survival as a tool for hunting, but here hunting is portrayed primarily as a sport and a mode for engaging nature. Yet again, the gun is playful.

The playfulness of guns continues through the museum, with a video presentation of a reality TV show where the hosts recreate movie and TV shooting scenes to determine if the scenes accurately represent the filmed guns' powers. We watch clips from *Hollywood Weapons*, the Outdoor Chanel reality TV show where the hosts recreate famous movies and TV firearms scenes. We watch a stuntman recreate a scene of Jason Bourne spraying a giant window with bullets to see if the glass will shatter as they did in a movie; in another clip the same stuntman replays a *Starsky and Hutch* scene with the heroes hiding behind a Ford Gran Torino door as the bad guys shoot to see if Starsky and Hutch would, in fact, survive. And again, there is an exhibit of highly decorated firearms presented to heads of state as luxurious gifts. Throughout the museum, the use of firearms is characterized as much by the playfulness of the instruments as by their place and time.

WAR

In a significant shift from the previous iteration of the museum, and importantly even within the curated version currently in place, the CFM appears to be much more forthright about the uses of firearms in violent conflicts, with specific attention to war. Occupying the center of the museum, a large, square, multisensory exhibit explores the costs and impacts of war and the role firearms have played in shifting modes of waging armed conflict. Drawing the visitor in by martial music, the exhibit showcases a video monitor filled with compelling images related to the "cost of war." Via engaging displays of weapons and other military accoutrement, this display urges visitors to attend carefully to the role of firearms in military conflict and the costs of conflict in society (fig. 25).

Figure 25. The *Cost of War* exhibit. Photograph by Greg Dickinson.

War was a constant theme in the previous museum as well. In that version, the design was driven by what we called an "exercise in taxonomy." Firearms were organized by manufacturer, caliber, and country and time of origin. The previous museum's designers used time markers as the weapons' historical contexts. Time and history served as an exercise in a very spare mode of categorization. The dates of wars often served as the time markers for organizing two-dimensional displays of the museum's archive. In the previous essay, we wrote this about the historical organization of the weapons:

The Civil War (1840–1865), The War of 1812 (1812–1814), The Mexican War (1846–1848), The American Revolution (1775–1783), The Colonial Wars (1689–1763), and The Conquest of North America (1520–1676). Though much of the historical signage in the CFM corresponds to specific armed conflicts . . . , it does not explain or contextualize those events. So, though the word "war" appears on several of the exhibition cases, the signifieds of war (i.e., battlefields, soldiers, bloodshed) are utterly absent, having been replaced with the signifieds of art (i.e., beauty, aura, skilled craftsmanship). Wars, like the guns in the museum, are sanitized—form without content. Consequently, to all but aficionados, the individual firearms are distinguishable only as a result of their minute differences in contour and design. Thus, even as the CFM's

164 Chapter 7

practices of classification invite a scientific, objective gaze, the focus on the subtle differences between the guns prompts close examination and appreciation of their craftsmanship.

Throughout the old museum, then, war was named and then forgotten, signified and then ignored. This maneuver—to mention and then ignore—is what led us, in that previous essay, to begin seriously grappling with the museum's glances, its efforts to "look awry" at the object of desire. The powerfully desirable force of guns was regularly, even obsessively named. The museum pointed to the warlike elements of the gun, its uses in "settling" the land (the Conquest of North America). The names were enough, we suggested, to trigger a desiring relationship among at least some viewers, the firearms, the museum. And, at the same time, by looking awry, the museum could preserve the desire, hidden in plain sight.

The new version of the museum moves in a different direction. Here wars are not simply named. Instead, the *Cost of War* exhibit compellingly demonstrates the ways firearms changed the nature of war, discusses changing military formations, and the remaking of battlefield strategy. The design places weapons in exhibits filled with other battlefield gear, urging the viewer to imagine the firearm in use. These exhibits briefly describe the importance of the items displayed—changing wartime tactics, the significance of the battles lost and won, and the difficult decisions about how to think about undeclared wars like the military conflict in Vietnam.

The most forceful contextualizing component of the exhibit, however, is the multimedia installation in the center of the square. Most folks who move into the space—and in our observation, most visitors do attend to the space—pause for a spell with this part of the exhibit. Under the large title *The Cost of War* the subtitle reads, "Few human endeavors are as costly as armed conflict." Twelve black and white photos surround this display title. Symmetrical grave markers marching serenely up from foreground to background anchor the bottom of the display, providing a visual and moral grounding. Flag-covered coffins, a closeup of a POW-MIA baseball style cap, a World War I–era hospital ward, and three soldiers with an automatic weapon frame the top of the wall. The center includes images of a beach landing and a Civil War–era casualty. As a reminder, we briefly discuss the curatorial decision making that lead to this wall in chapter 2.

The largest of the images in the left of center of the glossy wall is a photograph of a snow covered, barren landscape, made even more pronounced by the use of minimal humans in the foreground with an open yet stark background, making it the only image of the twelve that appears as though you are looking through a window onto a vast and barren landscape. The image is shot from a low angle. In the right foreground, a dark-haired woman in a long coat walks away from us. Her coat is blowing out to the sides, conjuring winter winds. Two more people in winter coats occupy the center of the image. Barracks frame the left and the giant butte occupies most of the background. A fine example of modernist photography with crisp lines and intriguing forms—a mix of linear, human made buildings, with flowing fabric, and the hardscape of a rock butte—the image is visually and aesthetically compelling. Reading it as a mnemonic of the cost of war, however, requires substantial cultural knowledge and is thus different than nearly all the images on the panel. Although two images on the bottom right are equally untethered to obvious war iconography, most of the images are clearly shot within the context of war. The cemetery photograph along the bottom of the montage is easily understood as that of a military graveyard. The scene in the upper-right corner contains an emaciated man framed by two men in military uniform and so on. Regardless, there are no written descriptions of the images to orient viewers. The large picture with the snow-covered landscape's visual references to war is far slimmer than most of the other photographs on this wall. The buildings on the left can be understood as military-style barracks. Beyond that, the picture is not easily placed in the context of the display.

Though nearly bereft of the visual signs of war's costs, this barren landscape photograph is nonetheless filled with mnemonic power. The striking butte in the background will trigger recognition in visitors familiar with the northern Wyoming landscape as that of Heart Mountain Butte. More directly related to the cost of war, the photo is an affectively charged mnemonic for those of us familiar with the history of Japanese American internment in the United States, for this image is in fact an evocative photograph of the Heart Mountain Relocation Center.

Heart Mountain Relocation Center was one of ten concentration camps that held Japanese American detainees in remote, mostly western locations. By early December 1941, when Japanese war planes attacked Pearl Harbor, FDR's administration had already formulated extensive plans for the possible internment of Japanese Americans. Drawing on long-held racist tropes, the administration asserted that Japanese Americans—unlike German Americans or Italian Americans— were suspect because of their race. As Greg Robinson argues, Roosevelt and those around him accepted and argued for a fundamental "Oriental" character that made Japanese Americans unassimilable to US cultural values and inherently risky.[31] Executive Order 9066, signed by FDR on February 19, 1942, allowed military leaders to designate military areas on the West Coast and then detain anyone deemed a threat to national security. While the executive order does not name Japanese Americans explicitly, it is clear the purpose of the order was to authorize the imprisonment of Japanese Americans in/from the western United States. And, indeed, that was the effect of the order. As Robinson writes, "In the spring of 1942, the army removed 100,000 Japanese Americans from their West Coast homes. They could only take with them what they could carry, thus losing land, homes, farms, cars."[32] The internees were imprisoned in one of the ten camps scattered around the Intermountain West. The Heart Mountain Relocation Center was bounded by barbed wire and guard towers, though this barbed wire was installed after the internees had moved into camp and the installation raised significant protests among the camp residents.[33]

The first detainees arrived at Heart Mountain in August 1942. The National Park Service describes the camp's location this way: "Heart Mountain was located on two terraces of the Shoshone River on a flat, treeless landscape covered in buffalo grass and sagebrush. The dry desert environment received only a small amount of precipitation annually, was hot in the summer, and cold and windy in the winter."[34] The photograph we are gazing at captures the winter's cold and wind. The image has the potential to trigger cascading recollections of the racism that underpinned the internment project. And it reminds the viewer that the cost of World War II in America included devastating losses of time, property, family, and fully embodied citizenship experienced by the Japanese Americans interred at Heart Mountain Relocation Center and elsewhere.

This photograph offers a trenchant critique of World War II. It invites those who feel the tug of its mnemonic hooks, to remember the conflict's sordid underbelly. Rather than the "Good War" we are often offered, the image reminds many of us of the racism that, though predating the declaration of war, was allowed to flourish in the name of pursuing military ends. Requiring substantial historical knowledge of the Japanese American internment during World War II and even more knowledge of the location of specific camps, the photograph's memory potential is deep but not wide, affectively powerful for the relatively small number of people who are "in the know." Still, this mnemonic anchor has the potential of guiding us to explore the other oppressions war can justify and materialize.

Each of us brings a different relationship to this photograph. Both Greg and Brian come to it having learned of the Japanese American internment as adults. Greg has a friend whose family was interred; but he only had conversations with him about this internment in graduate school. Brian knows only what he has read on his own. Eric's family history, on the other hand, includes family members imprisoned at Jerome and Rohwer, Arkansas, during World War II. Eric has searched the National Archives to find details of his grandparents, father, and uncles and aunties, finding such information as "Never in Japan," "Buddhists," and "Has Not Attended Japanese Language School" among other demographic and life details. As we talked through this photograph and the larger questions of the cost of war, these individual and family histories wove in and out of our responses to this picture, the display, and the full *Cost of War* installation. So, too, it would be for other visitors to this exhibit, the mnemonic force of the images weaving the aesthetic force of the colors and shapes and forms with the personal, familial, cultural, and national memories the images knit into.

We have been writing about the specific material, symbolic, affective memory hooks of the Heart Mountain photograph offering concrete performances of the abstract claim that material and symbolic mnemonics are at least plural if not radically unfixed across audiences. Some could use this claim—that mnemonic images and places can produce multiple meanings and affects—to sterilize critical assessment. The mixed emptiness and fullness of memory supported by the Heart Mountain photograph serve as a powerful example of dissociative contextualization. This photograph, the photographs surrounding it, and the larger *Cost of War* exhibit are powerful examples of dissociative contextualization. Here the CFM seems to want to look directly into the face of the horrors of war and the firearms that war demands and uses. And, at the same time, the images on the board are devoid of guns. What is more, because they are nearly absent of storytelling beyond the visual image, the display allows us—encourages us—to sit with the context of war and at the same time move into daydreams and nightmares. In fact, the video monitor's stories intersect with the images, including a brief slide stating "The U.S. & Canada detained more than 140,000 civilians of Japanese descent considered to be a security risk." The slide does not tell us that the photograph to the left is an affectively compelling image of this detention. It does not assert a fundamental truth—those detained were not just civilians, they were citizens. In the passive rendering of "considered to be a security risk," the slide elides the racism of both the decision and its implementation. The image and the monitor perform a powerful context, one that is linked to embodied and generational trauma. And it dissociates, moving from action to motion, from costs borne by specific bodies to "security risks." Here is the performance of dissociative contextualization. The memory of the trauma of Japanese American internment is fully available. And it is denied, given almost no voice, the image left to be felt by those whose trauma is already present.

There is a homology between the empty/fulness of the image and the text—the dissociative contextualization—and haunting as an affect and a critical resource. As we have argued, haunting is an affective state that weaves presence and absence. The affect of haunt is the sense that something forbidden, hidden, or repressed is still present. The image we have been discussing is haunting in this sense. It draws forward (for some) long-forgotten memories of a civic repression—the imprisonment of citizens and legal residents because of their "Oriental" character. Even for those Americans who do not have historical, familial, or other knowledge of the internment, the image has formal qualities of haunting: a stark landscape filled with (un)homes on the left and faceless bodies moving slowly away from the camera. The image materializes the multiple unhomeliness of the internment camps, of the treatment of Japanese Americans, and of citizenship. Centering a powerful image of Heart Mountain on this display offers an important critique of US war efforts and is particularly appropriate for a museum located just minutes from Heart Mountain. It matters that this is the one photograph of the entire display taken from the BBCW's own archives. This is a haunting that possesses at least the possibility of the ethical bite about which Avery Gordon writes. We laud this critical haunting. Our praise is tempered, though, by our recognition of the display's dissociative performance. In fact, Greg, who was the first to write about the image, needed some time away from the display before he recognized the photograph for what it was: a memory, ready to be recalled and also shunted aside, just out of mind.

Unlike the previous iteration of the CFM, the new museum addresses war directly. It imagines with us the cost of war; it contemplates the complex interactions of weapons, war fighting strategies, and culture; it pauses on the conundrum of US armed conflict outside of declared wars (like undeclared wars waged in Korea and Vietnam); and it addresses the immense monetary costs of war. This version of the CFM more fully contextualizes firearms as weapons and more specifically as instruments of war. But, as this chapter's thesis states, this contextualization is also always a form of dissociation through deferral and misdirection. The emphasis on guns and play contextualizes guns as similar to baseballs and skis, little more than tools to enable friendly or competitive sports. The recognition that firearms are central to acts of war and that war is costly in terms of lives, relationships, economics, and culture acknowledge the killing force of weapons. Yet even as the museum acknowledges these costs, it consistently directs our attention away from the oppressions war often entails and produces. Placing guns in their historical, social, cultural, and political contexts is a crucial step in more fully remembering the power of guns in everyday lives and recognizing those affected by such atrocities. At the same time, historical contextualization can also serve as an alibi, urging us to see guns as located in only specific historical moments and not others, helping us to imagine firearms' violent force as playfully neutral, as deferred to another museum/time/location—displacement captured in the abstractions of *The Cost of War* and represented as stark photographs of Heart Mountain where guns themselves never actually appear. In our most recent experience, increased contextualization made the museum more complex, more interesting, and more immersive. We appreciated our increased engagement and the deeper learning about firearms, and we recognized the critical impulse in the inclusion of the image of and information about the Japanese American internment camps. Again and again, as we traversed *The Cost of War*, we felt the haunting of firearm violence even as we were urged to dissociate the guns from their promised actions.

Haunting haunts the rest of the museum, but seldom with the same critical turn. As we wandered the museum, took notes, reflected together and alone on the new design, we also came to realize that the new design better diverted attention from but did not eliminate the haunting absences and silences. As in the previous museum's design, our bodies cued us to the fact that this new design was, intentionally or not, obscuring something. Our bodies reminded us that—even as we were seeing guns and their contextualization—just out of sight, in our peripheral vision, as we looked awry—we could *sense* the museum's hauntings. The forms of the new design's contextualization constituted for us a renewed and more complex form of "looking awry," which we have been calling dissociation. Dissociative contextualization is a different way of expressing many of the basic ideas in the earlier argument about the CFM. Spending a bit of time with that earlier argument would help the three of us think through—and feel through—the ways the previous museum's design remains a palimpsest for the new institution.

In our initial essay on the CFM, we engaged the space on two levels: that which was present and that which was absent. We acknowledged that analyzing that which is absent is extraordinarily difficult. If we think of absence as all the possible things, meanings, performances that are not in the museum, then the possible absences are infinite. However, we argued that absence is not presence's opposite, suggesting instead that meaningful absence can be understood as presence's barred Other. "The Imaginary—the field of images and appearances and of the signifier—is structured by the Symbolic, [that is] the field of the linguistic and the signified," we wrote. That which we see directly—the museum's objects, placards, displays, and so on—is in the field of the imaginary. But these images and objects are structured, organized, and given affective weight by the symbolic. The symbolic is expressed in the unconscious or, as we wrote, "the discourse of the Other and its concealed desires."[35] These discourses of the Other and the powerful tug of desire cannot be seen directly. Instead, we see them best askance and awry.

The previous iteration of the CFM was a scene of abjection, an abjection whose form is specific to US colonization. As Julia Kristeva argues, societies— towns, cities, nations—often create themselves through a violent rejection of the scene from which they came. We mark out our territory—geographically and politically—by creating and then removing an Other. We ascribe to that Other values and performances we are drawn to and which (we imagine) repulse us. We might imagine this Other to possess radically different spiritual structures and beliefs or repellently different sexualities. "Abjection reflects," we wrote, "a rather violent revolt against and repelling of the very thing that gives us being, the Other that we, at once, desire and abhor."[36] The profound absence of history, context, and representation of violence in the older version of the CFM was precisely this form of abjection, where the museum rejected and covered over that which so many of us desire and abhor.

And so it is in the new version of the museum. The older museum's motivations undergird the new museum, with meaningful absences consistently calling

170   Chapter 7

on our subjectivity. Given society's vigorous discussion of mass shootings and
a renewed attention to race in the United States (including concerns over representation of colonialism among museum professionals and others), the new
museum simply had to confront the violence of firearms. We can see this contested confrontation in the published conversation among museum professionals, in which Hlebinsky was required to address the ways the CFM represented
the firearms in the history of the West. In this conversation about how to display
firearms in museums, the discussion turned again and again to guns and violence. And, again and again, Hlebinsky acknowledged that firearms are used in
war and by violent criminals but dissociates the guns on display from violence
by asserting that most firearms are never used for violence.[37]

The museum that resulted from this set of principles expresses the dual understandings that firearms are and are not violent. We can look directly at the
firearms on display. We see guns and placards, costumes, and factory machines.
But if we attend to our affective responses, if we allow that which is visible and
felt, if we follow the directions to explore the force of weapons elsewhere, then
we begin to *feel* settler colonialism. Indeed, in the firearms and war section, just
to the left of the *Cost of War* display, one grouping of guns, clothing, images,
and placards addresses the "Plains Wars." These wars also show up in the linear
history of the firearms display nearby. In both areas, there is acknowledgment
that firearms were both a point of fact and mythmaking elements of the material, cultural, and symbolic processes of settler colonialism. One placard informs
visitors that Native Americans were often outgunned in the nineteenth-century
battles but also suggests that—because they did not fight with army-supplied
and often substandard weapons—Native Americans sometimes had superior
armament.

Crucially, however, the museum gestures to other times and places, as if the
visitor wants a deeper engagement with the intersection of firearms and, say, the
colonization of the West. In the history of the gun section, a placard in the display of guns used in the Plains Indian Wars tells visitors that the PIM narrates a
fuller story of this history.[38]

We sense in this iterative deferral the haunting of the BBCW. This wall is already a haunting repression of the embodied and emplaced tragedies of settler
colonialism. For the CFM to point visitors toward the PIM for a fuller understanding of the uses of firearms in the nineteenth-century settler colonial West
and into the present is (at least) a doubled performance of "looking awry." First,
the symbolic pointing from one museum to the next creates in us an embodied
desire to leave the CFM, wander through the center's atrium, down the long hall
to the PIM, and from there find the display tucked near the back of the PIM. But
we do not follow this impulse. Why not? The barriers to confronting that which
is dissociated are material and substantive—the process of leaving the current

space and walking to the other end of a large, multipart building stands in the way of the invited investigation.

In a second awry moment, were we to accept this invitation to leave the CFM for the PIM and find the display about the Plains Indian War, we would see, well, almost nothing. A few more guns. A bare description of the changes wrought across the Plains before and after the Civil War. A short description of the boarding schools to which many Plains Indian young people were sent, tearing them from their homes, culture, and language. The PIM does engage the nineteenth-century wars between Plains Indians and colonists. A long wall in the PIM offers a timeline of white incursion on Native land, including presentation of firearms typical of the wars. But we also noted earlier in this book that—especially compared to the immersive nature of the rest of the exhibits in the PIM—this wall narrates the settler colonial wars in the museal equivalent of the passive voice. The dispossessive violence of the nineteenth century is acknowledged, imaged, and imagined. But these acknowledgments are performed with and invite a flat and nearly neutral affect. The wall does little to explain the nature of the conflict, the stories of broken treaties, the series of landgrabs, the constant destruction of indigenous peoples and their ways of life. It is absolutely the case that Native People survived these wars—and in chapter 4 we explore the important rhetoric of survivance in the museum. Yet it is also the case that the wars and the politics that the wars performed depend on "the *dispensability* of the indigenous person in a settler colonial context."[39] This dispensability and the military campaigns that enforced and produced it are the cost of war in the Plains context. In place of honestly confronting this history, the museum's practice is an iterative regress in which the traumas of settler colonialism are acknowledged as a cost of war even as any embodied or affective engagement with the conflicts and its legacy is deferred. We are offered context that allows us to dissociate the weapons we are viewing from the violence and destruction of which they are a constitutive part.

In no case would we be invited to look deeply and squarely into the practices that make William Cody, the town of Cody, Wyoming, and the CFM, PIM, and the overall BBCW possible. Yet, at the same time, colonizing forces and practices are recognized throughout the museum and the center. The ghosts of settler colonialism are here—viscerally felt as the hair-tingling shiver in our embodied steps as we walk on through—walking beside us and urging an ethical engagement with the center that could foster justice even as the center works to avoid this reckoning.

The dissociative contextualization—or looking awry—has more prosaic forms as well. The history of the gun display we have been writing about also demythologizes the popular culture images of the "Gun That Won the West." As the placard correctly notes, "the gun that won the West" was a post–World War I marketing slogan that "was created to market and capitalize on nostalgic mythology after World War I rather than to incite a critical examination of the many types of firearms that were used during America's westward expansion." Here the museum substitutes one myth—that one specific firearm "won the West"—for a different version of much the same myth. Instead of one gun winning the West, many different guns undergirded "America's westward expansion." The promise of myth busting (ghost chasing?) is materialized in the CFM through the surrounding encyclopedic collection and display of guns used by white folks over the nineteenth century to take possession of Indian land. The colonizing force of the white use of firearms in this context is resisted and reinforced by the much smaller displays of Native American firearm use.

Placing firearms into their popular culture context serves as a major diversionary mode for the CFM, exploring the ways movies, TV shows, and advertising helped construct our understanding of guns and the West. In a substantial exhibit about guns and media, the museum notes that the idea of the Wild West was produced by entertainers like Buffalo Bill, Annie Oakley, and James Arness. The story behind the displayed weapons focuses on the marketing materials, the movie costumes, and the development of well-known stars. As one placard asserts, these popular culture representations make it "hard to distinguish the reality behind the myth." The CFM offers itself as a reality-based site, helping visitors distinguish between media-generated myth and CFM-reported reality. The museum repeatedly raises the possibility of a deep engagement with the reality of firearms in the world. But it also repeatedly veers away from the most difficult conversations into a discussion of fictional representations of firearms.

With what may be its most impactful move toward a deeper direction, at the near end of the CFM a framed, information board titled "The Gun Chronicles: A Story of America" stands next to an impressive, wall-sized *Time* mural. Presented in black-and-white, the mural depicts diverse people posed around the proverbial table of engagement (read: debate)—a table complete with microphones, factual notes, water glasses, and in this case, firearms. The mural conjures up classic photographic qualities, and this aesthetic is a distinct departure from the vibrant color palette used throughout the rest of the newly renovated CFM. The black-and-white coding also cultivates aesthetic associations with the US binary of race relations, as well as with printed history and/or historical news. The individuals depicted in this mural perform a wide array of engaged and animated nonverbal performances of emotions and body and facial postures, a visual performance that reinforces the centrality of firearms along with the debates they elicit as core values in US society.

The CFM information board accompanying the mural offers that "the Evolution of Firearms gallery explores the entirety of firearms history. It examines the histories of technology, war, sport, legislation, misuse, and defense. History can often be used as a means to understand the present." The information board also welcomes us "to visit www.time.com/guns-in-america to hear their stories." Once navigating to the Guns in America website, we learn (as is noted similarly on the information board):

> To create our "Guns in America" special report, *Time* collaborated with JR, the French artist and photographer known for his murals around the world that portray complex social issues. The goal: bring together a variety of voices in search of common ground on one of the nation's most divisive topics.
> In three U.S. cities profoundly affected by guns—Dallas, St. Louis and Washington, D.C.—we invited people to share their views and describe their experiences in a search for common ground. In all, JR filmed and photographed 245 people—hunters and activists, teachers and police officers, parents and children—to create this mural for *Time*'s November 5, 2018, cover.[40]

On the website, you can hover over each person's photo on the technological mural and tap and listen to a recorded snippet of their interview (i.e., their human voice) while they share their views, experiences, and positions on firearms. There are also prompts to "ADD YOUR VOICE TO THE CONVERSATION" through the partnership of StoryCorps and *Time*. The website states, "We encourage people across America to ask and answers questions like: 'Was there a moment, event, or person in your life that shaped your political views?' 'What is most hurtful to you about what people across the political divide say about people on your side and in your life?' 'Do you believe that there are some threads that bind us all together, even when it seems there is more that divides us? What do you think they are?' 'Can you think of any traits you admire in people on the other side of the political divide?'"[41] As we view both the CFM mural and website, firearms or guns no longer exist as the sterile artifacts of the original museum: here, guns are encoded with representational human agency through the mural, albeit generally without voice. That is, unless you make the extra effort to go onto the *Time* online site and listen to voiced narratives of the individuals depicted in the mural.

Having engaged the CFM's invitation to access the *Time* Guns in America site (but, only after we had left the museum), we became impacted, perhaps vocally haunted, by the lingering voices of the interviewed individuals, who otherwise would remain visually impactful in the CFMs photo mural, yet devoiced. This point noted, and with the dynamic interplay of on-site viewing of the mural with the offerings of modern-day technology to *listen in* to a deeper story of the voiced-agentic perspective of the people in the mural, human agency has been enhanced. Yet we assert that we remain in many ways safely at a distance from this emotional and contentious debate in US society, leaving us untethered from the emotions and intensity of value discourses that the mural (re)presents. We can walk away from viewing the mural feeling or believing that we have, in fact,

174   Chapter 7

engaged and done needed work to acknowledge that the debate exists. But for the visitor who does not choose to engage the Guns in America site or for the visitor who has been saturated with the high-color and diverse engagements we detailed in the earlier sections of the CFM, the takeaway may be one perhaps closer to dissociative contextualization.

The *Time* mural and the link to the website hold the potential to deepen the visualization and (re)presentation of human agency around firearms and the explosive visual nodes of human conflict depicted, but we, the visitor, have also moved through the *logical and more-enticing playful start* of the CFM exhibits before attending to this mural. We have already likely stood in alignment with the instructive floor-mapping early on (in an engaged posturing stance while learning ways to properly hold a firearm), engaged in museum *play* with a video-like gaming immersive exhibit, observed photos of firearms held by a range of sharpshooters, celebrated sports athletes, and walked through a presentation of firearms in association with war and history as well as popular culture scientific studies that look into whether or not (re)presentations of firearm use in Hollywood shootouts were in fact accurate. Thus, importantly, we approach the visually powerful black-and-white *Time* mural where human agency is (re) presented only after we have been saturated in color during our journey through the CFM's other displays and exhibits.

Through these earlier displays and exhibits, the museum enacts a larger cultural approach to firearms and our understanding of the West. We can see and feel throughout the CFM a desire to confront the concerns many of us have about the role of firearms in US society and about the injustices of settler colonialism. But the CFM, like many of us, is anxious about approaching these haunting stories too closely. The embodied narratives of hunting in the hunting lodge, the compelling story of industrial development in the reproduction of a gun factory, the emplacement of firearms in a clean and well-lit western general store, the in-depth exploration of guns as works of art all suture armament— and us as museum visitors—into deeply important narratives of conservation, mechanization, commerce, and aesthetics. The long discussion of the cost of war anchors these representations of firearms in a lineage of violence and costly destruction. The CFM draws us closer to the tragic consequences of firepower even as it strives to divert our gaze to advertising and mechanization, to hunting and entertainment, to games and art. Deep in our bones we understand that the museum is not lying to us. We feel that it obscures or downplays truths we—as individuals, citizens, and men—want more fully explored.

A MUSEUM TO ITSELF

We have been arguing that the redesigned museum draws on the palimpsestic remains of the older museum to produce newly created dissociative contextualization. Just as we developed the concept of dissociated contextualization from the museum curator's discussion of the museum, the idea that the older iteration of the museum structures the newer iteration is also derived from the redesign, for the newer iteration consistently refers to the earlier iteration. Even as the redesigned museum (partially) met our ongoing desire for a gun museum that more carefully explored the situatedness of firearms, others visiting the museum likely desired something very different. In talking with the former curator, we sensed that the CFM had a deeply loyal audience—mostly men, already knowledgeable about guns and committed to a western vision of gun ownership. The "gunquarium" version of the museum was ideal for this passionate audience. Displays were composed of beautiful arrangements of gun after gun, shining in museum lights. The museum offered little by way of explanation because little was required by the devoted antiquarians the museum invited in. In fact, as we argued in our analysis of the previous version of the museum, decontextualizing, domesticating, and sterilizing repression of firearms' bloody possibilities allowed visitors to revel in the mechanical and aesthetic beauty of the firearms.

Based on the museum's redesign, the current CFM clearly wants to acknowledge and appeal to the sensibilities and audiences for which the previous design was so well-suited. The CFM is a mnemonic machine for firearms often devoid of violent purpose or colonizing force, and it is also a mnemonic machine for itself. In remembering and reproducing its own past, the museum is also reproducing and remembering its past audiences. Thus, even as the museum invites and constitutes a new audience concerned with the social and cultural impacts of firearms, it remembers, invites, and constitutes an older version of the gun audience, one that is less inclined to historicize firearms. With a wink and a smile, the museum lets visitors familiar with the older version of the museum see and experience that museum as well as the redesigned space (fig. 26).

One of the most arresting displays of the earlier design was a giant fan or sunburst pattern of guns. In our previous commentary, we described the display this way: "The guns in this display are encased in protective glass like rare and precious artifacts; they are elaborately arrayed in a partial sunburst pattern suggestive of a flower in bloom. The twelve slender rifles and twelve stout handguns that comprise the display are positioned such that none of the guns' barrels are exposed. One can neither stand behind the guns as if in a position to shoot them nor stand in front of them as if in their line of sight (i.e., as a target)."[42] In our observations of visitor movement through the museum, nearly all visitors we observed at least paused at this dramatic display of firearms, replete with finely printed placards naming the guns, their age, and provenance.

Figure 26. Wall commemorating prior installation of the CFM. Photograph by Greg Dickinson.

The firearms that made up this original display are showcased in the redesigned museum as the introduction to the *Firearms in the American West* portion of the current design.[43] In place of the original dramatic three-dimensional display, however, the guns are now arranged in a more two-dimensional case, floating inches off a white wall. The guns cast complex shadows on the wall, giving the display depth and motion. Pistols are arranged horizontally on the far left of the case while rifles occupy much of the space and are arrayed in a pleasing wavelike pattern. Crucially, the guns displayed are associated with and often manufactured in the West.

The display is offered as an explicit memorial to the previous design. In one of two explanations of the exhibit, designers write that "firearms collections historically have been displayed in elaborate fans that are aesthetically pleasing to the eye. The old Cody Firearms Museum had a large fan of western firearms at the entrance to the museum that became iconic. As an homage to the original display, we have upgraded the fan here at the beginning of the Firearms of the West Gallery." The fan had become, curators write, an icon deserving of public veneration. More than the previous display is remembered, however. Remembered as well is the older museum and older museal practices. Interacting with this "upgraded" display, visitors are simultaneously introduced to the *Firearms of the West* gallery, which provides comforting images of the previous museum, and offers a very short history of how gun collections have been displayed in the past. In attending to this display, we came to understand that the redesigned museum employs the latest museum design practices as guideposts. We are also, at the same time, reminded that the curators have affection, even reverence, for the older modes of displaying guns, for the earlier design serves as the redesign's palimpsest.

This display case within the main body of the museum reinforces a narrative about the museum as a memorial to itself. Indeed, the admired fan form still welcomes visitors into the museum. On our left as we walk toward the museum, wall hangings offer a history of the CFM through a large introductory poster titled "A Matter of Record." What follows is a timeline tracing the CFM's collection from 1871 to the creation of the original, stand-alone museum in 1988. The timeline is populated with images from the collection, a 1959 exhibition of the Winchester collection in New York, the collection as exhibited in at the BBCW in 1976, and photographs of the 1988 wing.

With this detailed narrative of the museum's past, along with the revised, smaller fan serving as the introduction to the CFM, we are invited to understand the redesigned CFM as always, a memorial to itself, linked directly to its own past and to the museum's commitment to offering an encyclopedic display of firearms. We are asked to contextualize the material goods and symbolic narratives we will engage in through the rest of the museum in the story of the BBCW's commitment to the aesthetic and stylized display of guns. The images from the timeline remind us that the museum is committed to individual guns and groupings of weapons as aesthetic (and, thus, affective) material goods. At the exact same time and with the very same display techniques, the CFM wants us to know that this is a remarkable and remarkably complete collection of firearms. The amazing aesthetic displays of guns is made possible by the sheer abundance of firearms. Abundance—that is, the rhetorical trope of *copia*—serves as a crucial context of each firearm, as the weapons begin to make meaning in relation to each other and their sheer number certifies the importance of the CFM.

This aesthetically compelling abundance is emphasized over and over, with the innumerable pull-out displays on both the main floor and in the basement "firearms library." These vertical drawers serve as the museum's visible archive. They engage our whole bodies. We are asked to walk to the drawer, to tug on the drawer's handle. We feel the heft of the drawer and the silky movement of the heavy displays' slide on finely turned ball bearings. The drawer glides out and slides back in with the satisfying hum of a well-made, beautifully engineered domestic item. In short, the drawers are homologous with the firearms. Both are finely wrought, beautifully finished, and engagingly useful. We may not be able to handle the firearms, but with each pull of the drawers through our own agency we can, at least, manipulate the drawers in which they are stored. In this manipulation, we can appreciate the craft of the drawers as we are visually pulled into the beauty and craft of the guns. While the substantially increased historical and cultural contextualization of firearms that we address in the previous section actively moves away from the gunquarium model of firearm display, the gunquarium returns throughout the museum. Much of the CFM is an homage to this previous display practice and moral stance. The newly installed gun drawers link to the museum's self-story as a comprehensive collection and deepens the commitment to firearm display as aesthetic and acontextual.

The museum's memorial to its own development is interesting in and of itself. What makes this self-memorializing even more fascinating is that the other museums of the BBCW do not engage in this practice. Over the course of the two decades we have studied the BBCW, designers have completely redesigned both the BBM and the Whitney. The Draper was in construction when we first visited. The PIM had only recently been completed upon our first visit. None of these museums—those that have been redesigned and those that have not—comment on their own past. Nowhere in the current BBM is there a reflection on the previous version, nor does the Whitney work to actively invoke its previous installations. There is something special about the CFM that generated the need and desire to contextualize the current display in the museum's history.

The rhetorical effects of this self-referential memorialization are at least threefold. First and most obvious is the invitation to understand the CFM as a leading narrator of firearms in the United States. The memorialization reminds visitors that the collection is old—dating to the late nineteenth century—and incomparably large. What is more, by distinguishing the current design from the previous one, the CFM invites visitors to know that the CFM is on the front edge of firearms display. And so, we are in the presence of an outstanding collection, carefully presented, with the most current museal approaches grounding the display. We can feel assured that our time spent in the CFM is well worth it, for we are in a world-class institution.

Second, this contextualization—that is, the excellence of the collection and creativity of the displays—invites us to imagine firearms as items of collection. As such, firearms become cultural capital. Knowledge about gun changes, aesthetic shifts, relative rarity, the worth of particular firearms, and the awesomeness of the size of the collection all become crucial groundings for understanding firearms. In short, the museum urges us to partially shift our attention from firearms as woven into historical endeavors—hunting, war, crime, security—and toward collection and appreciation. Since these are the very first stories we are told as we enter the museum, this contextualization of the museum qua museum surely provides crucial rules for rhetorical understanding. Much as we discussed in the previous section, the CFM's performance consistently functions to treat firearms not as instruments of violence but as other sorts of objects. In this case, firearms are objects of desire for collection, display, and knowledge. Firearms in this setting deserve the same museal weight as the art in the Whitney, the anthropological and historical artifacts in the PIM and the BBM, and the natural history artifacts in the Draper. The CFM elevates firearms to artifacts of cultural, historical, and economic importance.

Third, the museum's constant referencing of its own past resonates with the nostalgia often attached to firearms themselves. As the CFM notes, and as we wrote about earlier in the chapter, "The Gun That Won the West" was a nostalgically driven slogan built for the post–World War I era. The museum devotes substantive time and space to firearms and western movies, TV shows, and entertainers. These exhibits are themselves wrapped in nostalgia. They offer a warmly hued look at films and TV shows from the post–World War II period. These films and TV shows were themselves nostalgic representations of a seemingly simpler time, the nineteenth-century West. Even as the museum casts a critical eye on these representations, regularly suggesting that the myth and fact about the Wild West are so intertwined that pulling them apart is difficult, the immediate experience is of nostalgia itself. As the museum showcases, here are the costumes worn by favorite western stars; here, too, are the rifles and sidearms they carried onto the sets and into our living rooms and theaters of the 1950s and beyond. Here are the posters that advertised the movies. Sure, the placards informing us that this image of the West is riven with myth are telling the truth about media's mythmaking, but by the time we read the placards the affective force of this nostalgia has worked its rhetorical invitation of dissociative contextualization.

The rhetoric of the CFM's memorialization of its past enactments serves to secure the authenticity and comprehensive quality of the museum, places firearms into a museological context, and reinforces a nostalgic affective relationship to the Wild West. As such, this memorialization weaves with the CFM's larger rhetorical structures that deepen the dissociated firearms through deep, wide, and consistent contextualization of firearms in their historical, cultural, economic, and political context.

HAUNTING GUNS, HAUNTED SELVES

When we began writing about the Buffalo Bill center in 2002, we quickly realized that we would need to write separate essays about each of the museums. The last essay we wrote in the original cycle of five essays was the one that would eventually form the basis for this chapter—the essay about the CFM. This museum has caused us the most resistance, presented the greatest challenge. As we settled into writing about the museum in its former incarnation, we realized that this resistance was the key to our analysis. The museum kept hiding from us, or, differently and more on point, we kept hiding from the museum. As we talked together about our experience in the older museum, we commented about how depressed or anxious we felt when we visited it. We came to understand that we were affectively responding to the museum's rhetorically meaningful absences. In our bodies we could feel the pull of the repressed violence, we could sense poignant and powerful absences. Present absences like those we wrote about in 2011 have a way of being depressing. Remaining just out of view, repressed and hidden emotions are outside of our agency, beyond the reach of our engagement, lodged deeply in our souls in ways that demand and resist attention. Our effort in that original essay was to look—to feel—askew and askance at and with the museum. We wanted to and worked to pull into emotive and affective range that which the museum contained and hid.

Our response to the CFM's demand that we attend even more carefully to our embodied engagement with the space (precisely because at the time the CFM was by far the least immersive experience) came to represent a set of critical shifts on our part. As this project about the center developed over the years, so too have our approaches to doing criticism of memory places. All three of us, because of this work and work we were doing in our independent research projects, became more and more convinced of the importance of the body, materiality, context, contextualization, and affect as crucial components of communitive interaction and, thus, of communication criticism. We have returned to the center, its museums, and our responses to these spaces with a deeper focus on our entanglement with the spaces. Following the urging of one of our reviewers, we are moving from a critic-as-god perspective to more fully engaged participants with the museums and their visitors.[44]

We began this essay with our reflections about our childhood memories of guns. We narrated our most recent journey to Cody amid the COVID-19 pandemic and only a week away from the 2020 presidential election. Our writing about the CFM and the center is influenced by our participation in and responses to our larger contexts. Over the twenty years of going to Cody to explore the center and the CFM, we have found the trips and the museums intersecting with our deeply held values and concerns. When we were finishing the 2011 essay on the CFM, we reflected on the presences and absences of the museum and the rise of birtherism and Tea Party activism. We were finalizing revisions of that essay just after Gabby Giffords was shot in Tucson, Arizona, in January 2011.

We are concluding this essay in 2021—a decade and what feels like a lifetime later—after birtherism made possible the white masculinist nationalism of Donald Trump. We write in the midst of the constant drumbeat of mass shootings and the middle of the powerful movement of Black Lives Matter in response to state-sanctioned police violence against people of color. We write in the aftermath of the January 6, 2021, insurrection and in the middle of a pandemic prolonged in the United States and elsewhere by antivaccine beliefs and actions. We weave together our affective global entanglements with our personal histories, our embodied predilections and positionalities as we write this (and the other) essays. As we left the center and the CFM after our last visit, we reflected on how discouraging the museum continued to be. We contemplated how badly we want a stronger commitment from the museum to address mass shootings (indeed, the museum has undertaken no such effort) and the use of weapons in settler colonialism in the West. As we composed this essay over the months following that visit, we engaged in long-distance conversations about Japanese American internment and our differing histories of this event. Even as we are positioned to desire these engagements, others wish to ignore and forget these concerns and want to attend instead to others: the beauty of the guns, the fascination with the industrial design, the pleasure in gun ownership and use. These issues do not move us in the way they move others. This longing for a deeper engagement with these issues in the museum is as much—more—about us as it is about the museum.

We find, nonetheless, mnemonic hooks in the museum that trigger in us ghostlike memories. The haunting of the CFM—of the BBCW—is in the museum's design and in ourselves. For example, the delayed recognition by Greg that the stark photograph on the *Cost of War* display was of Japanese American internment captures this haunting quite well. He spent much time over two days looking at this display, taking pictures, wandering by, watching the video presentation. He recognized that the image of Heart Mountain Relocation Center was the affective center of the collected images of his experience with the CFM. And as he began to write, he spent more and more time with his images of the display and then with this photograph. At the beginning there was but a pinprick of recognition, a faint call of conscience. This call became louder with more reflection, more time. The haunting ghost become a painful but welcome guest and, in conversing with this past, a shifting ethical commitment.

This is the power of the CFM. The haunting call toward justice is, while repressed and partially hidden, still part of the museum. These rhetorically meaningful absences offer triggers that at least make possible an assignation with the (in)justices firearms have made possible. As we discussed in the introduction, dissociation from painful memories and traumatic pasts reminds us that those memories are available. Thus, displays that acknowledge the misuse of firearms remind us that firearms are too often misused. The small but present recognition of the use of firearms in violent confiscation of land from Native Peoples reminds us that the land we are on in the museum is stolen. The displays that prominently feature women and people of color remind us that guns are primarily the provenance of white men and often serve to support white masculinity's oppressive power. As we moved through the museum, we felt this double call. We felt called to see firearms as useful tools of daily life, especially in the American West. We could understand this call with our own experiences of hunting, gun play, and gun ownership. And we sensed the museum's efforts to see and acknowledge the costs of firearm violence. We wove this with our own experiences of white masculinist power, power to which we have differential access and wish to reject. Throughout our visit and our writing, we kept knotting the narratives of the CFM with the narratives of settler colonialism, of school shootings, of the toxic flowering of white nationalism in the Trump era.

The CFM contextualizes firearms in social, cultural, and political history. It also plays firearms into a museological narrative, with the current instantiation of the museum as an exemplar of contemporary firearm display. In each case, we have argued, the redesigned museum more fully investigates the development and use of firearms in the West than did the previous version. In so doing, the CFM more clearly nods to and recognizes the kinds of injustices the weapons often supported and continue to support. Still, completely absent are investigations of police shootings of people of color or, alternatively, the uses of weapons by Black Panthers and other people of color to fight for justice. Mostly hidden, but partially present, are older injustices like western settler colonialism (and the use of firearms by Native Americans to resist their dislodging from the land), the imprisonment of Japanese Americans in the western United States, and the burdensome costs of armed conflict on society. Dissociative contextualization, then, is like haunting. The haunting memories, the memories from which we are dissociated, are available in the audiences of the museum and in the museum itself.

We remain haunted by the CFM. The displays of thousands of guns circulate in our daydreams and our nightmares. And we are continuously drawn to the steely beauty of the machines, pulled by the historical significance of these seemingly inert objects, and fascinated by the deep and passionate commitments so many have to these particular things over all the others in the world. We have ended our analysis of the museums with this critical discussion of the CFM because the museum continues to draw us in and repel us. It refuses our careful analysis and frustrates our ability to make linear arguments.

In the next chapter—the conclusion—we will once more take up the entwined concerns of the book and of this chapter. We will revisit haunting as a mode of knowing and feeling. We will return to methodological concerns that have driven our writing about the built environment and places of memory. And we will reflect again on our own commitments to rhetorical and communication criticism as a mode of engaged citizenship.

Conclusion

Living by the Spirit

"Follow me," urges William Cody's ghost at the entrance to the BBM. It is not an actual ghost, of course, but the image of an actor playing Cody, which has been projected onto a vapor screen—a thin layer of mist—at the museum's entrance that invites us to enter and explore his life. Importantly, this ghostly image encourages us to be guided by the spirit of the West, a spirit that we are told the real-life "Buffalo Bill" Cody embodied and exemplified. The image is, in every sense of the word, haunting. After two decades of visits and hundreds of hours of writing, talking, and thinking about the BBCW, we remain haunted by the site, by the spirits that invite us in, and by the spirit of the West that motivates the center and radiates outward into the West as we know it today.

In this book, we have endeavored to reflect on those hauntings. We have attended to our moments of joy and frustration with the center. We have pondered our comforts and anxieties as we have visited the space. We have considered our inclinations and hesitancies as we have talked with wide-ranging audiences about the center. From the beginning of the project, our affective engagement with the center and with its various iterations has guided our work. We have seen in this space a condensation of so many of the things that the West has come to mean to us. The appeals to masculinity, to whiteness, and to heteronormativity were already familiar to us. The center's references to and creation of symbolic and material landscapes of the West resonated with our long-held, deeply embodied experiences as men born and raised (for two of us) and living (all three of us for most of this project) in the West. Our adult lives, along with our maturation as scholars, teachers, and citizens, have been entwined with our study of the center and with our disparate experiences of the West. The site has been a center in our individual and institutional lives over the last twenty years. The pages that precede this conclusion are the barest expression of our embodied relationship to the center, to each other, and to the world.

We have argued that the BBCW enacts a rhetoric of haunting. Our approach to the center as haunt and haunted is inspired by the center itself. It takes seriously the center's slogan to "Celebrate the Spirit of the American West." We recognize that by "spirit," the authors likely intended something akin to "the animating or vital principle in man (and animals); that which gives life to an organism, in contrast to its purely material elements; the breath of life."[1] Spirit in this sense is a life-giving force, tied to national identity. But any appeal to identity, whether individual or collective, is rooted in exclusions. The self always entails—always carries with it—the barred and repressed Other. Spirit, then, is simultaneously about presence and absence, about what is remembered and celebrated, as well as what is forgotten and ignored. "Spirit" may animate our present-day selves, but only because we are haunted by "spirits," by the often-terrifying rem(a)inders of past/cast off selves. And so it is with the BBCW. Thus, we sought to engage both the spirit the center openly celebrates and the spirits it wishes to relegate to a forgotten past.

For us, both senses of "spirit" are evident in the ghostly Buffalo Bill projected onto mist at the entrance of the BBM. On the one hand, the mist-made Cody is playfully ghostlike. He rises from the grave to address visitors directly. He wishes, it seems to us, to offer his own funeral oration. In the best epideictic tradition, he wants to commemorate the values he represented. The designers, we suspect, were not trying to conjure a frightening ghost for museumgoers. Much more likely, they were trying to find a novel way of engaging visitors and celebrating a series of core "American" values. On the other hand, the technologically inspired apparition of Buffalo Bill—and what he represents—haunts the center, the West, and the whole of the nation. In short, even as the installation executes the center's invitation to celebrate a set of ideals—of Platonic truths—about what it means to be "American," it invokes a darker, repressed history and legacy of nation-building related to settler colonialism.

That the center broadly and this installation specifically does both things—that it affords and appeals to a set of enduring "American" values and calls forth repressed memories of material violence—does not mean that it treats or values them equally. The center's preference, it seems to us, is to engage in untroubled commemoration, to tell a story of nation-building that is celebratory, one that moves and inspires its visitors. Toward that end, it engages in a series of practices unique to museums: collection, preservation, exhibition, and representation strategically crafted to encourage an inspiring set of meanings and messages. But as much as the center may work to produce a coherent and compelling set of messages about the past, messages that erase or, at least, markedly downplay the violence on which the nation is founded, it cannot succeed. That this is so is due in no small measure to the fact that places of public memory enlist our fully embodied and emplaced selves.

Consequently, in attempting to make "sense" of the center, which entails analyzing its meaning and presence effects, we have worked to attend carefully to rhetoric's always twined dimensions: its symbolicity and materiality.[2] This has meant analyzing not just the BBCW's objects and displays, its placards and videos but also its rhythms and punctuations, its sounds and the smells, its colors and the lights, and its spatial aesthetics. The movement of bodies through the space, the arresting of eyes and ears and the proprioceptive shifts accompanying changes in building materials make the center's rhetorical invitations powerful. In sum, the rhetorical force of the center is a product of a full range of symbolic inducements and concrete, fully embodied enactments of the West.

We also approached the center's symbolic and material rhetoric as consequential. We acknowledge that its rhetorical invitations urge us to imagine and support a world in which embodied violence protects white masculinity, Indigenous people are subjected to the whims of dominant culture, and the natural world is subjected to the forces of extractive economics. We take these material consequences of the center's suasory force seriously and, indeed, we are convinced that directing our attention to "spirit" is one of the ways the center secures its rhetorical efficacy. It directs us, among other things, to treat the space as a haunt and, subsequently, we suggest, as haunted.

For us, haunts function rhetorically. They involve a return, a trek to a familiar place like a childhood home or old hangout. At a minimum, that trek enlists our memories, imaginations, and physical selves. While this return can be comforting and/or disconcerting, it is registered as an embodied response to a place's structured invitations. Folding past, present, and future, knitting memory and sensation, a haunt is both meaningful and affective. While haunts often invoke warm memories and comforting feelings, they can also be haunted by repressed memories, which make returning "home" unhomely. Whether as comfort or fear, a haunt is felt, first, in the body as an affective response to place. Only after the body registers this affective response does it take on an emotive imprint available to cognitive structures for symbolic (re)working. As we have worked to make "sense" of the spirit of the American West throughout the book, we have explored how spirit is actively enlisted in meaning and presence effects. That is, we have explored how it is symbolically depicted in the built environment and materially realized in the body as an affect of reassurance and/or fear.

We came to our argument about haunts and haunting primarily through our own direct contact with the site, making this book the result of empirical study. We began with empirical communication questions: What are the attitudes, beliefs, and values conveyed by the Buffalo Bill Center of the West? What are the rhetorical mechanisms and devices that the center enlists to communicate these messages and move visitors? What identities and performances does the space engender and disavow? We proceeded to investigate them by way of empirical investigation. Taking our bodies to the site, we spent hours and days spread over years and decades looking at, smelling, touching, tasting, walking through, talking about the BBCW. In short, we experienced the BBCW and its landscapes. As we argue in chapter 2, experience is best understood as conducting a trial or engaging in empirical testing of the world. From this close-to-the-ground position, we began to develop our understandings of haunting, experiential landscapes, and the other conceptual terms that guided our work.

We began our critical investigation of the BBCW with the BBM, for this is the museum and the home that is the authorizing gesture for the rest of the center. We started with the BBM in part because the efforts to memorialize Buffalo Bill served as the founding gestures for the BBCW. But starting with BBM also allowed us to limn most carefully the white masculinity that serves as the longed-for cultural and political structures the BBCW offers as "the Spirit of the West." We then took up the PIM, the Whitney, and the Draper, ending our analysis with the CFM, the most recently redesigned space of the five. In each museum, we were struck by the powerful relationship between presence and absence and by the ways these apparent opposites filter through the whole institution. The BBM explores Cody's roles as a scout and family man, but it is (nearly) silent about his exploits as a bison hunter and Indian killer. The PIM investigates the history and culture of Indigenous peoples, but it is (nearly) silent about western colonization. The CFM traces the technological development of firearms, but it is (nearly) silent about the unique culture of gun violence in the United States. And so it goes.

This presence/absence relationship is but one manifestation of the awkward relationship between the two meanings of haunt we have woven throughout this book. Comfort and fear, security and anxiety are tied together in the complex relationships our present selves have with the past. The desire for a secure and securing past depends on—and is responsive to—the past's repressed challenges. And this, in short, is the haunt. Haunt(ing) is built of memory, it is woven of presence and absence, and it has material manifestations in the built environment and in our bodies.

In this conclusion, we will reflect on two broadly conceived issues. First, we consider again the importance of engaging the built environment as experiential landscape. Considering all that we have written about each of the individual museums, we grapple with how these specific experiences enrich our understanding of this term. Second, we return to the importance of the haunt. We work through the ways haunt has not only enlivened our understanding of the BBCW but also impacted our understanding of this very particular present moment into which the BBCW always inserts itself and of which the center is constitutive.

EXPERIENTIAL LANDSCAPES

We initially developed the concept of experiential landscapes in 2006 for the purpose of writing an essay about the PIM.[3] The issue we sought to address with the concept was a seemingly simple one having to do primarily with understanding the boundaries of our object of study. We had become increasingly dissatisfied with analysis of only the "text." After several trips to the center, it was clear to us that its rhetorical force and consequentiality had much to do with the surrounding landscape and the very real difficulty of actually "getting to" Cody. But, as with many ideas, the more we reflected on this matter, the more complex it became. We began to realize that the influential landscapes were not simply the material ones surrounding the center such as Yellowstone and Wyoming but also the mental landscapes we brought with us as a consequence of growing up and living in the West, as well as being exposed to constructions of the West in US popular culture.

So, when we began working on a book-length project about the center and our twenty-plus years spent studying it, we sought to rework the concept. In doing so, we took more seriously than we had in the past the "experiential" dimension, which reflected our growing interest in rhetoric's materiality across a series of both individual and collective projects. Seeking to better understand and engage built spaces like museums prompted us to be more attentive to the extra-symbolic and often nonsignifying aspects of places. We were convinced by Lefebvre, who wrote, "A spatial work (monument or architectural project) attains a complexity fundamentally different from the complexity of a text, whether prose or poetry. As I pointed out earlier, what we are concerned with here is not texts but texture. . . . The actions of social practice are expressible but not explicable through discourse; they are, precisely, *acted*—and *not read*."[4] This led to a much more thorough engagement with the materiality of the center and its surrounding environs. At the same time, we were also convinced that each museum did its rhetorical work as part of a larger complex of symbolic structures. We certainly could have treated this "larger complex" simply as context or intertext(uality), but both of these terms bound us to a "textual" understanding of museums that seemed limiting.

Our own engagement with the museums reinforced for us the ways that textuality was a poor entrée into the analysis of the center. Our bodies and our minds let us know that context and intertextuality would not suffice. We needed, instead, a term or phrase that was attuned more fully to sensation and the human sensorium. And we wanted a phrase that would help us think through the specificity of the West. This set of reflections led us to proffer the notion of experiential landscapes. As we explicate in chapter 2, experience allowed us to take seriously Lefebvre's recognition that space is acted upon, as well as his recognition, along with that of many others, that space is always embodied. Meanwhile,

188 Conclusion

experience also allowed us to think carefully about the ways individual and social and past, present, and future fold together.

The West, we also knew, was already overdetermined as an experience partly through the surfeit of painted, photographed, filmed, and written landscapes. The West, as John Dorst teaches us, is already a way of looking, at least within the white imagination and experience.[5] The risk of landscape, we knew, was that our readers would also be overdetermined by Bierstadt paintings and Adams photographs. And yet the homology between landscape as a way of seeing, landscape as a way of experiencing, and landscape as a human intervention in the natural world was strong enough that we remain willing to risk this simplification.

What is more, when taken together, the notions of "experiential" and "landscape" work to reshape one another. Landscape modifies experience by reminding us that experience is always emplaced. Experience's constant testing of the world is really a testing of space. Experience is a pushing up against material and cultural relationality, sensing how the world pushes back, with the engagement reshaping the contours of the world and of ourselves. Likewise, experience modifies landscape, transforming it from a distant and static canvas into a present and lived engagement with spatiality. Tagged with ongoing testing, landscape does not simply appear or preexist inhabitance but coproduces the material world. Being in and through landscapes changes them. Not only does the movement wear grooves in the world, but the movement in some real senses produces the landscape as landscape. Even more deeply, since humans are—like their landscapes—natural, our being in and experiencing of the landscape is a small but constitutive part of the landscape itself. Most obviously in this case, the visitors to the center and its museums are part of the museal experience. The museum as museum depends at least in part on its audiences. Likewise, the drive to and from Cody, our time in the town, in Wyoming, and in the West, as well as our movement into and out of Yellowstone, are all constitutive of the landscape and of our experience.

MUSEAL AND CRITICAL CHANGE

The more time we spent at/with the center and the more times we traveled to and from Cody, the more complex became our understanding of experiential landscapes. Our experiences as scholars and friends and as citizens of the West wove with our visions of the Wind River Canyon through which we traveled again and again. Our deepening understanding of the cowboy and of violence and of colonization as represented and repressed in the center impacted our teaching in Fort Collins and Springfield and shifted our ways of seeing politics and people in our hometowns and our nation. The well-worn route between Fort Collins and Cody, the well-known movement from idea to presentation, and the well-rehearsed working through of self as scholar, friend, and teacher all accreted our places in the world. We have come to understand what Doreen Massey meant when she wrote, "We are always, inevitably, making spaces and places. The temporary cohesions of articulations of relations, the provisional and partial closures, the repeated practices that chisel their way into being established flows, these spatial forms mirror the necessary fixings of communication and identity."[6] We have used the idea of experiential landscape to explore the BBCW's efforts at chiseling into established flows and also our own forms and fixings of communication and identity.

But the fixing and forms are always, also, under revision. Visiting the BBCW for twenty years enabled us to track the center's and its museums' constant and continual change. We were struck repeatedly by the conundrum of studying material places. Made of concrete and stone, material places are nevertheless malleable, changing, ever in flux. As we have traced throughout this book—but especially in the chapters on the BBM, the Whitney, and the CFM—the museums of the BBCW have undergone crucial and extensive revisions. The displays have been reimagined and redesigned. These changes are responsive to and constitutive of other changes. The new designs allow the museums to display new and different pieces of their vast collection. Indeed, when we arrived first at the BBCW in the early 2000s, the PIM had just reopened and the new design allowed the museum to more fully display a collection that had grown and diversified from that which was first displayed in the 1970s.

Museums also change because museal design and display practices evolve in response to cultural trends and technological innovations. We highlight several of these forces of change in chapter 5. In the BBCW, we experienced museums becoming more interactive and immersive. The PIM and the Draper, for instance, which were both completed during the span of our many visits, were the first museums to embrace a more immersive design aesthetic. This aesthetic was later evident in the redesigned BBM and CFM as well. The experience of embodied immersion created through light, sound, smell, and directed movement coincided with an effort to offer visitors deeper historical contextualization of the displayed objects. Shunning a merely classificatory approach to various animals, for example, the Draper narrates the relations among animals, plants, climate, and humans.

And, of course, museums change for political and ethical reasons. The Whitney's new design was clearly attentive to the shift in art museums away from simple veneration of great art, which often meant the art of white men, to art as embedded in and creative of culture. In this case, the new design allowed the museum to hang its increasingly diverse collection and also to call into question the aesthetic and political assumptions of the art displayed. In the immediate aftermath of George Floyd's murder, the Whitney added signage at the museum's entrance engaging questions of diversity in the collection and on the museum walls. Likewise, the CFM recognized that guns can be instruments of violence, especially in relation to armed conflicts among nation states.

But we, too, have changed. As we noted in the introduction, we began this project as junior scholars just a few years out of our PhD programs. We were settling into our rhythms as teachers, scholars, and citizens. We were getting to know each other as friends and colleagues. Over the years, our travel to and writing about the BBCW has punctuated our friendship. Our presentations of this work to our departmental colleagues, to university communities, and to the discipline have shaped our own experiences and those of our colleagues. We have interacted with our readers. Students have joined our graduate programs because of this work. We have continued to read in rhetorical theory and criticism, public memory studies and museum studies, western history, ethnographic and autoethnographic approaches to studying communication, and in the areas relevant to specific museums (Indigenous studies, art history, guns, etc.). This reading, these conversations, in short, our continued practice as scholars has transformed us and has done so in at least four ways.[7]

First, we have revisited our positionality as critics. As one of the book's reviewers astutely noted, we too often adopted a critic-as-God stance in writing about the museums. This stance asserts certain knowledge, views the critical object from afar, and tolerates little disagreement. While this positionality is typical of scholars trained in the 1990s, it does not fit well with the stated commitments of this book or who we are in the process of becoming as scholars and people. Though we have sought to offer clear and compelling assessments of the museums that comprise the BBCW—assessments that are rooted in the structured rhetorical invitations of those places—we are also clearer throughout the book that these assessments are ours and that they come from our positions as variously identifying men each with particular backgrounds, trainings, and experiences. As such, we more thoroughly acknowledge alternative ways of feeling, sensing, and knowing the center.

Second, over the decades, we have engaged scholarship and scholars outside of the white and masculine tradition. Our citations are more diverse than when we began. This is not, exactly, about citing more voices. It is, instead, part of the process of remaking our identities from certainty to provisionality, from singularity to multiplicity. In our analysis of the PIM, for instance, we are far more alert to the rhetorics of survivance than when we first wrote about the museum. Similarly, we are more generous toward the CFM than we might otherwise be.

Third, we have deepened our commitment to this work as engaged and engaging. While the second chapter may feel a bit of a slog if the reader is not familiar with the debates around museums, criticism, and haunting, we have tried to be reflective about the heuristic value and utility of this work. Museums are so popular and so powerfully persuasive that careful, ongoing study of them matters. Making these studies approachable to nonspecialists also really matters. We have imagined our audience as undergraduate and graduate students, ready to be turned on to studying space and place, excited about leaving the classroom for the museum (and the memorial and the downtown and the suburb). We hope this book can foster that excitement.

And this leads to our fourth critical change. We have become more vulnerable and open. Throughout the book, we have shifted from language about visitors and their relationships to the museums to one that more fully encodes our own relationship to the museum and thereby to memory, citizenship, and the West. In this fourth shift, we have returned to our changing understandings of ourselves as critics. Here we see ourselves as fully involved museumgoers, citizens, friends, teachers, and passionate writers. We are implicated in the rhetorical invitations offered by the center, by Cody, by Wyoming, by the West. And we are implicated in our own writing, implicated in our own commitments as they show up in our book.

Taken together, these four transformations offer important lessons to ourselves and, we hope, to our readers. Often our writing—by "our" we mean the three of us but also the "our" of the discipline—scrubs out the appearance of our writerly, scholarly, and citizenry commitments. Frequently, we eliminate from the final essays the starts and stops of the drafting process. We remove the signs of the changing argument, the shifting knowledges we bring as critics to our tasks, the wrong turns we make as thinkers, the rabbit holes into which we often descend. In this way, published scholarship—like museums—erases the signs of scholarship's older versions. This is true of all the museums at the BBCW except the CFM, which openly reflects on its previous iteration. In place of this purifying impulse, we have wanted to reflect on how we have changed as critics because these changes have influenced our writing and shed light on critical processes. In several of the chapters, we have discussed the old argument and then offered the new one to give a sense of the roughness that lies behind the final glossy surface of scholarly essays. Our regular reflection on both museal and scholarly change has altered our writing and deepened our understanding of ourselves. Our regular reflection on ourselves as teachers, friends, colleagues, and citizens has also informed our writing in this book.

We want to reveal at least some of these changes; we want to perform the contingencies that lie behind making arguments. Perhaps readers of the book can, in the revealed cracks and in the obvious change over time, see a space for their own critical entry into the spaces of their lives as citizens, community members, students, and scholars. We hope we have shown that as citizens and critics, friends, and teachers, we can speak before we have a final perfect statement to make. If someone reading this book can find inspiration in it to perform their own (provisional) criticism of the landscapes around them, then the book

192 Conclusion

will have succeeded. If we can offer some resilience and a call for patience (we have been working on this book for twenty years!), then we will feel rewarded.

HAUNTS AND HAUNTING

In this process, we have come to experience the haunt and the haunting of the West. While we began to write about experiential landscapes early in this project, haunt(ing) came later. While many in the humanities and social sciences have written about haunts and haunting as a powerful way to explore social relations for some time, our own invocation of the terms is more recent. The appeal originated with our experience; that is, we constantly felt a haunting affect. Eric and Greg, in particular, felt the rural, cowboy West as a familiar haunt, having grown up in the rural West and embedded in communities of ranchers and farmers. But all of us also felt a haunting that Avery Gordon describes well when she portrays haunting as a "seething presence, acting on and often meddling with taken-for-granted realities."[8] When a local townsperson observed during our first trip to Cody, "Y'all aren't from around here, are you?" we felt this seething presence as our western-ness, our (non)whiteness, and our masculinities were called into question. Suddenly a space that could or should feel like home was askew. We felt the uncanniness that arises when ghosts return to haunt us.

Ghosts spoke to us when we tried to make sense of the *Encounters* display in the PIM. When, in the BBM, we stepped between the young Bill Cody and the American bison family, we were called by the ghosts of missing Plains Indians. When we toggled between two radically different visions of the Battle of Greasy Grass/Custer's Last Stand in the Whitney, we felt spirits moving us. The oil derricks and water wells and chaotically plunging bison in the Draper whispered of death, destruction, and renewal. And, in the designs of the CFM, we felt the tendrils of those lost to gun (and other) violence, from the attempted destruction of Plains People in the nineteenth century to the violent deaths of people of color at the hands of police in the twenty-first. Where, we wondered, was this affect located? These affects, these ghosts were located in a space just aside from the direct glance and felt like a seething presence to which we were determined to attend.

As we contemplated the idea of a book that examined all the center's museums and spaces, we turned to haunt to help us understand how the BBCW does its rhetorical work. Drawn to the powerful push and pull of comfort and anxiety, of presence and (near) absence, of home and un-home that the idea of haunt signals, we recognized we were writing about and writing through a haunted experiential landscape. As we visited a center that offered itself as a site of comfort and meaning, as a place to secure our fundamental Spirit, we found ourselves anxious and avoidant. Bringing together these embodied experiences of the landscape with theoretical understandings of haunts and haunting, our book has held the two sides of the haunt in constant tension. We have felt the space's comforts and its concerns, we have lived its simplicities and acknowledged its ghosts.

Our job has not been to rid the space of its ghosts. Instead, like Joshua Gunn, we are "learning to live with ghosts," which "entails the recognition that the Other does not have to be the Same."[9] It seems to us the case that the BBCW wishes to expel the Other or turn the Other into the Same. But despite its best efforts, the center can neither expel nor reduce the Other. Those open to recognizing the ghosts as inhabitants of the place can take from the center a powerful ethical hope: "the Other does not have to be the Same." In this way, the two haunting affects circle back on one another, for there is a deep and abiding comfort in the recognition that the Other need not be the Same, and there is a powerful way of being in this ability to accept the radical difference that is (human) life. Perhaps against its own intentions and efforts, the center offers the opportunity to accept—indeed, to welcome—the Other as different. Here is a chance to welcome into the (national) home its ghosts, to live beside these ghosts without turning them into us. Or, at least, that is our hope for ourselves and our nation.

Notes

Preface

1. Buffalo Bill Historical Center, "Mission," online, accessed June 28, 2012.

2. Numerous authors have engaged the BBCW or its museums. See Richard A. Bartlett, *From Cody to the World: The First Seventy-Five Years of the Buffalo Bill Memorial Association* (Cody, WY: Buffalo Bill Historical Center, 1992); Liza Nicholas, "Wyoming as America: Celebrations, a Museum, and Yale," *American Quarterly* 54 (2002): 437–65; Nicholas, *Becoming Western: Stories of Culture and Identity in the Cowboy State* (Lincoln: University of Nebraska Press, 2006), especially chaps. 2 and 4; John Dorst, "A Walk through the Shooting Gallery," *Museum Anthropologist* 17 (1993): 7–13; and Jane Tompkins, *West of Everything: The Inner Life of Westerns* (New York: Oxford University Press, 1992), especially chap. 9.

3. We have inscribed "America" in quotation marks to highlight the problematic nature of this term. For the most part, we will use US or United States to refer to the nation throughout the book. But there are times when we deliberately use "America" because we intend to refer to the myth that is America.

4. Bartlett, *From Cody to the World*, 4.

5. Charles Chamberlain, "From 'Haunts' to 'Character': The Meaning of Ethos and Its Relation to Ethics," *Helios* 11 (1984): 101.

6. We use the nomenclature of "Native American" and "Indigenous Peoples" throughout the book, generally, and more particularly use the label "Plains Indians" as specific to the BBCW's use, along with other nomenclature used by the BBCW and/or as used in source materials.

7. We use the appellation "Euro American" and "white" for general use throughout the book to describe the national identity of the dominant ethnic/racial group in the United States. We also use the phrase (Euro) American to highlight many texts and sources we rely on that use the single term "American" as the colloquial national term of use.

8. Avery Gordon, *Ghostly Matters: Haunting and the Sociological Imagination* (Minneapolis: University of Minnesota Press, 2008), 134.

9. Amy Lonetree, *Decolonizing Museums: Representing Native America in National and Tribal Museums* (Chapel Hill: University of North Carolina Press, 2012) 5.

Chapter 1

1. Emilene Ostlind, "The Bighorn Basin: Wyoming's Bony Back Pocket," wyohistory

(website), accessed March 20, 2014; Lynn Johnson Houze, "Cody, Wyoming," wyohistory (website), accessed March 20, 2014.

2. Jill St. Germain, *Broken Treaties: United State and Canadian Relations with the Lakotas and the Plains Cree, 1868–1885* (Lincoln: University of Nebraska Press, 2009), 1.

3. St. Germain, *Broken Treaties*, 1–5.

4. Jane Tompkins, *West of Everything: The Inner Life of Westerns* (New York: Oxford University Press, 1992), 6; John Dorst, *Looking West* (Philadelphia: University of Pennsylvania Press, 1999): 13–16; Liza Nicholas, "Wyoming as America: Celebrations, a Museum, and Yale," *American Quarterly* 54 (2002): 439.

5. Accounts of Buffalo Bill are innumerable. The most recent and best account of his life is Louis S. Warren, *Buffalo Bill's America: William Cody and the Wild West Show* (New York: Alfred A. Knopf, 2005).

6. Richard White, "Frederick Jackson Turner and Buffalo Bill," in *The Frontier in American Culture: An Exhibition at the Newberry Library, August 26, 1994–January 7, 1995*, ed. Richard White, Patricia Nelson Limerick, and James R. Grossman (Berkeley: University of California Press, 1994), 11.

7. Much has been written about Buffalo Bill and more specifically on his Wild West Show. For recent treatments of the Wild West Show, see Joy S. Kasson, *Buffalo Bill's Wild West: Celebrity, Memory, and Popular History* (New York: Hill and Wang, 2000); and Warren, *Buffalo Bill's America*. And for a recent treatment of the role of Native Americans in the Wild West see Linda Scarangella McNenly, *Native Performers in Wild West Shows: From Buffalo Bill to Euro Disney* (Norman: University of Oklahoma Press, 2012), 21–38.

8. Richard Slotkin, *Gunfighter Nation: The Myth of the Frontier in Twentieth-Century America* (New York: Atheneum, 1992), 81–82.

9. *Buffalo Bill Museum*, catalog (Cody, WY: Buffalo Bill Historical Center, 1995), 31.

10. White, "Frederick Jackson Turner and Buffalo Bill," 7; also Slotkin, *Gunfighter Nation*, 67–68.

11. Tompkins, *West of Everything*, 179; Howard Roberts Lamar, ed., *The Reader's Encyclopedia of the American West* (New York: Crowell, 1977), 230.

12. *Buffalo Bill Museum*, 28; *Treasures of Our West*, catalog (Cody: Buffalo Bill Historical Center, 1992), 8.

13. Will Wright, *The Wild West: The Mythic Cowboy and Social Theory* (London: Sage Publications, 2002), 2.

14. Slotkin, *Gunfighter Nation*, 10.

15. Slotkin, 11–12.

16. Warren, *Buffalo Bill's America*, xi.

17. Warren, x.

18. Liza J. Nicholas, *Becoming Western: Stories of Culture and Identity in the Cowboy State* (Lincoln: University of Nebraska Press, 2006), 102–3. By the mid-1920s, Coe owned Cody's TE Ranch. In the 1950s he made contributions that helped found both the Yale and the University of Wyoming American Studies programs as distinctly anticommunist efforts.

19. Nicholas, *Becoming Western*, xiii.

20. Nicholas, *Becoming Western*, 50.

21. Nicholas, *Becoming Western*, 36–37; See also Richard A. Bartlett, *From Cody to the World: The First Seventy-Five Years of the Buffalo Bill Memorial Association* (Cody, WY: Buffalo Bill Historical Center, 1992), 46–53.

22. Bartlett, *From Cody to the World*, 57.

23. Bartlett, 56.

24. Nicholas, "Wyoming as America," 449.

25. Bartlett, 117–18.

26. Coe, quoted in Nicholas, "Wyoming as America," 452; Nicholas, "Wyoming as America," 459.

27. Bartlett, 152–54. The museum continues to depend almost exclusively on private financing from entrance fees, donations, and grants. State and federal funds have served a minor role in funding it (J. Hedderman, personal communication, March 8, 2004).

28. Bartlett, 122–51.

29. Robert Windler, "Museum Is Set Up for Buffalo Bill: Half-Finished Structure in Wyoming Is Dedicated," *New York Times*, July 5, 1968.

30. *Treasures from Our West* (Cody, WY: Buffalo Bill Historical Center, 1992), 44.

31. John Dorst, "A Walk through the Shooting Gallery," *Museum Anthropology* 17 (1993): 8.

32. Ed Christopherson, "New Art Collection Records the Great West," *New York Times*, May 24, 1959, XX 25 (travel section).

33. Windler, "Museum Is Set Up for Buffalo Bill," 22.

34. Ruth Rudner, "Wyoming Prospects," *New York Times*, September 18, 1983, section 10 (travel), page 22 ; Jim Robbins, "Cody Displays Art and Relics of the West: Where Buffalo Bill's Not Defunct," *New York Times*, July 26, 1987, section 10 (travel), page 19.

35. Edward Rothstein, "At the Buffalo Bill Museum, a Showdown between History and Myth," *New York Times*, August 4, 2012.

36. Rothstein, "At the Buffalo Bill Museum."

37. Rothstein.

38. Robbins, "Cody Displays Art and Relics of the West."

39. Bartlett, 4.

40. Rothstein.

41. "The Mission of the Center of the West," Center of the West (website), accessed April 23, 2014.

42. "Mission of the Center of the West."

43. "Mission of the Center of the West."

44. "Mission of the Center of the West."

45. "Mission of the Center of the West."

46. "Mission of the Center of the West."

47. Edward Tabor Linenthal, *Sacred Ground: Americans and Their Battlefields*, 2nd ed. (Urbana: University of Illinois Press, 1993).

48. Anthony Vidler, *The Architectural Uncanny: Essays in the Modern Unhomely* (Cambridge: MIT Press, 1992); Sigmund Freud, "The Uncanny," in *The Uncanny*, trans. David McLintock (London: Penguin Books, 2003), 123–62.

Chapter 2

1. Roy Rosenzweig and David P. Thelen, *The Presence of the Past: Popular Uses of History in American Life* (New York: Columbia University Press, 1998), 19–21.

2. Bernard J. Armada, "Memorial Agon: An Interpretive Tour of the National Civil Rights Museum," *Southern Journal of Communication* 63, no. 3 (1998): 235–43. The surge in interest in museums in rhetoric is evidenced by a number of book-length studies on museums. See Bernard-Donals, *Figures of Memory: The Rhetoric of Displacement at the United States Holocaust Memorial Museum* (Albany: State University of New York Press, 2016); Steven C. Dubin, *Displays of Power: Memory and Amnesia in the American Museum* (New York: New York University Press, 1999); Dubin, *Transforming Museums: Mounting Queen Victoria in a Democratic South Africa* (New York: Palgrave Macmillan, 2006); Amy Lonetree, *Decolonizing Museums: Representing Native America in National and Tribal Museums* (Chapel Hill: University of North Carolina Press, 2012); Elizabeth M. Weiser, *Museum Rhetoric: Building Civic Identity in National Spaces* (University Park: Penn State University Press, 2017).

3. Roberta Chevrette and Aaron Hess, "Unearthing the Native Past: Citizen Archaeology and the Modern (Non)Belonging at the Pueblo Grande Museum," *Communication and Critical/Cultural Studies* 12, no. 2 (2015): 139–58; Victoria J. Gallagher, "Remembering Together?" *Southern Communication Journal* 60, no. 2 (1995): 109–19; Marouf Hasian and Rulon Wood, "Critical Museology (Post)Colonial Communication, and the Gradual Mastering of Traumatic Pasts at the Royal Museum for Central Africa (RMCA)," *Western Journal of Communication* 74, no. 2 (2010): 128–49; Nicole Maurantonio, "Material Rhetoric, Public Memory, and the Post-It Note," *Southern Communication Journal* 80, no. 2 (2015): 83–101; Aaron T. Phillips, "Eliding Extraction, Embracing Novelty: The Spatio-Temporal Configuration of Natural History," *Environmental Communication* 8, no. 4 (2014): 452–67; Carly S. Woods et al., "A Matter of Regionalism: Remembering Brandon Teena and Willa Cather at the Nebraska History Museum," *Quarterly Journal of Speech* 99, no. 3 (2013): 341–63.

4. James W. Loewen, *Lies across America: What Our Historic Sites Get Wrong* (New York: New Press, 2010); Dubin, *Displays of Power*; Vivien Green Fryd, *Art and Empire: The Politics of Ethnicity in the United States Capitol, 1815–1860* (New Haven: Yale University Press, 1992); Liza Nicholas, "Wyoming as America: Celebrations, a Museum, and Yale," *American Quarterly* 54 (2002): 437–65.

5. The list of rhetorically oriented books engaging museums is growing. See in particular, Bernard-Donals, *Figures of Memory*; Lisa King, *Legible Sovereignties: Rhetoric, Representations, and Native American Museums* (Corvallis: Oregon State University Press, 2017); Lonetree, *Decolonizing Museums*; Weiser, *Museum Rhetoric*; Dubin, *Transforming Museums*; Michael Bowman makes a strong case for rhetoric's purchase on museums. Michael Bowman, "Tracing Mary Queen of Scots," in

Places of Public Memory: The Rhetoric of Museums and Memorials, ed. Greg Dickinson, Carole Blair, and Brian L. Ott (Tuscaloosa: University of Alabama Press, 2010), 191–215.

6. Collected memory, as we use it here, is different from the use of the same term by Jeffrey K. Olick. For Olick, collected memory is one epistemology within memory studies that imagines public memory to be individual and psychological rather than a form of deeply structured sociality. See Jeffrey K. Olick, "Collective Memory: The Two Cultures," *Sociological Theory* 17, no. 3 (November 1999): 333–48.

7. Danny Michael, email correspondence with Greg Dickinson, August 8, 2021.

8. Barry Edmund Gaither, "'Hey, That's Mine:' Thoughts on Pluralism and American Museums," in *Museums and Communities: The Politics of Public Culture*, ed. Ivan Karp, Christine Mullen Kreamer, and Steven D. Lavine (Washington, DC: Smithsonian Press, 1992), 61.

9. Susan A. Crane, "Introduction," *Museums and Memory* (Stanford: Stanford University Press, 2000), 9.

10. Gaynor Kavanagh, "Making Histories, Making Memories," in *Making Histories in Museums* (London: Leicester University Press, 1996), 6; Barbie Zelizer, "Reading the Past against the Grain: The Shape of Memory Studies," *Critical Studies in Media Communication* 12, no. 2 (1995): 224.

11. Carole Blair, "Contemporary US Memorial Sites as Exemplars of Rhetoric's Materiality," in *Rhetorical Bodies*, ed. Jack Selzer and Sharon Crowley (Madison: University of Wisconsin Press, 1999), 30–50; Pierre Nora, "Between Memory and History: Les Lieux de Mémoire," *Representations* 26 (Spring 1989): 13; Zelizer, "Reading the Past against the Grain," 232.

12. Sandra Dudley, "Introduction: Museum and Things," in *The Thing about Museums: Objects and Experience, Representation and Contestation*, ed. Sandra Dudley et al. (London: Routledge, 2012), 7; Rosenzweig and Thelen, *Presence of the Past*, 21.

13. Dudley, "Introduction," 7.

14. Kavanagh, "Making Histories, Making Memories," 6; Helen Rees Leahy, "Exhibiting Absence in the Museum," in Dudley et al., *Thing about Museums*, 250.

15. Tiffany Jenkins, *Contesting Human Remains in Museum Collections: The Crisis of Cultural Authority* (New York: Routledge, 2011): 5–7; Heather J. H. Edgar and Anna L. M. Rautman, "Contemporary Museum Policies and the Ethics of Accepting Human Remains," *Curator: The Museum Journal* 57, no. 2 (April 2014): 237–47.

16. Chip Colwell, *Plundered Skulls and Stolen Spirits: Inside the Fight to Reclaim Native America's Culture* (Chicago: University of Chicago Press, 2017): 5. Robert E. Bieder, "The Representations of Indian Bodies in Nineteenth-Century American Anthropology," in *Repatriation Reader: Who Owns American Indian Remains*, ed. Devon A. Mihesuab (Lincoln: University of Nebraska Press), 19–36.

17. Devon A. Mihesuab, "Introduction," in Mihesuab, *Repatriation Reader*, 1–2.

18. Bieder, "Representations of Indian Bodies," 19–20.

19. Colwell, *Plundered Skulls and Stolen Spirits*, 6.

20. "Native American Graves Protection and Repatriation Act," National Park Service website, accessed December 3, 2021.

21. "Hansen Resigns, West Leads Plains Indian Museum," *Cody Enterprise*, May 14, 2014.

22. "Notice of Intent to Repatriate Cultural Items: Buffalo Bill Center of the West, Plains Indian Museum," National Park Service July 19, 2019, Federal Register (website), accessed December 2, 2021.

23. In a blog post in 2015, the BBCW addressed the NAGPRA as a crucial component of PIM's governance. Rebecca West, the curator of the PIM at the time, wrote, "Consultation visits have always been welcome opportunities for Center staff and tribal representatives to connect. The objects are what bring everyone together for a time that is full of anticipation, emotion, and sharing of information. The tribal delegations that have visited sometimes consist of elders and multiple generations, both men and women, NAGPRA coordinators, tribal and spiritual leaders, historic preservation officers, and families. Center staff abides by the belief that the tribal delegations tell us how they would like to spend time with the objects, what they would like to see, and how much they wish to share with us."

24. G. J. Ashworth, "Conservation as Preservation or Heritage: Two Paradigms and Two Answers," *Built Environment* 23, no. 2 (1997): 92–93. We have chosen *preservation* as the term to capture the practices that protect objects from harm. Others use the term *conservation*. As Ashworth points out, these two terms and others like *heritage* are used loosely and often synonymously. Regardless of the term used, we mean to capture those practices that help maintain the material remnants of the past. For further discussion on the distinction between preservation and conservation, see Miriam Clavir, *Preserving What Is Valued: Museums, Conservation, and First Nations* (Vancouver: University of British Columbia Press, 2002); Suzanne Keene, *Managing Conservation in Museums*, 2nd ed. (Oxford: Butterworth-Heinemann, 2002), 24.

25. Jan Schall, "Curating Ephemara: Responsibility and Reality," in *(Im)permanence: Cultures in/out of Time*, ed. Judith Schachter and Stephen Brockmann (Pittsburgh: Center of the Arts in Society, Carnegie Mellon University, 2008), 16.

26. Jacques Derrida, *Archive Fever: A Freudian Impression*, trans. Eric Prenowitz (Chicago: University of Chicago Press, 1998), 4.

27. Sarah E. Boehme, *Whitney Gallery of Western Art* (Cody, WY: Buffalo Bill Historical Center, 1997), 7.

28. Zelizer, "Reading the Past against the Grain," 223.

29. Patrick H. Hutton, *History as an Art of Memory* (Hanover, NH: University Press of New England, 1993), 78.

30. Hans Ulrich Gumbrecht, *Production of Presence: What Meaning Cannot Convey* (Stanford: Stanford University Press, 2004), 17; Julia Petrov, "Playing Dress-Up: Inhabiting Imagined Spaces through Museum Objects," in Dudley et al., *Thing about Museums*, 232.

31. Erika Suderburg, "Introduction: On Installation and Site Specificity," in *Space, Site, Intervention: Situating Installation Art*, ed. Erika Suderburg (Minneapolis: University of Minnesota Press, 2000), 4.

32. Carole Blair and Neil Michel, "Commemorating in the Theme Park Zone:

Reading the Astronauts Memorial," in *At the Intersection: Cultural Studies and Rhetorical Studies*, ed. Thomas Rosteck (New York: Guilford Press, 1999), 58–59.

33. Armada, "Memorial Agon," 236; Didier Maleuvre, *Museum Memories: History, Technology, Art* (Stanford, CA: Stanford University Press, 1999), 1.

34. Tony Bennett, *The Birth of the Museum: History, Theory, Politics* (New York: Routledge, 1995), 180–86; Crane, "Introduction," 4; Suderburg, "Introduction," 5.

35. Bennett, *Birth of the Museum*, 59–86.

36. United States Holocaust Museum, "Mission and History" (website), accessed September 11, 2020. On the rhetorical force of the United States Holocaust Memorial and Museum see Bernard-Donals, *Figures of Memory*.

37. Diane Marie Keeling, "Of Turning and Tropes," *Review of Communication* 16, no. 4 (2016): 317–33.

38. Carole Blair, Greg Dickinson, and Brian L. Ott, "Introduction: Rhetoric/Memory/Place," in Dickinson, Blair, and Ott, *Places of Public Memory*, 24–25.

39. Henri Lefebvre, *The Social Production of Space*, trans. Donald Nicholson-Smith (Oxford, UK: Blackwell, 1991), 174.

40. Francis A. Yates, *The Art of Memory* (Chicago: University of Chicago Press, 1966), 46.

41. Charles Chamberlain, "From 'Haunts' to 'Character': The Meaning of *Ethos* and Its Relation to Ethics," *Helios* 11, no. 2 (1984): 98; Michael J. Hyde, "Introduction: Rhetorically, We Dwell," *The Ethos of Rhetoric*, ed. Michael J. Hyde (Columbia: University of South Carolina Press, 2004): xii–xxviii.

42. The rhetorical and communication literature on intersections of space, place, and memory is rapidly growing and too significant to fully cite here. Here is a representative selection of recent work beyond that which we have already cited and will cite in the coming chapters. Emma Frances Bloomfield, "Ark Encounter as Material Apocalyptic Rhetoric: Contemporary Creationist Strategies on Board Noah's Ark," *Southern Communication Journal*, 82 (2017): 263–77; Laura Michael Brown, "Flyover States, No Man's Land, and the Bible Belt: Introducing Critical Regionalism for Rhetorical Analysis," *Communication Teacher* 34 (2020): 198–203; Anthony C. Cavaiani, "Rhetoric, Materiality, and the Disruption of Meaning: The Stadium as a Place of Protest," *Communication and Sport* 8 (2020): 473–88; Jordin Clark, "Daddy Pence Come Dance": Queer(ing) Space in the Suburbs," *Western Journal of Communication* 85 (2021): 168–87; E. Cram, "Queer Geographies and the Rhetoric of Orientation," *Quarterly Journal of Speech* 105 (2019): 98–115; Joshua Daniel-Wariya, "Welcome to Decision Points Theater: Rhetoric, Museology, and Game Studies," *Rhetoric Society Quarterly* 49 (2019): 387–408; Justin Eckstein and Amy Young, "WastED Rhetoric," *Communication and Critical/Cultural Studies* 15 (2018): 274–91; Joshua P. Ewalt, "Visibility and Order at the Salt Lake City Main Public Library: Commonplaces, Deviant Publics, and the Rhetorical Criticism of Neoliberalism's Geographies," *Communication and Critical/Cultural Studies* 16 (2019): 103–21; Alyson Farzad-Phillips, "Huddles or Hurdles? Spatial Barriers to Collective Gathering in the Aftermath of the Women's March," *Women's Studies in Communication* 43 (2020): 247–70; Brenda Helmbrecht, "Revisiting Missions: Decolonizing Public

Memories in California," *Rhetoric Society Quarterly* 49, no. 5 (2019): 470–94; Elinor Light, "Playing in Cyberspace: The Social Performative on Heidelberg Street," *Critical Studies in Media Communication* 36 (2019): 207–20; Amy J. Lueck, "Haunting Women's Public Memory: Ethos, Space, and Gender in the Winchester Mystery House," *Rhetoric Review* 40 (2021): 107–22; Kevin Marinelli, "Placing Second: Empathic Unsettlement as a Vehicle of Consubstantiality at the Silent Gesture Statue of Tommie Smith and John Carlos," *Memory Studies* 10 (2017): 440–58; J. David Maxson, "Second Line to Bury White Supremacy': Take 'Em Down Nola, Monument Removal, and Residual Memory," *Quarterly Journal of Speech*, 106 (2020), 48–71; Scott A. Mitchell, "Spaces of Emergent Memory: Detroit's 8 Mile Wall and Public Memories of Civil Rights Injustice," *Communication and Critical/Cultural Studies* 15 (2018): 197–212; Lauren Obermark, "'Assurance That the World Holds Far More Good Than Bad': The Pedagogy of Memory at the Oklahoma City National Memorial Museum," *Rhetoric Review* 38 (2019): 93–107; Jesse J. Ohl and Jennifer E. Potter, "Traumatic Encounters with Frank Mechau's Dangers of the Mail," *Communication and Critical/Cultural Studies* 16 (2019): 26–42; Nicholas S. Paliewicz, "The Country, the City, and the Corporation: Rio Tinto Kennecott and the Materiality of Corporate Rhetoric," *Environmental Communication* 12 (2018): 744–62; Vincent N. Pham, "Drive-By Cinema's Drive-Outs and U-Turns: Materiality, Mobility, and the Reconfiguring of Forgotten Spaces and Absurd Borders," *Women's Studies in Communication* 41 (2018); 370–82; Kendall R. Phillips and Connah Podmore, "The Scale of Our Memory: Spectacle in the Commemoration of Gallipoli," *Rhetoric Society Quarterly* 50, no. 1 (2020): 35–52; Sarah Pinto et al., eds., *Interdisciplinary Unsettlings of Place and Space* (Singapore: Springer, 2019); Jennifer H. Rice et al., "Memory and Lost Communities: Strange Methods for Studying Place," *Review of Communication* 20 (2020): 144–51; Emily Robinson, "Objects, Documentation, and Identification: Materiality and Memory of American Indian Boarding Schools at the Heard Museum," *Rhetoric Society Quarterly* 51 (2021): 94–108; Carl Schlachte, "Material Inertia: The Sedimented Spatial Rhetoric of Public School Buildings," *Rhetoric Review* 39 (2020): 317–29; Kate Siegfried, "Making Settler Colonialism Concrete: Agentive Materialism and Habitational Violence in Palestine," *Communication and Critical/Cultural Studies* 17 (2020): 267–84; Sara Vartabedian, "No Cause for Comfort Here: False Witnesses to 'Peace,'" *Southern Communication Journal* 82 (2017): 250–62; Andrew F. Wood, "Haunting Ruins in a Western Ghost Town: Authentic Violence and Recursive Gaze at Bodie, California," *Western Journal of Communication*, 84 (2020): 439–56.

43. *Oxford English Dictionary*, 3rd ed., s.v. "experience," accessed June 25, 2014, online. Definition 1a is "The action of putting to the test; trial." Definition 1b is "A tentative procedure; an operation performed in order to ascertain or illustrate some truth; an experiment." While these are obsolete definitions, it is not hard to see how they move into definition 3, "The actual observation of facts or events, considered as a source of knowledge."

44. Alva Nöe, *Varieties of Presence* (Cambridge, MA: Harvard University Press, 2012), 2–3.

45. Nöe, *Varieties of Presence*, 24. See also Brian Massumi, *Parables for the Virtual:*

Movement, Affect, Sensation (Durham, NC: Duke University Press, 2002), 180; and Massumi, *Semblance and Event: Activist Philosophy and the Occurrent Arts* (Cambridge, MA: MIT Press, 2011), 1.

46. Jane Bennett, "The Force of Things: Steps Toward an Ecology of Matter," *Political Theory* 32, no. 2 (2004): 360.

47. Andy Clark, *Being There: Putting Brain, Body, and World Together Again* (Cambridge, MA: Bradford Books, 1997), 18, 22–23.

48. Nöe, 2–3.

49. Weiser, 3–4.

50. Nöe, 190.

51. Nöe, 5.

52. The emplacedness of experience wraps together several components of contemporary non-Cartesian understandings of mind. These rely on what some have called the four "e"s: mind as embodied, embedded, enacted, and extended. We address the first of these in our first principle of experience. The idea that experience is emplaced weaves the complicated relations among embedded (that our material world co-constitutes cognition), enacted (that cognition includes the actions and practices of the entire human), and extended (that cognition is extended beyond the brain and even beyond the subject). See Mark Rowlands, *The New Science of the Mind: From Extended Mind to Embodied Phenomenology* (Cambridge, MA: MIT Press, 2010): 3–4, 51–84.

53. Nöe, 5. It is this perceptual process by which we, Nöe argues, become "at home in the world."

54. Nöe, 31.

55. Doreen Massey, *For Space* (Los Angeles: Sage, 2005), 30.

56. Sharon Zukin, *Landscapes of Power: From Detroit to Disney World* (Berkeley: University of California Press, 1991), 18.

57. Amy Mills, *Streets of Memory: Landscape, Tolerance, and National Identity in Istanbul* (Athens: University of Georgia Press, 2010), 83.

58. Mills, *Streets of Memory*, 209.

59. Massey, *For Space*, 9.

60. Massey, 130.

61. Massey, 130.

62. Massey, 130.

63. Lefebvre, *Social Production of Space*, 189.

64. Lefebvre, 189.

65. Barry Brummett, *Rhetoric in Popular Culture* (New York: St. Martin's Press, 1994), 80.

66. Lefebvre, 222. He goes on to write: "The actions of social practice are expressible but not explicable through discourse; they are, precisely, acted—and not read. A monumental work, like a musical one, does not have a "signified" (or "signifieds"); rather, it has a horizon of meaning: a specific or indefinite multiplicity of meanings, a shifting hierarchy in which now one, now another meaning comes momentarily to the fore, by means of—and for the sake of—a particular action."

67. Blair and Michel, "Commemorating in the Theme Park Zone," 58–59.

68. Meaghan Morris, "Things to Do with Shopping Centres," in *Grafts: Feminist Cultural Criticism*, ed. Susan Sheridan (New York: Verso, 1988), 224n17.

69. Lefebvre, 222.

70. Blair and Michel, 58.

71. Kavanagh, 3–4.

72. Victor Burgin, *In/Different Spaces: Places and Memory in Visual Culture* (Berkeley: University of California Press, 1996), 28.

73. William Deverell, "Fighting Words: The Significance of the American West in the History of the United States," in *A New Significance: Re-Envisioning the History of the American West*, ed. Clyde A. Milner II (New York: Oxford University Press, 1996), 37.

74. Philip Joseph Deloria, *Playing Indian* (New Haven: Yale University Press, 1998), 4–7. The literature on non–Native American uses of images of Indianness is vast. See S. Elizabeth Bird, "Introduction: Constructing the Indian, 1930s–1990s," in *Dressing in Feathers: The Construction of the Indian in Popular Culture*, ed. S. Elizabeth Bird (Boulder, CO: Westview Press, 1996), 1–12; Martin Barker and Roger Sabin, *The Lasting of the Mohicans: History of an American Myth* (Jackson: University Press of Mississippi, 1995); Richard Drinnon, *Facing West: The Metaphysics of Indian-Hating and Empire-Building* (Minneapolis: University of Minnesota Press, 1980); Renard Strickland, *Tonto's Revenge: Reflections on American Indian Culture and Policy* (Albuquerque: University of New Mexico Press, 1997), 17–45, 63–75.

75. See Michel de Certeau, *The Practice of Everyday Life*, trans. Steven Rendall (Berkeley: University of California Press, 1984), 82–90; Morris, "Things to Do with Shopping Centres," 206.

76. Blair and Michel, 67, 71.

77. John Darwin Dorst, *Looking West* (Philadelphia: University of Pennsylvania, 1999), 96.

78. Maurice Charland, "Constitutive Rhetoric: The Case of the *Peuple Québécois*," *Quarterly Journal of Speech* 73, no. 2 (May 1987): 138.

79. Lefebvre, 194.

80. Ian Buchanan, "Heterophenomenology, or de Certeau's Theory of Space," in "Michel de Certeau," ed. Ian Buchanan, special issue, *Social Semiotics* 6, no. 1 (1996): 126.

81. Dorst, *Looking West*, 167.

82. Greg Dickinson and Giorgia Aiello, "Being through There Matters: Materiality, Bodies, and Movement in Urban Communication Research," *International Journal of Communication* 10 (2016): 1296. For one explanation of at least Brian's and Greg's skepticism of method in rhetorical criticism, see Brian L. Ott and Greg Dickinson, "Entering the Unending Conversation: An Introduction to Rhetorical Criticism," in *The Routledge Reader in Rhetorical Criticism*, ed. Brian L. Ott and Greg Dickinson (New York: Routledge, 2013): 4.

83. Greg Dickinson and Brian L. Ott, "Neoliberal Capitalism, Globalization, and

Lines of Flight: Vectors and Velocities at the 16th Street Mall," *Cultural Studies ↔ Critical Methodologies* 13 (2013): 531.

84. Avery Gordon, *Ghostly Matters: Haunting and the Sociological Imagination* (Minneapolis: University of Minnesota Press, 2008), 8.

85. Joshua Gunn, "Mourning Speech: Haunting and the Spectral Voices of Nine-Eleven," *Text and Performance Quarterly*, 24 (2004): 97.

86. Gunn, "Mourning Speech," 97.

87. Chamberlain, "From 'Haunts' to 'Character,'" 98.

88. Chamberlain, 101.

89. The classic formulation of the uncanny as a sense of unhomliness caused by the return of the repressed is Sigmund Freud, "The Uncanny," in *The Uncanny*, trans. David McLintock (London: Penguin Books, 2003), 123–62. See also Anthony Vidler, *The Architectural Uncanny: Essays in the Modern Unhomely* (Cambridge, MA: MIT Press, 1992).

90. Gordon, *Ghostly Matters*, xvi.

91. Gordon, 206.

92. Lorenzo Veracini, *Settler Colonialism: A Theoretical Overview* (Houndmills, UK: Palgrave Macmillan: 2010), 77.

93. Varacini, *Settler Colonialism*, 76.

94. Warren Cariou, "Haunted Prairie: Aboriginal 'Ghosts' and the Spectres of Settlement," *University of Toronto Quarterly* 75 (2006): 727–28.

95. Gordon, xix.

96. Barry Brummett, "Rhetorical Theory as Heuristic and Moral: A Pedagogical Justification," *Communication Education* 33 (1984): 97–107.

Chapter 3

Epigraph. Actor voice-over accompanying the ghostly, water vapor visual image at the entrance into the Buffalo Bill Museum (an in-situ transcription, May 22, 2013).

1. "The Center's Mission, Vision, and Grounding Principles," Buffalo Bill Center of the West, accessed December 8, 2015, web.

2. Drawing a distinction between "function" and "atmosphere," Gernot Böhme discusses how "functionally considered, all bookshops are alike: they are terminals of the major retail booksellers. But in their atmosphere they are not alike at all. On the contrary: their functional sameness permits and indeed necessitates the differences in their aesthetic presentation." Gernot Böhme, "Staged Materiality," *Interstices: Journal of Architecture and Related Arts* 14 (2013): 94.

3. With some context-specific exceptions, from here on out we will refer to both Buffalo Bill Cody and William F. Cody as "Cody," recognizing that the two identities are deeply woven together.

4. Ben Anderson details a working of atmospheres: "On the one hand, atmospheres require completion by the subjects that 'apprehend' them. They belong to the perceiving subject. On the other hand, atmospheres 'emanate' from the ensemble

of elements that make up the aesthetic object. They belong to the aesthetic object. Ben Anderson, "Affective Atmospheres," *Emotion, Space and Society* 2 (2009): 79.

5. Since the nineteenth century, this haunting longing has most often been figured as nostalgia. Like haunting, nostalgia has both enabling and disabling modes. A pathology that undermines the sufferer's ability to be content in the present time/place, it can also be a powerfully comforting rhetorical mode. Svetlana Boym, *The Future of Nostalgia* (New York: Basic Books, 2001); Greg Dickinson, *Suburban Dreams: Imagining and Building the Good Life* (Tuscaloosa: University of Alabama Press, 2015).

6. Gaston Bachelard, *The Poetics of Space*, trans. Maria Jolas (Boston: Beacon Press, 1994).

7. Another way of thinking about the duality of home and haunt along with the body's materiality may be found in the neurobiological study of trauma. In the face of a traumatic or painful present experience, the body often strives to return home, even if home has itself been a site of trauma and other, safer environments are available. The body/mind is programmed to seek comfort in home haunts even if the home is haunted. Bessel Van Der Kolk, *The Body Keeps the Score: Brain, Mind, and Body in the Healing of Trauma* (New York: Viking, 2014).

8. Greg Dickinson, Brian L. Ott, and Eric Aoki, "Memory and Myth at the Buffalo Bill Museum," *Western Journal of Communication* 69, no. 2 (2005): 85–108.

9. Jane Bennett, "The Force of Things: Steps toward an Ecology of Matter," *Political Theory* 32, no. 3 (2004): 348.

10. Brian Massumi, "The Autonomy of Affect," *Cultural Critique* 31 (1995): 85; Giorgia Aiello and Greg Dickinson, "Beyond Authenticity: A Visual-Material Analysis of Locality in the Global Redesign of Starbucks Stores," *Visual Communication* 13, no. 3 (2014): 316; Greg Dickinson and Giorgia Aiello, "Being through There Matters: Materiality, Bodies, and Movement in Urban Communication Research," *International Journal of Communication* 10 (2016): 1295.

11. Massumi, "Autonomy of Affect," 85.

12. Dickinson and Aiello, "Being through There Matters," 1304.

13. Charles B. Hosmer Jr., *Presence of the Past: A History of the Preservation Movement in the United States before Williamsburg* (New York: G. P. Putnam's Sons, 1965), 44–46; William J. Murtagh, *Keeping Time: The History and Theory of Preservation in America*, rev. ed. (New York: John Wiley and Sons, 1997), 78–79, 28–30.

14. Patricia West, *Domesticating History: The Political Origins of America's House Museums* (Washington, DC: Smithsonian Institution Press, 1999), 1–2.

15. West, *Domesticating History*, 1.

16. West, 44–46.

17. West, 43.

18. Winchester notes that the log cabin built in Cody was not, in fact, a replica of the TE Ranch house but rather an "idealized construction of the place that Mrs. Allen would have had Cody call home." Juti A. Winchester, "Log Cabin Dreams: Women, Domesticity and Museums in the Early Twentieth Century," *Points West: Journal of the Buffalo Bill Historical Center*, Summer 2003, 20.

19. Sandra K. Sagala, *Buffalo Bill on Stage* (Albuquerque: University of New Mexico Press, 2008), 83.

20. Winchester, "Log Cabin Dreams," 22.

21. Mac E. Berrick, "The Log House as Cultural Symbol," *Material Culture* 18, no. 1 (1986): 8–11.

22. Richard A. Bartlett, *From Cody to the World: The First Seventy-Five Years of the Buffalo Bill Memorial Association* (Cody, WY: Buffalo Bill Historical Center, 1992), 151, 153.

23. Robert Windler, "Museum Is Set Up for Buffalo Bill: Half-Finished Structure in Wyoming Is Dedicated," *New York Times*, July 5, 1968.

24. Liza Nicholas, "Wyoming as America: Celebrations, a Museum, and Yale," *American Quarterly* 54 (2002): 439. By the time of his death, in 1975, Coe had donated $1.85 million to the Buffalo Bill Historical Center. Bartlett, *From Cody to the World*, 116.

25. *Buffalo Bill Museum*, catalog (Cody, WY: Buffalo Bill Historical Center, 1995), 31, 28.

26. Dickinson, Ott, and Aoki, "Memory and Myth," 87.

27. "The Credo of the Buffalo Bill Center of the West" includes "We believe in a spirit, definable and intellectually real, called "the Spirit of the American West." See "The Center's Mission, Vision, and Grounding Principles," Buffalo Bill Center of the West, accessed August 14, 2015, web.

28. Ungulates like the North American bison are understood to have been a keystone species in the development of the both the shortgrass prairies of the western Great Plains and the tallgrass prairies of the eastern Great Plains. Bison grazing on the Great Plains increases plant biodiversity and distributes and fixes soil nutrients. In short, bison served as a keystone species that created the pre–Euro American Great Plains ecosystem. Alan K. Knapp et al., "The Keystone Role of Bison in North American Tallgrass Prairie: Bison Increase Habitat Heterogeneity and Alter a Broad Array of Plant, Community, and Ecosystem Processes," *Bioscience* 49 (1999): 39–50; Dan Flores, "Bison Ecology and Bison Diplomacy: The Southern Plains from 1800 to 1850," *Journal of American History* 78 (1991): 465–85; Pekka Hämälinen, "The Rise and Fall of Plains Indian Horse Cultures," *Journal of American History* 90 (2003): 833–62.

29. Flores, "Bison Ecology," 466.

30. Roxanne Dunbar-Ortiz, *An Indigenous Peoples' History of the United States* (Boston: Beacon Press, 2014), 137–61.

31. Flores, 467.

32. Ken Zontak, "Hunt, Capture, Raise, Increase: The People Who Saved the Bison," *Great Plains Quarterly* 15, no. 2 (1995): 135.

33. David Nesheim, "How William F. Cody Helped Save the Buffalo without Really Trying," *Great Plains Quarterly* 27 (2007): 163–64.

34. Nesheim, "How William F. Cody Helped Save the Buffalo," 164.

35. John Dorst, "Skin Remembers: Animal Trophies as Material Memory," *Cultural Studies* ↔ *Critical Methodologies* 13 (2013): 36.

36. Buffalo herds are complex organizations but, at the very least, they are composed of groups of cows, calves, and juvenile males and more or less separate herds of bulls. What is more, once the cow weens the calf, social associations are random. David F. Lott and Steven C. Minta, "Random Individual Association and Social Group Instability in American Bison (*Bison bison*)," *Zeitschrift für Tierpsychologie* 61 (1983): 153–72.

37. The creation of a nuclear family with father, mother, and child or children in dioramas is not unique to the BBCW. According to a museum designer at Chicago's Field Museum interviewed by Stephen T. Asma, "If you look at the bear exhibits, there's always the mom, the dad, and the babies and in real life the mom would drive the dad away because he would kill the babies." See Asma, *Stuffed Animals and Pickled Heads: The Culture and Evolution of Natural History Museums* (Oxford: Oxford University Press, 2001), 224.

38. Dunbar-Ortiz, *Indigenous Peoples' History*, 142–44.

39. Emma I. Hansen, *Memory and Vision: Arts, Cultures, and Lives of Plains Indian People* (Seattle: University of Washington Press, 2007), 211–13.

40. In situ transcription of a museum sign in the BBM, May 22, 2013.

41. Placards inform us that the Game of Buffalo Bill (1896), was "sold by Parker Bros.," and that "Buffalo Bill's Wild West Show in 6 Acts," "consisted of thirty-eight paper cutouts, distributed in American Tobacco Company cigarette packs, a game board, and a 'program.'" This game illustrates the immense popularity of Buffalo Bill, the ways his image and the *Wild West* offered endless marketing opportunities, and the manner in which the settling of the West as narrated by Cody had in it the kernel of a game—that is, the game of Cowboys and Indians.

42. "Buffalo Bill Museum – Window on the West – feature 1," YouTube video, 1:52, posted by "Buffalo Bill Center of the West," June 17, 2011, accessed July 17, 2016.

43. See "Buffalo Bill," Buffalo Bill Center of the West, accessed August 10, 2015, web.

44. "The Center's Mission, Vision, and Grounding Principles," Buffalo Bill Center of the West, accessed September 1, 2015, web.

45. Jacques Derrida, *Specters of Marx: The State of the Debt, the Work of Mourning, and the New International*, trans. Peggy Kamuf (New York: Routledge, 1994), xvii.

46. Roland Barthes, *Mythologies*, translated by Anne Lavers (New York: Hill and Wang), 1972.

Chapter 4

1. Quoted in Robert J. Moore, *Native Americans: The Art and Travels of Charles Bird King, George Catlin and Karl Bodmer* (Edison, NJ: Chartwell Books, 2002), 125.

2. Brian W. Dippie, "The Visual West," in *The Oxford History of the American West*, ed. Clyde A. Milner II, Carol A. O'Connor, and Martha A. Sandweiss (New York: Oxford University Press), 682.

3. Moore, *Native Americans*, 8.

4. Moore, *Native Americans*, 147.

Notes 209

5. For a more extended discussion of the challenges associated with "speaking for" and "speaking about" others, see Linda Alcoff, "The Problem of Speaking for Others," *Cultural Critique*, no. 20 (1991): 5 -32. The three of us have had many discussions over the years about how best to refer to indigenous peoples. While no approach is perfect, we are largely compelled by Roxanne Dunbar-Ortiz's perspective. Commenting on terminology, she writes, "I use 'Indigenous,' 'Indian,' and 'Native' interchangeably in the text. Indigenous individuals and peoples in North America on the whole do not consider 'Indian' a slur. Of course, all citizens of Native nations much prefer that their nations' names in their own language be used, such as Diné (Navajo), Haudenosaunee (Iroquois), Tsalagi (Cherokee), and Anishinaabe (Ojibway, Chippewa). I have used some of the correct names combined with more familiar usages, such as 'Sioux' and 'Navajo.' Except in material that is quoted, I don't use the term 'tribe.' 'Community,' 'people,' and 'nation' are used instead and interchangeably. I also refrain from using 'America' and 'American' when referring only to the United States and its citizens. Those blatantly imperialistic terms annoy people in the rest of the Western Hemisphere, who are, after all, also Americans. I use 'United States' as a noun and 'US' as an adjective to refer to the country and 'US Americans' for its citizens." Roxanne Dunbar-Ortiz, *An Indigenous Peoples' History of the United States* (Boston: Beacon Press, 2014), xiii–xiv.

6. Quoted in Dippie, "Visual West," 685.

7. Amy Lonetree, *Decolonizing Museums: Representing Native America in National and Tribal Museums* (Chapel Hill: University of North Carolina Press, 2012): 1.

8. Emma I. Hansen, *Memory and Vision: Arts, Cultures, and Lives of Plains Indian People*, with contributions by Beatrice Medicine et al. (Seattle: University of Washington Press, 2007). 205

9. Hansen, *Memory and Vision*, 9.

10. Ryan E. Burt, "'Sioux Yells' in the Dawes Era: Lakota 'Indian Play,' the Wild West, and the Literatures of Luther Standing Bear," *American Quarterly* 62, no. 3 (2010): 618.

11. Hansen, *Memory and VIsion*, 9.

12. Rebecca West, "Roundtable Discussion: 'The Legacy of Buffalo Bill and the Center of the West," Buffalo Bill Centennial Symposium, Buffalo Bill Center of the West, August 2–3, Cody, Wyoming, retrieved September 23, 2021, online video. For the quoted portions, see 19:25 to 20:14 of the video.

13. Hansen, 9.

14. The PIM advisory board consisted of Arthur Amiotte (Lakota), Custer, South Dakota; Silas S. Cathcart, Lake Forest, Illinois; Mrs. Henry H. R. Coe, Cody Wyoming; Dr. Michael D. Coe, New Haven, Connecticut; Robert D. Coe II, Cody, Wyoming; Garrett E. Goggles (Northern Arapaho), Fort Washakie, Wyoming; Joe Medicine Crow (Crow), Lodge Grass, Montana; Lloyd K. New (Cherokee), Santa Fe, New Mexico; Harold Ramser Jr., Murrieta, California; Kenneth Ryan (Assiniboine), Box Elder, Montana; Harriet Stuart Spencer, Long Lake, Minnesota; Abraham Spotted Elk (Northern Cheyenne), Ethete, Wyoming; Darwin J. St.Clair (Shoshone), Fort

Washakie, Wyoming; Curly Bear Wagner (Blackfeet), Browning, Montana; Margo Grant Walsh (Chippewa), New York.

15. *Treasures from Our West* (Cody, WY: Buffalo Bill Historical Center, 1992), 34; *Visitor's Guide: Buffalo Bill Historical Center* (Cody, WY: Buffalo Bill Historical Center, 2000).

16. According to museum curators, "most visitors to the Plains Indian Museum come with little or no knowledge about Plains Indian cultures; if anything, they come with familiar and erroneous stereotypes of American Indians" (*Plains Indian Museum Buffalo Bill Historical Center: A Reinterpretation* [Cody, WY: Buffalo Bill Historical Center, 2002], 5). While the original 1979 installation did little to challenge these views, the "reinterpretation" represents a "major shift in interpretive focus by providing a significantly greater humanities interpretation" (*Plains Indian Museum*, 7).

17. *Plains Indian Museum*, 9.

18. *Plains Indian Museum*, 9.

19. Recognizing that "interpretation is always contingent upon . . . the audience," we have limited our critical claim to the experience of white visitors. See Helene A. Shugart, "Reinventing Privilege: The New (Gay) Man in Contemporary Popular Media," *Critical Studies in Media Communication* 20 (2003): 68; see also Stanley E. Fish, "Interpreting the *Variorum*," in *Reader-Response Criticism: From Formalism to Post-Structuralism*, ed. Jane P. Tompkins (Baltimore, MD: Johns Hopkins University Press, 1980), 182. While it would certainly be interesting and informative to know how American Indians understand the PIM, our concern in this study is with how the museum addresses white visitors. Located as it is in a state that, according to the US Census Bureau, is 92.1 percent "White," the PIM is a key site in constructing memory of western settlement in the "white imagination." Although the BBHC maintains geographic data about visitors to the museum, it does not maintain specific demographics regarding ethnicity (personal communication from J. Hedderman, March 8, 2004).

20. According to Kenneth Burke, human beings can (symbolically) address guilt in one of three ways—mortification, victimage, or transcendence. The first two ways stress punishment of either the self (through atonement) or someone else (through scapegoating). Transcendence, by contrast, is a strategy of avoidance, in which public discourse (such as a museum) shifts the "terms" of a conflict or debate, erecting a new, nobler social hierarchy. In the new hierarchy, the guilt-producing actions are no longer sources of guilt. Kenneth Burke, *Attitudes toward History*, 3rd ed. (Berkeley: University of California Press, 1984), 80–105.

21. Gernot Böhme, "The Theory of Atmospheres and Its Applications," trans. A.-Chr. Engels-Schwarzpaul, *Interstices* 15 (2014): 93–94. The guilt to which we are referring is, in many cases, deeply repressed. We see its return in the "imperialist nostalgia" about which Renato Rosaldo writes in *Culture and Truth: The Remaking of Social Analysis* (Boston: Beacon Press, 1989), 69. Laurie Anne Whitt argues that the marketing of Native American spirituality in particular serves to assuage this Euro American guilt over destroying the lifeworld of Native Americans (see Laurie Anne Whitt, "Cultural Imperialism and the Marketing of Native America," *American Indian*

Culture and Research Journal 19 [1995]: 7). Richard Drinnon asserts that the making of American identity depends on metaphysics of Indian hating, a metaphysics that the PIM attempts to ignore through its rhetoric of transcendence (*Facing West: The Metaphysics of Indian-Hating and Empire-Building* [Minneapolis: University of Minnesota Press, 1980], 463–64). Philip Deloria argues that the violence against Indians so central to American identity continues to influence "a long night of American dreams" (Deloria, *Playing Indian* [New Haven: Yale University Press, 1998], 191).

22. The critical literature on the National Museum of the American Indian is large and growing. See Amy Lonetree and Amanda J. Cobb, *The National Museum of the American Indian: Critical Conversations* (Lincoln: University of Nebraska Press, 2008). This book collects original essays and essays published in special issues in a wide variety of journals, in particular the special issues published in *American Indian Quarterly*, 30, 3–4 (2006): 507–600, edited by Amy Lonetree.

23. Gerald Vizenor, *Native Liberty: Natural Reason and Cultural Survivance* (Lincoln: University of Nebraska Press, 2009), 1.

24. Vizenor, *Native Liberty*, 2.

25. Vizenor, 3.

26. Emily C. Burns, "Circulating Regalia and Lakhota Survivance, c. 1900," *Arts* 8 (2019): 146; Jordan Christiansen, "The Water Protectors at Standing Rock: Survivance Strategies for Gendered Relinking," *Women's Studies in Communication* 44 (2021): 278–300; Valerie N. Wieskamp and Courtney Smith, "'What to Do When You're Raped': Indigenous Women Critiquing and Coping through a Rhetoric of Survivance," *Quarterly Journal of Speech* 106 (2020): 72–94; Ashley Noel Mack and Tiara R. Na'puti, "'Our Bodies Are Not Terra Nullius': Building a Decolonial Feminist Resistance to Gendered Violence," *Women's Studies in Communication* 42 (2019): 347–70.

27. Vizenor, 99.

28. Tiara R. Na'puti, "Speaking of Indigeneity: Navigating Genealogies against Erasure and #RhetoricSoWhite," *Quarterly Journal of Speech* 105 (2019): 495.

29. Scott Richard Lyons, "Rhetorical Sovereignty: What Do American Indians Want from Writing?" *CCC* 51 (2000): 457–58.

30. Lyons, "Rhetorical Sovereignty," 462.

31. Renato Rosaldo, "Imperialist Nostalgia," *Representations* (1989): 107–22.

32. *Plains Indian Museum*, 9.

33. Micaela di Leonardo, *Exotics at Home: Anthropologies, Others, American Modernity* (Chicago: University of Chicago Press, 1998), 8.

34. Vine Deloria, writing about the relationship between American Indians and anthropologists, notes, "Into each life, it is said, some rain must fall. . . . But Indians have been cursed above all people. Indians have anthropologists" (*Custer Died for Your Sins: An Indian Manifesto* [New York: Avon, 1969], 87).

35. di Leonardo, *Exotics at Home*, 33–34.

36. Gernot Böhme, "Atmosphere as Mindful Physical Presence in Space," *OASE* 91 (2013): 31.

37. Kenneth Burke, "Four Master Tropes," *Kenyon Review* 3, no. 4 (1941): 424.

Burke goes on to write the metonymy connects to the most "'materialistic' term of all, 'motion' (a key strategy in Western materialism has been the reduction of 'consciousness' to 'motion')" (425).

38. Böhme, "Theory of Atmospheres," 94. Here, Böhme speaks of both light and sound as the most important contributors acknowledged since 1900 as well as more specifically light and sound as "music and illumination" (94).

39. This migration display is set up in a sort of migratory pattern that leads the visitor from the display of the traditional house to the display honoring the hunting of the buffalo. Here the voices start only when the visitor pauses under the speaker to view the display.

40. Kay Anderson and Mona Domash, "North American Spaces/Postcolonial Stories," *Cultural Geographies* 9 (2002): 125–28.

41. Victoria J. Gallagher, "Memory and Reconciliation in the Birmingham Civil Rights Institute," *Rhetoric and Public Affairs* 2 (1999): 314.

42. Michael Kammen, *Mystic Chords of Memory: The Transformation of Tradition in American Culture* (New York: Vintage, 1993), 6.

43. The discourse of progress underlies the rhetoric of at least two of the other museums in the BBCW, the Draper Natural History Museum and the Cody Firearms Museum.

44. Arthur Amiotte, "Transformation and Continuity in Lakota Culture: The Artwork of Standing Bear and Arthur Amiotte," Buffalo Bill Centennial Symposium, BBCW, August 2–4, 2017, Cody, Wyoming.

45. Amiotte, "Transformation and Continuity in Lakota Culture."

46. Vizenor, 3.

47. As is the case in other parts of the museum, the narrative and the visuals work to reinforce familiar gender stereotypes. Young men go on vision quests and hunt, while women teach girls domestic arts that will make them desirable marriage partners. In contrast to the gender stereotypes motivated by the museum, the lived experiences and voices of Plains Indian women are far more complex. See, for example, the work of Joy Harjo, a member of the Creek (Muscogee) tribe: Joy Harjo, *How We Become Human: New and Selected Poems* (New York: W. W. Norton, 2002); Harjo, *The Spiral of Memory: Interviews*, ed. Laura Coltelli (Ann Arbor: University of Michigan Press, 1996); Harjo, *In Mad Love and War* (Middletown, CT: Wesleyan University Press, 1990); and Joy Harjo and Stephen Strom, *Secrets from the Center of the World* (Tucson: University of Arizona Press, 1989).

48. Randall Lake, "Between Myth and History: Enacting Time in Native American Protest Rhetoric," *Quarterly Journal of Speech* 77 (1991): 127.

49. Lake, "Between Myth and History," 126. As Michael Kammen argues, this emphasis on progress is fundamental to American culture and is also crucial to understanding the contours of memory in the United States. Kammen further argues that discourses of progress are often also discourses of amnesia, or at least deeply selective memory. All pasts that conflict with the larger ideology of progress are shunted aside (Kammen, *Mystic Chords*, 13, 704).

50. Vizenor, 88.

51. Mark Rifkin, *Beyond Settler Time: Temporal Sovereignty and Indigenous Self-Determination* (Durham: Duke University Press, 2017), x.

52. The fire is convincing enough that nearly all the visitors we observed approached it and held out their hands to determine whether it was giving off any heat. The fire is made compelling through a combination of technological devices. The wood looks partially burned, the light from the fire flickers realistically, and the river home is filled with soft, crackling sounds.

53. Burns, "Circulating Regalia and Lakhota Survivance," 146.

54. Kammen, *Mystic Chords*, 13.

55. Lonetree, *Decolonizing Museums*, 6.

56. Anderson and Domash, "North American Spaces," 126.

57. John Belohlavek, "Race, Progress, and Destiny: Caleb Cushing and the Quest for American Empire," in *Manifest Destiny and Empire: American Antebellum Expansionism*, ed. Sam W. Haynes and Christopher Morris (College Station: Texas A&M University Press, 1997), 24.

58. Anderson and Domash, 126.

59. Anderson and Domash, 126.

60. See Gallagher, "Memory," 307–8; see also Kammen, 704.

61. Rosaldo, *Culture and Truth*, 69.

62. Rosaldo, 70.

63. Michael J. Hyde, "Introduction: Rhetorically, We Dwell," in *The Ethos of Rhetoric*, ed. Michael J. Hyde (Columbia: University of South Carolina Press, 2004), xxi.

64. Carole Blair and Neil Michel, "The Rushmore Effect: Ethos and National Collective Identity," in Hyde, *Ethos of Rhetoric*, 158–59.

65. Lonetree, 5.

Chapter 5

1. Sarah E. Boehme, *Whitney Gallery of Western Art* (Cody, WY: Buffalo Bill Historical Center, 1997).

2. Gernot Böhme, "The Theory of Atmospheres and Its Application," *Interstices: Journal of Architecture and Related Arts* 15 (2014): 93, 97.

3. Thomas Rickert, *Ambient Rhetoric: The Attunements of Rhetorical Being* (Pittsburgh: University of Pittsburgh Press, 2013): 8, 29, 146.

4. As will become clear in the analysis, the gallery can be thought through a range of musical forms: theme and variations will be the most apparent. We choose hymn, however, for two reasons. First, the gallery's conclusion is a cathedral-like window that visually and materially asserts the sacredness of the space and the images both inside and outside the museum. Second, since hymn is also a verb (meaning to sing in praise of someone of something), we can bring into focus the ways the gallery invites visitors to hymn the West.

5. Margaret Headstrom and Anna Perricci, "It's Only Temporary," in *(Im)permanence: Cultures in/out of Time*, ed. Judith Schachter and Stephen Brockmann (Pittsburgh: Center for the Arts in Society, Carnegie Mellon, 2008), 26–40.

6. Carole Blair, Greg Dickinson, and Brian L. Ott, "Introduction: Rhetoric/Memory/Place," in *Places of Public Memory: The Rhetoric of Museums and Memorials*, ed. Greg Dickinson, Carole Blair, and Brian L. Ott (Tuscaloosa: University of Alabama Press, 2010), 6.

7. Steven C. Dubin, *Transforming Museums: Mounting Queen Victoria in a Democratic South Africa* (New York: Palgrave Macmillan, 2006).

8. Dubin, *Transforming Museums*, 6.

9. Bernard J. Armada, "Memory's Execution: (Dis)Placing the Dissident Body," in Dickinson, Blair, and Ott, *Places of Public Memory*, 216–37. Armada is writing about the revised National Civil Rights Museum, which effectively silenced the protests of Jacqueline Smith, and asserts that these museum changes can be thought of as "memory's execution," that is, its performance *and* its destruction (217).

10. Boehme, *Whitney*, 4–5.

11. Elizabeth Martin, *Architecture as a Translation of Music* (New York: Princeton Architectural Press, 1994), 8.

12. Marvin Trachtenberg, "Architecture and Music Reunited: A New Reading of Dufay's 'Nuper Rosarum Flores' and the Cathedral of Florence," *Renaissance Quarterly* 54, no. 3 (2001): 740–75.

13. Martin, *Architecture as a Translation*, 8–9.

14. Doreen Massey, *For Space* (Los Angeles: Sage, 2005), 63.

15. Rickert, *Ambient Rhetoric*, 29.

16. Kenneth Burke, *Counter-Statement* (Berkeley: University of California Press, 1931), 31.

17. Bruce Baugh, "Body," in *The Deleuze Dictionary*, ed. Adrian Parr (Edinburgh: Edinburgh University Press, 2010), 35.

18. William W. Savage Jr., *The Cowboy Hero: His Image in American History and Culture* (Norman: University of Oklahoma Press, 1979).

19. Boehme, 42.

20. Emma I. Hansen, *Memory and Vision: Arts, Cultures, and Lives of Plains Indian People* (Seattle: University of Washington Press, 2008), 205.

21. Philip J. Deloria, *Indians in Unexpected Places* (Lawrence: University of Kansas Press, 2004), 6.

22. Of course, visitors may fill the absence in multiple ways. Some viewers, primed with a critical vision of US history, may imagine the colonizing acts that destroyed Native American lives and culture and produced radical changes to the natural landscape. It is possible, then, for this art to trigger more critical imaginings of First Peoples. However, there seems to be little in these paintings and sculptures that would enthymematically trigger these possibilities.

23. Manship's sculpture is mythological in two senses. First, it draws on classical images of mythological stories and so is mythological in a commonsense way. Second, the figures are mythological in Roland Barthes's more technical sense, in which an image can turn history into Nature and serve an ideological function.

24. T. Tolles, "Paul Manship, *Indian and Pronghorn Antelope*," in *Timeless Treasures: 50 Favorites from the Whitney Western Art Museum* (Cody, WY: Buffalo Bill

Historical Center, 2008), 53; Roland Barthes, *Mythologies*, trans. Anne Lavers (New York: Hill and Wang, 1972).

25. Brian W. Dippie, *Custer's Last Stand: The Anatomy of an American Myth* (Lincoln: University of Nebraska Press, 1994), 1.

26. Nathan Stormer, "Addressing the Sublime: Space, Mass Representation, and the Unrepresentable," *Critical Studies in Media Communication* 21, no. 3 (2004): 219.

27. Stormer, "Addressing the Sublime," 215.

28. Ned O'Gorman, "Eisenhower and the American Sublime," *Quarterly Journal of Speech* 94, no. 1 (2008): 68.

29. O'Gorman, "Eisenhower and the American Sublime," 67.

30. Boehme, *Whitney* 25.

31. Stephen Greenblatt, "Resonance and Wonder," *Bulletin of the American Academy of Arts and Sciences*, 43 (1990): 11–34.

32. Stormer, 233.

33. Burke, *Counter-Statement*, 30.

34. This painting can be viewed online at the BBCW's website, accessed April 1, 2020.

35. Greenblatt, "Resonance and Wonder," 19.

36. Greenblatt, 19–20.

37. Karen B. McWhorter, "Expanded Horizons: Promoting Diversity in the Whitney," *Points West: Black Cowboys in America* (Spring 2021): 8–11.

Chapter 6

1. The three of us intermittently voiced our shared notion of atmospheric awe in what Gernot Böhme ("The Theory of Atmospheres and Its Applications," *Interstices: Journal of Architecture and Related Arts* 15 [2014]: 92–99) notes would otherwise make the experience meaningless: "atmospheres can be produced and, further, that what they produce (namely a certain mood pervading the performance space, the so-called *Klima*) is something quasi-objective, or better, intersubjective" (94). While they are "attuned spaces" of "something *external* and thereby accessible to many subjects," Böhme clarifies that while an atmosphere is sometimes shared, "the atmosphere that prevails in a space" is also arguable (93).

2. We use the sublime here in the sense articulated by Nathan Stormer. Sublime images of nature can serve, Stormer argues, to "demarcate the boundaries of the self" while at the same time creating "the space of the appearance for a *mass subject*" ("Addressing the Sublime: Space, Mass Representation, and the Unpresentable," *Critical Studies in Media Communication* 21, no. 3 2004]: 219–20). See also our discussion of the sublime in chap. 5.

3. "Buffalo Bill Historical Center: Voice of the American West," BBCW, accessed January 18, 2007, web. Emphasis in original.

4. Charles Chamberlain, "From 'Haunts' to 'Character': The Meaning of Ethos and Its Relation to Ethics," *Helios* 11 (1984): 97.

5. Chamberlain, "From 'Haunts' to 'Character,'" 97–98.

6. Chamberlain, 97–98.

7. Chamberlain, 99.

8. Donna Haraway, *Primate Visions: Gender, Race, and Nature in the World of Modern Science* (New York: Routledge, 1989), 1.

9. Stephen T. Asma, *Stuffed Animals and Pickled Heads: The Culture and Evolution of Natural History Museums* (Oxford: Oxford University Press, 2001).

10. Contemporary scholarship continues to explore the role of natural history museums as sites of science pedagogy. See Asma, Asma, *Stuffed Animals and Pickled Heads*; Karen A. Rader and Victoria E. M. Cain, *Life on Display: Revolutionalizing U.S. Museums of Science and Natural History in the Twentieth Century* (Chicago: University of Chicago Press, 2014); Bill Watson and Shari Rosenstein Werb, "One Hundred Strong: A Colloquium on Transforming Natural History Museums in the Twenty-First Century" *Museum Journal* 58 (2013): 255–65.

11. Michel de Certeau, *The Practice of Everyday Life*, trans. Steven Randall (Berkeley: University of California, 1984), 117.

12. de Certeau, *Practice of Everyday Life*, 117.

13. de Certeau, 117.

14. de Certeau calls this "saying" of space an enunciation. See *Practice of Everyday Life*, 19, 97–98.

15. In this evocative passage, de Certeau writes:

> In our examination of the daily practices that articulate that experience, the opposition between "place" and "space" will rather refer to two sorts of determinations in stories: the first, a determination through objects that are ultimately reducible to the *being-there* of something dead, the law of a "place" (from the pebble to the cadaver, an inert body always seems, in the West, to found a place and give it the appearance of a tomb); the second, a determination through *operations* which, when they are attributed to a stone, tree, or human being, specify "spaces" by the actions of historical *subjects* (a movement always seems to condition the production of a space and to associate it with a history). Between these two determinations, there are passages back and forth, such as the putting to death (or putting into a landscape) of heroes who transgress frontiers and who, guilty of an offense against the law of the place, best provide its restoration with their tombs; or again, on the contrary, the awakening of inert objects (a table, a forest, a person that plays a certain role in the environment) which, emerging from their stability, transforms the place where they lay motionless in to the foreignness of their own space (118).

16. Stephen Greenblatt, *Marvelous Possessions: The Wonder of the New World* (Chicago: University of Chicago Press, 1991), 135.

17. John Berger, writing of the Renaissance European nude, argues that this new way of seeing women quite precisely objectifies them, turning women into objects to be surveyed and in the surveying, judged. See Berger, *Ways of Seeing* (New York: Viking Press, 1973), 46–47.

18. Greenblatt, *Marvelous Possessions*, 81–83.

19. Greenblatt, *Marvelous Possessions*, 81–83.

20. Doreen Massey, *For Space* (Los Angeles: Sage, 2005), 20–30.

21. Roxanne Dunbar-Ortiz, *Not a Nation of Immigrants: Settler Colonialism,*

White Supremacy, and a History of Erasure and Exclusion (Boston: Beacon Press, 2021), 21. See also Allan Greer, "Settler Colonialism and Empire in Early America," *William and Marty Quarterly* 76 (2019): 383–90; and Patrick Wolfe, "Settler Colonialism and the Elimination of the Native," *Journal of Genocide Research* 8 (2006): 387–409.

22. Greenblatt, *Marvelous Possessions*, 135.

23. On the appearance of zoos and their importance in modernity, see John Berger, *About Looking* (New York: Vintage International, 1980), 20–28; and Akira Mizuta Lippit, *Electric Animal: Toward a Rhetoric of Wildlife* (Minneapolis: University of Minnesota Press, 2000), 3–4.

24. Donna Haraway, *Primate Visions: Gender, Race, and Nature in the World of Modern Science* (New York: Routledge, 1989), 30.

25. For Haraway, taxidermy's "most *ecstatic* and skillful moment joins ape and man in visual embrace" (26), emphasis added. Note how, like Greenblatt's reading of Early Modern travel literature, the movement across difference (here, human and ape) is negotiated through ecstasy, which is related to the marvelous and wonder. The taxidermied animals are visually wonderful, allowing for an ecstatic communion that at once emphasizes similarity *and* difference.

26. Barry Mackintosh, *The National Parks: Shaping the System*, 3rd ed. (Washington DC: National Park System, 2000), 13.

27. By comparison, over 4.5 million people visit the Grand Canyon National Park each year. National Parks Service, accessed July 12, 2023, website.

28. Richard Grusin, *Culture, Technology, and the Creation of America's National Parks* (Cambridge, UK: Cambridge University Press, 2004), 13.

29. About the city, Victor Burgin writes, "The city in our actual experience is at the same time an actually existing physical environment, and a city in a novel, a film, a photograph, a city seen on television, a city in a comic strip, a city in a pie chart, and so on." Similarly, Burgin writes about films that "collecting such metonymic fragments [of posters, reviews, trailers, conversations] in memory, we may come to feel familiar with a film we have not actually seen. Clearly this 'film'—a heterogeneous psychical object, constructed from image scraps scattered in space and time, arbitrarily anchored in a contingent reality (a newspaper interview, a review)—is a very different object from that encountered in the context of 'film studies.'" Parks, cities, films, and museums, then, in our "actual experience" are not simply our experience with the material text; rather, they reflect the accumulation of memorized fragments. *In/Different Spaces: Place and Memory in Visual Culture* (Berkeley: University of California Press, 1996), 28, 23.

30. The pedagogical mission of the museum is not unusual. For analysis of the pedagogical goals and design of other natural history museums, see Ann Reynolds, "Visual Stories," in *The Visual Culture Reader*, ed. Nicholas Mirzoeff, 2nd ed. (New York: Routledge, 2002), 326, 330–31. As our analysis will show, however, while the museum certainly is pedagogical, it is less clear that it investigates "the ways in which nature and human cultures influence one another."

31. It is possible to enter the museum from a lower entrance. In our experience, few visitors do so.

32. It is tempting to read "narrative" as necessarily transforming "place" into "space." And yet, as de Certeau argues, "Stories thus carry out a labor that constantly transforms places into spaces or spaces into places" (118).

33. The BBHC website states that "the scrims were created from digital photographs. They were produced by a company called Color X, 33 East 17th Street, New York, NY 10003." "Buffalo Bill Historical Center: Voice of the American West," accessed January 18, 2007.

34. Dunbar-Ortiz, *Not a Nation of Immigrants*. See also de Certeau, 91–92.

35. Kristin Atman and Gretchen Henrich, "Explorer's Guide for Families," Draper Museum of Natural History (Cody, WY: Buffalo Bill Historical Center, n.d.), 10–11.

36. Gernot Böhme asserts that "sound, noise and music are amongst the main generators of atmospheres" and "Sound installations create acoustic environments and thereby spatial atmospheres" ("Theory of Atmospheres," 97).

37. Grusin, *Culture, Technology*, 81.

38. This is one of the few places in the museum that directly addresses change over time.

39. Atman and Henrich, "Explorer's Guide," 7.

40. Jean Baudrillard, "Simulacra and Simulations," in Mirzoeff, *Visual Culture Reader*, 146.

41. Victor W. Turner, *Dramas, Fields, and Metaphors: Symbolic Action in Human Society* (Ithaca, NY: Cornell University Press, 1974).

42. Haraway, *Primate Visions*, 30.

43. We use "man" here and later to indicate the role of patriarchy and masculinity in the kind of vision we are analyzing. See Haraway, 26.

44. See Jean Baudrillard, "The Animals: Territory and Metamorphoses," in *Simulation and Simulacra*, trans. Sheila Faria Glaser (Ann Arbor: University of Michigan Press, 1994), 134–35. Baudrillard asserts, "Those who used to sacrifice animals did not take them for beasts. . . . They held them to be guilty: which was a way of honoring them. We take them for nothing, and it is on this basis that we are 'human' with them. We no longer sacrifice them, we no longer punish them, and we are proud of it, but it is simply that we have domesticated them, worse: that we have made of them a racially inferior world, no longer even worthy of our justice, but only of our affection and social charity, no longer worthy of punishment and death, but only of experimentation and extermination like meat from the butchery" (134–35).

45. Baudrillard, *Simulation and Simulacra*, 3.

46. Gernot Böhme, "Staged Materiality," *Interstices: Interstices: Journal of Architecture and Related Arts* 14 (2013): 94–99.

47. On the importance of barbed wire fencing in the West, see Henry D. McCallum and Frances T. McCallum, *The Wire That Fenced the West* (Norman: University of Oklahoma Press, 1965).

48. Assuming the visitor accepts the museum's invitation to travel from top to bottom.

49. Draper Natural History Museum, "Monarch of the Skies," accessed November 11, 2021, web.

Notes 219

50. Greenblatt, *Marvelous Possessions*, 135.

51. Roland Barthes writes, "The myth of the human 'condition' rests on a very old mystification, which always consists of placing Nature at the bottom of History" (*Mythologies*. Trans. Annette Lavers [New York: Hill and Wang, 1972], 101).

Chapter 7

1. Victor Burgin, *In/Different Spaces: Place and Memory in Visual Culture* (Berkeley: University of California Press, 1996). See also Carole Blair and Neil Michel, "Commemorating in the Theme Park Zone: Reading the Astronauts Memorial," in *At the Intersection: Cultural Studies and Rhetorical Studies*, ed. Thomas Rosteck (New York: Guilford Press, 1999), 59–60. On a related note, Eric is named after one of his father's favorite western actors, Eric Fleming, from the television show *Rawhide* (1951).

2. We believe it is important to be reflexive about the unique set of experiences each of us *brings* to (and thus potentially reads into) the museum. The interpretation of texts such as the CFM is certainly influenced not only by the design and display practices of the museum itself but also by the history and experience of the critic or visitor (see Blair and Michel, "Commemorating in the Theme Park Zone," 59). Though the focus of this essay is principally on the former (i.e., design and display practices of the museum), we readily acknowledge that our interpretation (as with *all* interpretations) is filtered by our own backgrounds and experiences. It is our intent to write a second, more autoethnographic account of the CFM at some point.

3. Ocularcentric describes "the epistemological privileging of vision that begins at least as early as Plato's notion that ethical universals must be accessible to the 'mind's eye' and continue with the Renaissance, the invention of printing, and the development of modern sciences" (Georgia Warnke, "Ocularcentrism and Social Criticism," in *Modernity and the Hegemony of Vision*, ed. David Michael Levin [Berkeley: University of California Press, 1993], 287).

4. The dialectic between presence and absence is central to what Lawrence J. Prelli has termed *rhetorics of display*. According to Prelli, "the meanings manifested rhetorically through display are functions of particular, situated resolutions of the dynamic between revealing and concealing" ("Rhetorics of Display: An Introduction," in *Rhetorics of Display*, ed. Lawrence J. Prelli [Columbia: University of South Carolina Press, 2006], 2).

5. Brian L. Ott, Greg Dickinson, and Eric Aoki, "Ways of (Not) Seeing Guns: Presence and Absence at the Cody Firearms Museum," *Communication and Critical/Cultural Studies*, 8 (2011): 216. John Dorst published a scholarly interpretation of the CFM soon after the museum opened, "A Walk through a Shooting Gallery," *Museum Anthropology* 17 (1992): 7–13.

6. Our understanding of the violent force of firearms in the West draws on Michael A. Bellesiles, *Arming America: The Origins of a National Gun Culture* (New York: Alfred A. Knopf, 2000); Richard Slotkin, *Regeneration through Violence: The Mythology of the American Frontier 1600–1860* (Norman: University of Oklahoma

Press, 1973). We understand the American West as a site of settler colonialism. See Lorenzo Veracini, *Settler Colonialism: A Theoretical Overview* (Houndmills, UK: Palgrave Macmillan. 2010); Patrick Wolfe, "Settler Colonialism and the Elimination of the Native, "*Journal of Genocide Research* 8 (2006): 387–409; Alvin J. Primak, "You Are Not the Father: Rhetoric, Settler Colonial Curiosity, and Federal Indian Law," *Review of Communication* 20 (2020): 27–46; Tiara R. Na'puti, "Rhetorical Contexts of Colonization and Decolonization," in *Oxford Research Encyclopedia of Communication*, 2020, online. Lindsey Schneider argues that "settler colonialism has tended to consider land in the abstract, treating it as generic and equivalent without regard for *place*." Lindsey Schneider, "'There's Something in the Water': Salmon Runs and Settler Colonialism on the Columbia River," *American Indian Research Journal* 37 (2013): 149.

7. Brian L. Ott and Eric Aoki, "The Politics of Negotiating Public Tragedy: Media Framing of the Matthew Shepard Murder," *Rhetoric and Public Affairs* 5, no. 3 (2002): 483–505.

8. Brett French, "Cody Firearms Museum More Hands-on with $12M Remodel," *Billings Gazette*, July 19, 2019; T. Logan Metesh, "The Newly Renovated Cody Firearms Museum Is Open!" *Range 365*; Mathew Moss, "Touring the Newly Refurbished Cody Firearms Museum," *American Rifleman*, August 9, 2019; Michael Welton, "Renovating Cody Firearms Museum," *Architects and Artisans*.

9. Edward Rothstein, "Handled with Care," *Wall Street Journal*, September 27, 2019.

10. Metesh reports that museum professionals named museums like the CFM before the redesign "gunquariums."

11. The quoted passages from Ashley Hlebinsky are taken from a roundtable discussion published as Jennifer Tucker et al., "Display of Arms: A Roundtable Discussion about the Public Exhibition of Firearms and Their History," *Technology and Culture* 59 (July 2018): 731. It is crucial that Hlebinsky focuses on "feelings" about firearms and draws attention to the historical development of specific feelings toward the technology. The museum itself seldom directly engages the way we feel about firearms, even as it regularly notes the difference between myths and realities about them.

12. Tucker et al., "Display of Arms," 731.

13. Agnes van Rees, *Dissociation in Argumentative Discussions* (Berlin: Springer, 2009): 4–5.

14. Kenneth Burke, *A Rhetoric of Motives* (Berkeley: University of California Press, 1969), 149–54.

15. Kenneth Burke, *Permanence and Change: An Anatomy of Purpose*, 3rd ed. (Berkeley: University of California Press, 1984).

16. Kenneth Burke, *The Philosophy of Literary Form*, 3rd ed. (Berkeley: University of California Press, 1973), 9.

17. *APA Online Dictionary*, accessed August 3, 2021.

18. American Psychiatric Association, "Dissociative Disorder," in *Diagnostic and Statistical Manual of Mental Disorders (DSM-5)*, American Psychiatric Publishing (2013): 291.

Notes

19. American Psychiatric Association, "Dissociative Disorder," 291–307.

20. Rebecca Seligman and Laurence J. Kirmayer, "Dissociate Experience and Cultural Neuroscience: Narrative, Metaphor and Mechanism," *Cultural Medical Psychiatry*, 32 (2008): 31–64.

21. Seligman and Kirmayer, 35.

22. Giulia Lara Poerio and Jonathan Smallwood, "Daydreaming to Navigate the Social World: What We Know, What We Don't and Why It Matters," *Social and Personality Compass* 10 (2016): 605–18. "Daydreaming . . . can be defined as mental content that is stimulus-independent and task-unrelated" and "is unrelated to the progression or completion of one's current total(s) related to the environment" (606).

23. Brian L. Ott and Greg Dickinson, "Redefining Rhetoric: Why Matter Matters," *Berlin Journal of Critical Theory* 3 (2019): 66.

24. Joshua Gunn argues that psychoanalytic terms can be effectively used to perform cultural criticism despite the efforts of some to hold psychoanalytic terms as only useful for individuals on analysis. Joshua Gunn, *Perversion: Rhetorical Aberration in the Time of Trumpeteering* (Chicago: University of Chicago Press, 2021), 23. Dissociation is not, typically, a term in psychoanalysis. Using dissociation as an affective mode, however, draws us toward understanding drives in ways homologous to Gunn's psychoanalytic approach.

25. Chandra Ann Maldonado, "Commemorative (Dis)Placement: On the Limits of Textual Adaptability and the Future of Public Memory Scholarship," *Rhetoric and Public Affairs* 24 (2021): 244–45.

26. The debate regarding context is more extensive than we need to review here. For at least one way of thinking the controversies around text and context, see the *Western Journal of Speech Communication* 1990, "Special Issue on Rhetorical Criticism." Part of an ongoing decennial consideration of rhetorical criticism, this special issue turned on questions of object (text) and context. Issues of context and text are still prevalent in the 2020 *Western Journal of Communication* special issue on rhetorical criticism. See in particular Kent Ono, "Contextual Fields of Rhetoric," *Western Journal of Communication* 84 (2020): 264–79.

27. "The defining characteristic of dissociative amnesia is an inability to recall important autobiographical information that 1) would be successfully stored in memory and 2) ordinarily would be readily remembered. Dissociative amnesia differs from permanent amnesias due to neurological damage or toxicity that prevent memory storage or retrieval in that it is always potentially reversible because the memory has bas been successfully stored." *DSM-5*, 298.

28. Kim Parker et al., *America's Complex Relationship with Guns: An In-Depth Look at the Attitudes and Experiences of U.S. Adults*, Pew Research Center, June 22, 2017, pp. 5–6. Thanks to Jordin Clark for her research on gun attitudes in the United States.

29. Parker et al., *America's Complex Relationship with Guns*, 6.

30. Parker et al., 53.

31. Greg Robinson, *By Order of the President: FDR and the Internment of Japanese Americans* (Cambridge, MA: Harvard University Press, 2001), 6.

32. Robinson, *By Order of the President*, 4.

33. Bill Hosokawa, "The Sentinel Story," in *Remembering Heart Mountain: Essays on Japanese American Internment in Wyoming*, ed. Mike Mackey (Powell, WY: Western History Publications, 1998), 70–71.

34. Heart Mountain Relocation Center (website), National Park Service, accessed April 11, 2021.

35. Ott, Dickinson, and Aoki, "Ways of (Not) Seeing Guns," 228.

36. Ott, Dickinson, and Aoki, 229.

37. Tucker et al., "Display of Arms," 763.

38. The CFM's basement contains much more of the museum's collection, offering much of it for view in slide-out plexiglass and metal displays. There is a small selection of guns used by Native Americans. In a placard entitled "Native Adopted Firearms," the museum informs us that "Native peoples adopted firearms, they used guns they could acquire including Winchester models in the nineteenth century. The used firearms in hunting, sport, and war, however, tribal nations were vulnerable to periods of firearm confiscated by the US government, notably at Wounded Knee and also during the early reservation period."

39. Lorenzo Veracini, *Settler Colonialism: A Theoretical Overview* (Houndmills, UK: Palgrave Macmillan, 2010), 8.

40. "Guns in America," *Time*, November 5, 2018, online.

41. "Guns in America."

42. Ott, Dickinson, and Aoki, 225.

43. The larger gallery is named *Firearms of the West*. Within that gallery is a specific exhibit called "Firearms in the American West."

44. For an important discussion of the position of the critic regarding the critical object and the audience of criticism, see Joshua Gunn, *Political Perversion: Rhetorical Aberration in the Time of Trumpeteering* (Chicago: University of Chicago Press, 2021), 25–46. In his chapter "On Critical Violence," Gunn traces the twentieth-century impulse of rhetorical critics to emulate science by creating a method that removed the critic and in particular the feeling, embodied critic from the critical act. He argues for a more engaged—humbler—version of criticism. Criticism should take our own bodies and our own feelings seriously (or humorously!), offering critical appraisals that have heuristic value but cannot claim universal or even provisional truth. "The key to moderation," Gunn writes, "is never believing interpretation is exhausted and maintain and cultivated uncertainty." He continues, "Critical rhythm is achieved not by the frame of pages or time, but rather by ceaseless and never-ending critique, playfulness, and (good) humor" (42).

Conclusion

1. s.v. "Spirit," Oxford English Dictionary, accessed August 8, 2017, web. The first definitions of "spirit" in the OED emphasize immateriality of the soul and the mind. The second definition reads, "The soul of a person, as commended to God, or passing out of the body, in the moment of death." The third definition is "a supernatural,

incorporeal, rational being or personality . . . frequently conceived as troublesome, terrifying, or hostile to mankind."

2. Brian L. Ott and Greg Dickinson, "Redefining Rhetoric: Why Matter Matters," *Berlin Journal of Critical Theory* 3, no. 1 (2019): 45–81.

3. Greg Dickinson, Brian L. Ott, and Eric Aoki, "Spaces of Remembering and Forgetting: The Reverent Eye/I at the Plains Indian Museum," *Communication and Critical/Cultural Studies* 3, no. 1 (2006): 27–47.

4. Henri Lefebvre, *The Social Production of Space*, trans. Donald Nicholson-Smith (Oxford: Blackwell, 1991), 222.

5. John D. Dorst, *Looking West* (Philadelphia: University of Pennsylvania Press, 1999).

6. Doreen Massey, *For Space* (Los Angeles: Sage, 2005), 175.

7. Avery Gordon, *Ghostly Matters: Haunting and the Sociological Imagination* (Minneapolis: University of Minnesota Press, 2008), 8.

8. Gordon, *Ghostly Matters*, 8. As we have written together, we have found many ways we are alike. We enjoy critical analysis, we believe in strong thesis statements, and we desire to write with passion and emotion. We have also found ways we are different. One of us loves lists of three characteristics. Another prefers lists of four. The third intentionally alternates between threes and fours. We are ending with four to avoid the force of the father, the son, and the holy ghost. We honor ghosts and write with spirit, but not *that* ghost or *that* spirit.

9. Joshua Gunn, "Review Essay: Mourning Humanism, or, the Idiom of Haunting," *Quarterly Journal of Speech* 92 (2006): 85.

Bibliography

Aiello, Giorgia, and Greg Dickinson. "Beyond Authenticity: A Visual-Material Analysis of Locality in the Global Redesign of Starbucks Stores." *Visual Communication* 13, no. 3 (2014): 303–21.

Alcoff, Linda. "The Problem of Speaking for Others." *Cultural Critique* 20, no. 20 (1991): 5–32.

American Psychiatric Association. "Dissociative Disorder." In *Diagnostic and Statistical Manual of Mental Disorders: Fifth Edition (DSM-5)*, 291–307. American Psychiatric Publishing, 2013. Online.

American Psychological Association. "Dissociation." Accessed August 3, 2021. Web.

Anderson, Ben. "Affective Atmospheres." *Emotion, Space and Society* 2 (2009): 77–81.

Anderson, Kay, and Mona Domash. "North American Spaces/Postcolonial Stories." *Cultural Geographies* 9 (2002): 125–28

Aoki, Eric, Greg Dickinson, and Brian L. Ott. "The Master Naturalist Imagined: Directed Movement and Simulations at the Draper Museum of Natural History" In Dickinson, Blair, and Ott, *Places of Public Memory*, 238–65.

Armada, Bernard J. "Memorial Agon: An Interpretive Tour of the National Civil Rights Museum." *Southern Journal of Communication* 63, no. 3 (1998): 235–43.

———. "Memory's Execution: (Dis)Placing the Dissident Body." In Dickinson, Blair, and Ott, *Places of Public Memory*, 216–37.

Ashworth, G. J. "Conservation as Preservation or Heritage: Two Paradigms and Two Answers." *Built Environment* 23, no. 2 (1997): 92–102.

Asma, Stephen T. *Stuffed Animals and Pickled Heads: The Culture and Evolution of Natural History Museums*. Oxford: Oxford University Press, 2001.

Atman, Kristin, and Gretchen Henrich. "Explorer's Guide for Families." Draper Museum of Natural History. Cody, WY: Buffalo Bill Historical Center, n.d.

Bachelard, Gaston. *The Poetics of Space*. Translated by Maria Jolas. Boston: Beacon Press, 1994.

Barker, Martin, and Roger Sabin. *The Lasting of the Mohicans: History of an American Myth*. Jackson: University Press of Mississippi, 1995.

Barthes, Roland. *Mythologies*. Translated by Anne Lavers. New York: Hill and Wang, 1972.

Bartlett, Richard A. *From Cody to the World: The First Seventy-Five Years of the Buffalo Bill Memorial Association*. Cody, WY: Buffalo Bill Historical Center, 1992.

Baudrillard, Jean. "The Animals: Territory and Metamorphoses." In *Simulation and Simulacra*, 129–43.

———. "Simulacra and Simulations." In Mirzoeff, *Visual Culture Reader*, 145–46.

———. *Simulation and Simulacra*, translated by Sheila Faria Glaser, 129–43. Ann Arbor: University of Michigan Press, 1994.

Baugh, Bruce. "Body." In *The Deleuze Dictionary*, edited by Adrian Parr, 35–37. Edinburgh: Edinburgh University Press, 2010.

Bellesiles, Michael A. *Arming America: The Origins of a National Gun Culture*. New York: Alfred A. Knopf, 2000.

Belohlavek, John. "Race, Progress, and Destiny: Caleb Cushing and the Quest for American Empire." In *Manifest Destiny and Empire: American Antebellum Expansionism*, edited by Sam W. Haynes and Christopher Morris, 21–47. College Station: Texas A&M University Press, 1997.

Bennett, Jane. "The Force of Things: Steps toward an Ecology of Matter." *Political Theory* 32, no. 2 (2004): 347–72.

Bennett, Tony. *The Birth of the Museum: History, Theory, Politics*. New York: Routledge, 1995.

Berger, John. *About Looking*. New York: Vintage International, 1980.

———. *Ways of Seeing*. New York: Viking Press, 1973.

Bernard-Donals, Michael. *Figures of Memory: The Rhetoric of Displacement at the United States Holocaust Memorial Museum*. Albany: State University of New York Press, 2016.

Berrick, Mac E. "The Log House as Cultural Symbol." *Material Culture* 18, no. 1 (1986): 1–19.

Bieder, Robert E. "The Representations of Indian Bodies in Nineteenth-Century American Anthropology." In Mihesuab, *Repatriation Reader*, 19–36.

Bird, S. Elizabeth. "Introduction: Constructing the Indian, 1930s–1990s." In *Dressing in Feathers: The Construction of the Indian in Popular Culture*, edited by S. Elizabeth Bird, 1–12. Boulder: Westview Press, 1996.

Blair, Carole. "Contemporary US Memorial Sites as Exemplars of Rhetoric's Materiality." In *Rhetorical Bodies*, edited by Jack Selzer and Sharon Crowley, 16–57. Madison: University of Wisconsin Press, 1999.

Blair, Carole, Greg Dickinson, and Brian L. Ott. "Introduction: Rhetoric/Memory/Place." In Dickinson, Blair, and Ott, *Places of Public Memory*, 1–54.

Blair, Carole, and Neil Michel. "Commemorating in the Theme Park Zone: Reading the Astronauts Memorial." In *At the Intersection: Cultural Studies and Rhetorical Studies*, edited by Thomas Rosteck, 29–83. New York: Guilford Press, 1999.

———. "The Rushmore Effect: Ethos and National Collective Identity." In Hyde, *Ethos of Rhetoric*, 156–96.

Bloomfield, Emma Frances. "Ark Encounter as Material Apocalyptic Rhetoric: Contemporary Creationist Strategies on Board Noah's Ark." *Southern Communication Journal* 82 (2017): 263–77.

Boehme, Sarah E. *Whitney Gallery of Western Art*. Cody, WY: Buffalo Bill Historical Center, 1997.

Böhme, Gernot. "Atmosphere as Mindful Physical Presence in Space." *OASE* 91 (2013): 21–32.

———. "Staged Materiality." *Interstices: Journal of Architecture and Related Arts* 14 (2013): 94–99.

———. "The Theory of Atmospheres and Its Applications." Translated by A.-Chr. Engels-Schwarzpaul. *Interstices: Journal of Architecture and Related Arts* 15 (2014): 93–100.

Bowman, Michael. "Tracing Mary Queen of Scotts." In Dickinson, Blair, and Ott, *Places of Public Memory*, 191–215.

Boym, Svetlana. *The Future of Nostalgia*. New York: Basic Books, 2001.

Brown, Laura Michael. "Flyover States, No Man's Land, and the Bible Belt: Introducing Critical Regionalism for Rhetorical Analysis." *Communication Teacher* 34 (2020): 198–203.

Brummett, Barry. *Rhetoric in Popular Culture*. New York: St. Martin's Press, 1994.

———. "Rhetorical Theory as Heuristic and Moral: A Pedagogical Justification." *Communication Education* 33 (1984): 97–107.

Buchanan, Ian. "Heterophenomenology, or de Certeau's Theory of Space." In "Michel de Certeau," edited by Ian Buchanan, special issue, *Social Semiotics* 6, no. 1 (1996): 111–32.

Buffalo Bill Center of the West. "Buffalo Bill." Center of the West (website). Accessed August 10, 2015.

———. "Buffalo Bill Historical Center: Voice of the American West." BBHC (website). Accessed January 18, 2007.

———. "Buffalo Bill Museum – Window on the West – Feature 1." Video, YouTube (website). Posted on June 17, 2011.

Buffalo Bill Historical Center. "Mission." Accessed June 28, 2012. Online.

Buffalo Bill Museum. Cody, WY: Buffalo Bill Historical Center, 1995. Catalog.

Burgin, Victor. *In/Different Spaces: Places and Memory in Visual Culture*. Berkeley: University of California Press, 1996.

Burke, Kenneth. *Attitudes toward History*. 3rd ed. Berkeley: University of California Press, 1984.

———. *Counter-Statement*. Berkeley, CA: University of California Press, 1931.

———. "Four Master Tropes." *Kenyon Review* 3, no. 4 (1941): 421–38.

———. *Permanence and Change: An Anatomy of Purpose*. 3rd ed. Berkeley: University of California Press, 1984.

———. *The Philosophy of Literary Form*. 3rd ed. Berkeley: University of California Press, 1973.

———. *A Rhetoric of Motives*. Berkeley: University of California Press, 1969.

Burns, Emily C. "Circulating Regalia and Lakhota Survivance, c. 1900." *Arts* 8 (2019): 146.

Burt, Ryan E. "'Sioux Yells' in the Dawes Era: Lakota 'Indian Play,' the Wild West, and the Literatures of Luther Standing Bear." *American Quarterly* 62, no. 3 (2010): 617–37.

Cariou, Warren. "Haunted Prairie: Aboriginal 'Ghosts' and the Spectres of Settlement." *University of Toronto Quarterly* 75 (2006): 727–34.

Cavaiani, Anthony C. "Rhetoric, Materiality, and the Disruption of Meaning: The Stadium as a Place of Protest." *Communication and Sport* 8 (2020): 473–88.

Certeau, Michel de. *The Practice of Everyday Life*. Translated by Steven Rendall. Berkeley: University of California Press, 1984.

Chamberlain, Charles. "From 'Haunts' to 'Character': The Meaning of Ethos and Its Relation to Ethics." *Helios* 11 (1984): 97–108.

Charland, Maurice. "Constitutive Rhetoric: The Case of the *Peuple Québécois*." *Quarterly Journal of Speech* 73, no. 2 (1987): 133–50.

Chevrette, Roberta, and Aaron Hess. "Unearthing the Native Past: Citizen Archaeology and the Modern (Non)Belonging at the Pueblo Grande Museum." *Communication and Critical/Cultural Studies* 12, no. 2 (2015): 139–58.

Christiansen, Jordan. "The Water Protectors at Standing Rock: Survivance Strategies for Gendered Relinking." *Women's Studies in Communication* 44 (2021): 278–300.

Christopherson, Ed. "New Art Collection Records the Great West." *New York Times*, May 24, 1959, XX 25 (travel section).

Clark, Andy. *Being There: Putting Brain, Body, and World Together Again*. Cambridge, MA: Bradford Books, 1997.

Clark, Jordin. "'Daddy Pence Come Dance': Queer(ing) Space in the Suburbs." *Western Journal of Communication* 85 (2021): 166–87.

Clavir, Miriam. *Preserving What Is Valued: Museums, Conservation, and First Nations*. Vancouver: University of British Columbia Press, 2007.

Colwell, Chip. *Plundered Skulls and Stolen Spirits: Inside the Fight to Reclaim Native America's Culture*. Chicago: University of Chicago Press, 2017.

Cram, E. "Queer Geographies and the Rhetoric of Orientation." *Quarterly Journal of Speech* 105 (2019): 98–115.

Crane, Susan A. "Introduction." In *Museums and Memory*, edited by Susan A. Crane, 1–13. Stanford: Stanford University Press, 2000.

Daniel-Wariya, Joshua. "Welcome to Decision Points Theater: Rhetoric, Museology, and Game Studies." *Rhetoric Society Quarterly* 49 (2019): 387–408.

Deloria, Philip Joseph. *Indians in Unexpected Places*. Lawrence: University of Kansas Press, 2004.

———. *Playing Indian*. New Haven: Yale University Press, 1998.

Deloria, Vine, Jr. *Custer Died for Your Sins: An Indian Manifesto*. New York: Avon, 1969.

Derrida, Jacques. *Archive Fever: A Freudian Impression*. Translated by Eric Prenowitz. Chicago: University of Chicago Press, 1998.

———. *Specters of Marx: The State of the Debt, the Work of Mourning, and the New International*. Translated by Peggy Kamuf. New York: Routledge, 1994.

Deverell, William. "Fighting Words: The Significance of the American West in the History of the United States." In *A New Significance: Re-Envisioning the History of the American West*, edited by Clyde A. Milner II, 29–55. New York: Oxford University Press, 1996.

Dickinson, Greg. *Suburban Dreams: Imagining and Building the Good Life*. Tuscaloosa: University of Alabama Press, 2015.

Dickinson, Greg, and Giorgia Aiello. "Being through There Matters: Materiality, Bodies, and Movement in Urban Communication Research." *International Journal of Communication* 10 (2016): 1294–308.

Dickinson, Greg, Carole Blair, and Brian L. Ott, eds. *Places of Public Memory: The*

Rhetoric of Museums and Memorials. Tuscaloosa: University of Alabama Press, 2010.

Dickinson, Greg, and Brian L. Ott. "Neoliberal Capitalism, Globalization, and Lines of Flight: Vectors and Velocities at the 16th Street Mall." *Cultural Studies ↔ Critical Methodologies* 13 (2013): 529–35.

Dickinson, Greg, Brian L. Ott, and Eric Aoki. "Memory and Myth at the Buffalo Bill Museum." *Western Journal of Communication* 69, no. 2 (2005): 85–108.

———. "(Re)Imagining the West: The Whitney Gallery of Western Art's Sacred Hymn." *Cultural Studies ↔ Critical Methodologies* 13, no. 1 (2013): 21–34.

———. "Spaces of Remembering and Forgetting: The Reverent Eye/I at the Plains Indian Museum." *Communication and Critical/Cultural Studies* 3, no. 1 (2006): 27–47.

Dippie, Brian W. *Custer's Last Stand: The Anatomy of an American Myth.* Lincoln: University of Nebraska Press, 1994.

———. "The Visual West." In *The Oxford History of the American West*, edited by Clyde A. Milner II, Carol A. O'Connor, and Martha A. Sandweiss, 675–706. New York: Oxford University Press, 1994.

Dorst, John. *Looking West.* Philadelphia: University of Pennsylvania Press, 1999.

———. "Skin Remembers: Animal Trophies as Material Memory." *Cultural Studies ↔ Critical Methodologies* 13 (2013): 35–46.

———. "A Walk through the Shooting Gallery." *Museum Anthropology* 17 (1993): 7–13.

Draper Natural History Museum. "Monarch of the Skies." Video, YouTube (website). Posted on February 7, 2018.

Drinnon, Richard. *Facing West: The Metaphysics of Indian-Hating and Empire-Building.* Minneapolis: University of Minnesota Press, 1980.

Dubin, Steven C. *Displays of Power: Memory and Amnesia in the American Museum.* New York: New York University Press, 1999.

———. *Transforming Museums: Mounting Queen Victoria in a Democratic South Africa.* New York: Palgrave Macmillan, 2006.

Dudley, Sandra. "Introduction: Museum and Things." In Dudley et al., *Thing about Museums*, 21–32.

Dudley, Sandra, Amy Jane Barnes, Jennifer Binnie, Julia Petrov, and Jennifer Walklate, eds. *The Thing about Museums: Objects and Experience, Representation and Contestation.* London: Routledge, 2012.

Dunbar-Ortiz, Roxanne. *An Indigenous Peoples' History of the United States.* Boston: Beacon Press, 2014.

———. *Not a Nation of Immigrants: Settler Colonialism, White Supremacy, and a History of Erasure and Exclusion.* Boston: Beacon Press, 2021.

Eckstein, Justin, and Amy Young. "WastED Rhetoric." *Communication and Critical/Cultural Studies* 15 (2018): 274–91.

Edgar, Heather J. H., and Anna L. M. Rautman. "Contemporary Museum Policies and the Ethics of Accepting Human Remains." *Curator: The Museum Journal* 57, no. 2 (2014): 237–47.

Ewalt, Joshua P. "Visibility and Order at the Salt Lake City Main Public Library:

Commonplaces, Deviant Publics, and the Rhetorical Criticism of Neoliberalism's Geographies." *Communication and Critical/Cultural Studies* 16 (2019): 103–21.

"Experience." OED (website). Accessed June 25, 2014.

Farzad-Phillips, Alyson. "Huddles or Hurdles? Spatial Barriers to Collective Gathering in the Aftermath of the Women's March." *Women's Studies in Communication* 43 (2020): 247–70.

Fish, Stanley E. "Interpreting the *Variorum*." In *Reader-Response Criticism: From Formalism to Post-Structuralism*, edited by Jane P. Tompkins, 164–84. Baltimore: Johns Hopkins University Press, 1980.

Flores, Dan. "Bison Ecology and Bison Diplomacy: The Southern Plains from 1800 to 1850." *Journal of American History* 78 (1991): 465–85.

French, Brett. "Cody Firearms Museum More Hands-On with $12M Remodel." *Billings Gazette*, July 1, 2019.

Freud, Sigmund. "The Uncanny." In *The Uncanny*, translated by David McLintock, 123–62. London: Penguin Books, 2003.

Fryd, Vivien Green. *Art and Empire: The Politics of Ethnicity in the United States Capitol, 1815–1860*. New Haven: Yale University Press, 1992.

Gaither, Barry Edmund. "'Hey, That's Mine:' Thoughts on Pluralism and American Museums." In *Museums and Communities: The Politics of Public Culture*, edited by Ivan Karp, Christine Mullen Kreamer, and Steven D. Lavine, 56–64. Washington, DC: Smithsonian Press, 1992.

Gallagher, Victoria J. "Memory and Reconciliation in the Birmingham Civil Rights Institute." *Rhetoric and Public Affairs* 2 (1999): 303–20.

———. "Remembering Together: Rhetorical Integration and the Case of the Martin Luther King, Jr. Memorial." *Southern Communication Journal* 60, no. 2 (1995): 109–19.

Gordon, Avery. *Ghostly Matters: Haunting and the Sociological Imagination*. Minneapolis: University of Minnesota Press, 2008.

Greenblatt, Stephen. *Marvelous Possessions: The Wonder of the New World*. Chicago: University of Chicago Press, 1991.

———. "Resonance and Wonder." *Bulletin of the American Academy of Arts and Sciences* 43 (1990): 11–34.

Greer, Allan. "Settler Colonialism and Empire in Early America." *William and Mary Quarterly* 76 (2019): 383–90.

Grusin, Richard. *Culture, Technology, and the Creation of America's National Parks*. Cambridge, UK: Cambridge University Press, 2004.

Gumbrecht, Hans Ulrich. *Production of Presence: What Meaning Cannot Convey*. Stanford, CA: Stanford University Press, 2004.

Gunn, Joshua. "Mourning Speech: Haunting and the Spectral Voices of Nine-Eleven." *Text and Performance Quarterly* 24 (2004): 91–114.

———. *Perversion: Rhetorical Aberration in the Time of Trumpeteering*. Chicago: University of Chicago Press, 2021.

———. "Review Essay: Mourning Humanism, or, the Idiom of Haunting." *Quarterly Journal of Speech* 92 (2006): 77–102.

"Guns in America." *Time* magazine website. Accessed March 11, 2022.

Hämäläinen, Pekka. "The Rise and Fall of Plains Indian Horse Cultures." *Journal of American History* 90 (2003): 833–62.

Hansen, Emma I. *Memory and Vision: Arts, Cultures, and Lives of Plains Indian People*. With contributions by Beatrice Medicine, Gerard Baker, Joseph Medicine Crow, Arthur Amiotte, and Bently Sprang. Seattle: University of Washington Press, 2007.

"Hansen Resigns, West Leads Plains Indian Museum." *Cody Enterprise*, Codyenterprise (website). May 14, 2014.

Haraway, Donna. *Primate Visions: Gender, Race, and Nature in the World of Modern Science*. New York: Routledge, 1989.

Harjo, Joy. *How We Become Human: New and Selected Poems*. New York: W. W. Norton, 2002.

———. *In Mad Love and War*. Middletown, CT: Wesleyan University Press, 1990.

———. *The Spiral of Memory: Interviews*. Edited by Laura Coltelli. Ann Arbor: University of Michigan Press, 1996.

Harjo, Joy, and Stephen Strom. *Secrets from the Center of the World*. Tucson: University of Arizona Press, 1989.

Hasian, Marouf, and Rulon Wood. "Critical Museology, (Post)Colonial Communication, and the Gradual Mastering of Traumatic Pasts at the Royal Museum for Central Africa (RMCA)." *Western Journal of Communication* 74, no. 2 (2010): 128–49.

Headstrom, Margaret, and Anna Perricci. "It's Only Temporary." In Schachter and Brockmann, *(Im)permanence*, 26–40.

Helmbrecht, Brenda. "Revisiting Missions: Decolonizing Public Memories in California." *Rhetoric Society Quarterly* 49, no. 5 (2019): 470–94.

Hosmer, Charles B., Jr. *Presence of the Past: A History of the Preservation Movement in the United States before Williamsburg*. New York: G. P. Putnam's Sons, 1965.

Hosokawa, Bill. "The Sentinel Story." In *Remembering Heart Mountain: Essays on Japanese American Internment in Wyoming*, edited by Mike Mackey, 63–74. Powell, WY: Western History Publications, 1998.

Houze, Lynn J. "Cody, Wyoming." Wyohistory (website). Accessed March 20, 2014.

Hutton, Patrick H. *History as an Art of Memory*. Hanover, NH: University Press of New England, 1993.

Hyde, Michael J. "Introduction: Rhetorically, We Dwell." In Hyde, *Ethos of Rhetoric*, xii–xxviii.

Hyde, Michael J., ed. *The Ethos of Rhetoric*, Columbia: University of South Carolina Press, 2004.

Jenkins, Tiffany. *Contesting Human Remains in Museum Collections: The Crisis of Cultural Authority*. New York: Routledge, 2011.

Kammen, Michael. *Mystic Chords of Memory: The Transformation of Tradition in American Culture*. New York: Vintage, 1993.

Kasson, Joy S. *Buffalo Bill's Wild West: Celebrity, Memory, and Popular History*. New York: Hill and Wang, 2000.

Kavanagh, Gaynor. "Making Histories, Making Memories." In *Making Histories in Museums*, 1–14. London: Leicester University Press, 1996.

Keeling, Diane Marie. "Of Turning and Tropes." *Review of Communication* 16, no. 4 (2016): 317–33.

Keene, Suzanne. *Managing Conservation in Museums*. 2nd ed. Oxford: Butterworth-Heinemann, 2002.

King, Lisa. *Legible Sovereignties: Rhetoric, Representations, and Native American Museums*. Corvallis: Oregon State University Press, 2017.

Knapp, Alan K., John M. Blair, John M. Briggs, Scott L. Collins, David C. Hartnett, Loretta C. Johnson, and E. Gene Towne. "The Keystone Role of Bison in North American Tallgrass Prairie: Bison Increase Habitat Heterogeneity and Alter a Broad Array of Plant, Community, and Ecosystem Processes." *Bioscience* 49 (1999): 39–50.

Lake, Randall. "Between Myth and History: Enacting Time in Native American Protest Rhetoric." *Quarterly Journal of Speech* 77 (1991): 123–51.

Lamar, Howard Roberts, ed. *The Reader's Encyclopedia of the American West*. New York: Crowell, 1977.

Leahy, Helen Rees. "Exhibiting Absence in the Museum." In Dudley et al., *Thing about Museums*, 270–82.

Lefebvre, Henri. *The Social Production of Space*. Translated by Donald Nicholson-Smith. Oxford: Blackwell, 1991.

Leonardo, Micaela di. *Exotics at Home: Anthropologies, Others, American Modernity*. Chicago: University of Chicago Press, 1998.

Light, Elinor. "Playing in Cyberspace: The Social Performative on Heidelberg Street." *Critical Studies in Media Communication* 36 (2019): 207–20.

Linenthal, Edward Tabor. *Sacred Ground: Americans and Their Battlefields*. 2n ed. Urbana: University of Illinois Press, 1993.

Lippit, Akira Mizuta. *Electric Animal: Toward a Rhetoric of Wildlife*. Minneapolis: University of Minnesota Press, 2000.

Loewen, James W. *Lies across America: What Our Historic Sites Get Wrong*. New York: New Press, 2010.

Lonetree, Amy. *Decolonizing Museums: Representing Native America in National and Tribal Museums*. Chapel Hill: University of North Carolina Press, 2012.

Lonetree, Amy, and Amanda J. Cobb. *The National Museum of the American Indian: Critical Conversations*. Edited by Amy Lonetree. Lincoln: University of Nebraska Press, 2008.

Lott, David F., and Steven C. Minta. "Random Individual Association and Social Group Instability in American Bison (*Bison bison*)." *Zeitschrift für Tierpsychologie* 61 (1983): 153–72.

Lueck, Amy J. "Haunting Women's Public Memory: Ethos, Space, and Gender in the Winchester Mystery House." *Rhetoric Review* 40 (2021): 107–22.

Lyons, Scott Richard. "Rhetorical Sovereignty: What Do American Indians Want from Writing?" *CCC* 51 (2000): 447–68.

Mack, Ashley Noel, and Tiara R. Na'puti. "'Our Bodies Are Not Terra Nullius': Building a Decolonial Feminist Resistance to Gendered Violence." *Women's Studies in Communication* 42 (2019): 347–70.

Mackintosh, Barry. *The National Parks: Shaping the System*. 3rd ed. Washington, DC: National Park System, 2000.

Maldonado, Chandra Ann. "Commemorative (Dis)Placement: On the Limits of Textual Adaptability and the Future of Public Memory Scholarship." *Rhetoric and Public Affairs* 24 (2021): 329–52.

Maleuvre, Didier. *Museum Memories: History, Technology, Art*. Stanford, CA: Stanford University Press, 1999.

Marinelli, Kevin. "Placing Second: Empathic Unsettlement as a Vehicle of Consubstantiality at the Silent Gesture Statue of Tommie Smith and John Carlos." *Memory Studies* 10 (2017): 440–58.

Martin, Elizabeth. *Architecture as a Translation of Music*. New York: Princeton Architectural Press, 1994.

Massey, Doreen. *For Space*. Los Angeles: Sage, 2005.

Massumi, Brian. "The Autonomy of Affect." *Cultural Critique* 31 (1995): 83–109.

——. *Parables for the Virtual: Movement, Affect, Sensation*. Durham, NC: Duke University Press, 2002.

——. *Semblance and Event: Activist Philosophy and the Occurrent Arts*. Cambridge, MA: MIT Press, 2011.

Maurantonio, Nicole. "Material Rhetoric, Public Memory, and the Post-It Note." *Southern Communication Journal* 80, no. 2 (2015): 83–101.

Maxson, J. David. "'Second Line to Bury White Supremacy': Take 'Em Down Nola, Monument Removal, and Residual Memory." *Quarterly Journal of Speech* 106 (2020): 48–71.

McCallum, Henry D., and Frances T. McCallum. *The Wire That Fenced the West*. Norman: University of Oklahoma Press, 1965.

McNenly, Linda Scarangella. *Native Performers in Wild West Shows: From Buffalo Bill to Euro Disney*. Norman: University of Oklahoma Press, 2012.

McWhorter, Karen B. "Expanded Horizons: Promoting Diversity in the Whitney." *Points West: Black Cowboys in America*, Spring 2021. Online.

Metesh, T. Logan. "The Newly Renovated Cody Firearms Museum Is Open!" Range 365 (website). Accessed March 3, 2020.

Mihesuab, Devon A. "Introduction." In *Repatriation Reader*, 1–2.

Mihesuab, Devon A., ed. *Repatriation Reader: Who Owns American Indian Remains*. Lincoln: University of Nebraska Press.

Mills, Amy. *Streets of Memory: Landscape, Tolerance, and National Identity in Istanbul*. Athens: University of Georgia Press, 2010.

Mirzoeff, Nicholas, ed. *The Visual Culture Reader*. 2nd ed. London: Routledge, 2002.

Mitchell, Scott A. "Spaces of Emergent Memory: Detroit's 8 Mile Wall and Public Memories of Civil Rights Injustice." *Communication and Critical/Cultural Studie* 15 (2018): 197–212.

Moore, Robert J. *Native Americans: The Art and Travels of Charles Bird King, George Catlin and Karl Bodmer*. Edison, NJ: Chartwell Books, 2002.

Morris, Meaghan. "Things to Do with Shopping Centres." In *Grafts: Feminist Cultural Criticism*, edited by Susan Sheridan, 168–81. New York: Verso, 1988.

Moss, Matthew. "Touring the Newly Refurbished Cody Firearms Museum." American Rifleman (website). Accessed August 9, 2019.

Murtagh, William J. *Keeping Time: The History and Theory of Preservation in America*. Rev. ed. New York: John Wiley and Sons, 1997.

Na'puti, Tiara R. "Rhetorical Contexts of Colonization and Decolonization." *Oxford Research Encyclopedia of Communication*, 2020. Online.

———. "Speaking of Indigeneity: Navigating Genealogies against Erasure and #RhetoricSoWhite." *Quarterly Journal of Speech* 105 (2019): 495–501.

National Park Service. Heart Mountain Relocation Center (website). Accessed April 11, 2021.

———. "Native American Graves Protection and Repatriation Act" (website). Accessed December 3, 2021.

———. "Notice of Intent to Repatriate Cultural Items: Buffalo Bill Center of the West, Plains Indian Museum." Federal Register (website), July 19, 2019.

———. "Park Facts" (website). Accessed July 8, 2023.

———. "Park Statistics" (website). Accessed July 8, 2023.

Nesheim, David. "How William F. Cody Helped Save the Buffalo without Really Trying." *Great Plains Quarterly* 27 (2007): 163–75.

Nicholas, Liza J. *Becoming Western: Stories of Culture and Identity in the Cowboy State*. Lincoln: University of Nebraska Press, 2006.

———. "Wyoming as America: Celebrations, a Museum, and Yale." *American Quarterly* 54 (2002): 437–65.

Nöe, Alva. *Varieties of Presence*. Cambridge, MA: Harvard University Press, 2012.

Nora, Pierre. "Between Memory and History: Les Lieux de Mémoire." *Representations* 26 (Spring 1989): 7–24.

Obermark, Lauren. "'Assurance That the World Holds Far More Good Than Bad': The Pedagogy of Memory at the Oklahoma City National Memorial Museum." *Rhetoric Review* 38 (2019): 93–107.

O'Gorman, Ned. "Eisenhower and the American Sublime." *Quarterly Journal of Speech* 94, no. 1 (2008): 44–72.

Ohl, Jesse J., and Jennifer E. Potter. "Traumatic Encounters with Frank Mechau's Dangers of the Mail." *Communication and Critical/Cultural Studies* 16 (2019): 26–42.

Olick, Jeffrey K. "Collective Memory: The Two Cultures." *Sociological Theory* 17, no. 3 (1999): 333–48.

Ono, Kent. "Contextual Fields of Rhetoric." *Western Journal of Communication* 84 (2020): 264–79.

Ostlind, Emilene. "The Bighorn Basin: Wyoming's Bony Back Pocket." Wyohistory (website). Accessed March 20, 2014.

Ott, Brian L., and Eric Aoki. "The Politics of Negotiating Public Tragedy: Media Framing of the Matthew Shepard Murder." *Rhetoric and Public Affairs* 5, no. 3 (2002): 483–505.

Ott, Brian L., and Greg Dickinson. "Entering the Unending Conversation: An Introduction to Rhetorical Criticism." In *The Routledge Reader in Rhetorical*

Criticism, edited by Brian L. Ott and Greg Dickinson, 1–14. New York: Routledge, 2013.

———. "Redefining Rhetoric: Why Matter Matters." *Berlin Journal of Critical Theory* 3 (2019): 45–81.

Ott, Brian, L., Greg Dickinson, and Eric Aoki. "Ways of (Not) Seeing Guns: Presence and Absence at the Cody Firearms Museum." *Communication and Critical/Cultural Studies* 8 (2011): 215–39.

Paliewicz, Nicholas S. "The Country, the City, and the Corporation: Rio Tinto Kennecott and the Materiality of Corporate Rhetoric." *Environmental Communication* 12 (2018): 744–62.

Parker, Kim, Juliana Horowitz, Ruth Igielnik, Baxter Oliphant, and Anna Brown. *America's Complex Relationship with Guns: An In-Depth Look at the Attitudes and Experiences of U.S. Adults.* Pew Research Center (website). June 22, 2017.

Petrov, Julia. "Playing Dress-Up: Inhabiting Imagined Spaces through Museum Objects." In Dudley et al., *Thing about Museums*, 250–61.

Pham, Vincent N. "Drive-By Cinema's Drive-Outs and U-Turns: Materiality, Mobility, and the Reconfiguring of Forgotten Spaces and Absurd Borders." *Women's Studies in Communication* 41 (2018): 370–82.

Phillips, Aaron T. "Eliding Extraction, Embracing Novelty: The Spatio-Temporal Configuration of Natural History." *Environmental Communication* 8, no. 4 (2014): 452–67.

Phillips, Kendall R., and Connah Podmore. "The Scale of Our Memory: Spectacle in the Commemoration of Gallipoli." *Rhetoric Society Quarterly* 50, no. 1 (2020): 35–52.

Pinto, Sarah, Shelly Hannigan, Bernadette Walker-Gibbs, and Emma Charlton, eds. *Interdisciplinary Unsettlings of Place and Space.* Singapore: Springer, 2019.

Plains Indian Museum Buffalo Bill Historical Center: A Reinterpretation. Cody, WY: Buffalo Bill Historical Center, 2002.

Poerio, Giulia Lara, and Jonathan Smallwood. "Daydreaming to Navigate the Social World: What We Know, What We Don't and Why It Matters." *Social and Personality Compass* 10 (2016): 605–18.

Prelli, Lawrence. "Rhetorics of Display: An Introduction." In *Rhetorics of Display*, edited by Lawrence J. Prelli, 1–38. Columbia: University of South Carolina Press, 2006.

Primak, Alvin J. "You Are Not the Father: Rhetoric, Settler Colonial Curiosity, and Federal Indian Law." *Review of Communication* 20 (2020): 27–46.

Rader, Karen A., and Victoria E. M. Cain. *Life on Display: Revolutionizing U.S. Museums of Science and Natural History in the Twentieth Century.* Chicago: University of Chicago Press, 2014.

Reynolds, Ann. "Visual Stories." In Mirzoeff, *Visual Culture Reader*, 324–38.

Rice, Jennifer H., et al. "Memory and Lost Communities: Strange Methods for Studying Place." *Review of Communication* 20 (2020): 144–51.

Rickert, Thomas. *Ambient Rhetoric: The Attunements of Rhetorical Being.* Pittsburgh: University of Pittsburgh Press, 2013.

Rifkin, Mark. *Beyond Settler Time: Temporal Sovereignty and Indigenous Self-Determination*. Durham, NC: Duke University Press, 2017.

Robbins, Jim. "Cody Displays Art and Relics of the West: Where Buffalo Bill's Not Defunct." *New York Times*, July 26, 1987, section 10 (travel), page 19.

Robinson, Emily. "Objects, Documentation, and Identification: Materiality and Memory of American Indian Boarding Schools at the Heard Museum." *Rhetoric Society Quarterly* 51 (2021): 94–108.

Robinson, Greg. *By Order of the President: FDR and the Internment of Japanese Americans*. Cambridge, MA: Harvard University Press, 2001.

Rosaldo, Renato. *Culture and Truth: The Remaking of Social Analysis*. Boston: Beacon Press, 1989.

———. "Imperialist Nostalgia." *Representations* 26 (1989): 107–22.

Rosenzweig, Roy, and David P. Thelen. *The Presence of the Past: Popular Uses of History in American Life*. New York: Columbia University Press, 1998.

Rothstein, Edward. "At the Buffalo Bill Museum, a Showdown between History and Myth." *New York Times*, August 4, 2012.

———. "Handled with Care." *Wall Street Journal*, September 27, 2019.

Rowlands, Mark. *The New Science of the Mind: From Extended Mind to Embodied Phenomenology*. Cambridge, MA: MIT Press, 2010.

Rudner, Ruth. "Wyoming Prospects," *New York Times*, September 18, 1983, section 10 (travel), page 22.

Sagala, Sandra K. *Buffalo Bill on Stage*. Albuquerque: University of New Mexico Press, 2008.

Savage, William W., Jr. *The Cowboy Hero: His Image in American History and Culture*. Norman: University of Oklahoma Press, 1979.

Schachter, Judith, and Stephen Brockmann, eds. *(Im)permanence: Cultures in/out of Time*. Pittsburgh: Center of the Arts in Society, Carnegie Mellon University, 2008.

Schall, Jan. "Curating Ephemera: Responsibility and Reality." In Schachter and Brockmann, *(Im)permanence*, 15–25.

Schlachte, Carl. "Material Inertia: The Sedimented Spatial Rhetoric of Public School Buildings." *Rhetoric Review* 39 (2020): 317–29.

Schneider, Lindsey. "'There's Something in the Water': Salmon Runs and Settler Colonialism on the Columbia River." *American Indian Research Journal* 37 (2013): 149–63.

Seligman, Rebecca, and Laurence J. Kirmayerm. "Dissociate Experience and Cultural Neuroscience: Narrative, Metaphor and Mechanism." *Cultural Medical Psychiatry* 32 (2008): 31–64.

Shugart, Helene A. "Reinventing Privilege: The New (Gay) Man in Contemporary Popular Media." *Critical Studies in Media Communication* 20 (2003): 67–91.

Siegfried, Kate. "Making Settler Colonialism Concrete: Agentive Materialism and Habitational Violence in Palestine." *Communication and Critical/Cultural Studies* 17 (2020): 267–84.

Slotkin, Richard. *Gunfighter Nation: The Myth of the Frontier in Twentieth-Century America*. New York: Atheneum, 1992.

———. *Regeneration through Violence: The Mythology of the American Frontier 1600–1860*. Norman: University of Oklahoma Press, 1973.

"Spirit." OED (website). Accessed August 8, 2017.

St. Germain, Jill. *Broken Treaties: United State and Canadian Relations with the Lakotas and the Plains Cree, 1868–1885*. Lincoln: University of Nebraska Press, 2009.

Stormer, Nathan. "Addressing the Sublime: Space, Mass Representation, and the Unrepresentable." *Critical Studies in Media Communication* 21, no. 3 (2004): 212–40.

Strickland, Renard. *Tonto's Revenge: Reflections on American Indian Culture and Policy*. Albuquerque: University of New Mexico Press, 1997.

Suderburg, Erika. "Introduction: On Installation and Site Specificity." In *Space, Site, Intervention: Situating Installation Art*, edited by Erika Suderburg, 1–22. Minneapolis: University of Minnesota Press, 2000.

Tolles, Thayer. "Paul Manship, *Indian and Pronghorn Antelope*." In *Timeless Treasures: 50 Favorites from the Whitney Western Art Museum*, 52. Cody, WY: Buffalo Bill Historical Center, 2008. Catalog.

Tompkins, Jane. *West of Everything: The Inner Life of Westerns*. New York: Oxford University Press, 1992.

Trachtenberg, Marvin. "Architecture and Music Reunited: A New Reading of Dufay's 'Nuper Rosarum Flores' and the Cathedral of Florence." *Renaissance Quarterly* 54, no. 3 (2001): 741–75.

Treasures of Our West. Cody, WY: Buffalo Bill Historical Center, 1992. Catalog.

Tucker, Jennifer, Glenn Adamson, Jonathan S. Ferguson, Josh Garrett-Davis, Erik Goldstein, Ashley Hlebinsky, David D. Miller, and Susanne Slavick. "Display of Arms: A Roundtable Discussion about the Public Exhibition of Firearms and Their History." *Technology and Culture* 59 (July 2018): 719–69.

Turner, Victor W. *Dramas, Fields, and Metaphors: Symbolic Action in Human Society*. Ithaca, NY: Cornell University Press, 1974.

United States Holocaust Museum. "Mission and History." Ushmm (website). Accessed September 10, 2020.

Van Der Kolk, Bessel. *The Body Keeps the Score: Brain, Mind, and Body in the Healing of Trauma*. New York: Viking, 2014.

Van Rees, Agnes. *Dissociation in Argumentative Discussions*. Berlin: Springer, 2009.

Vartabedian, Sara. "No Cause for Comfort Here: False Witnesses to 'Peace.'" *Southern Communication Journal* 82 (2017): 250–62.

Veracini, Lorenzo. *Settler Colonialism: A Theoretical Overview*. Houndmills, UK: Palgrave Macmillan. 2010.

Vidler, Anthony. *The Architectural Uncanny: Essays in the Modern Unhomely*. Cambridge, MA: MIT Press, 1992.

Visitor's Guide: Buffalo Bill Historical Center. Cody, WY: Buffalo Bill Historical Center, 2000.

Vizenor, Gerald. *Native Liberty: Natural Reason and Cultural Survivance*. Lincoln: University of Nebraska Press, 2009.

Warnke, Georgia. "Ocularcentrism and Social Criticism." In *Modernity and the Hegemony of Vision*, edited by David Michael Levin, 287–308. Berkeley: University of California Press, 1993.

Warren, Louis S. *Buffalo Bill's America: William Cody and the Wild West Show*. New York: Alfred A. Knopf, 2005.

Watson, Bill, and Shari Rosenstein Werb. "One Hundred Strong: A Colloquium on Transforming Natural History Museums in the Twenty-First Century." *Museum Journal* 58 (2013): 255–65.

Weiser, Elizabeth M. *Museum Rhetoric: Building Civic Identity in National Spaces.* University Park: Penn State University Press, 2017.

Welton, Michael. "Renovating Cody Firearms Museum." *Architects and Artisans*, architectsandartisans (website). Accessed March 3, 2020.

West, Patricia. *Domesticating History: The Political Origins of America's House Museums.* Washington, DC: Smithsonian Institution Press, 1999.

West, Rebecca. "Roundtable Discussion: 'The Legacy of Buffalo Bill and the Center of the West." Buffalo Bill Center of the West. Filmed August 2–3, 2017 at Buffalo Bill Centennial Symposium in Cody, Wyoming. YouTube video, 1:32:17.

White, Richard. "Frederick Jackson Turner and Buffalo Bill." In *The Frontier in American Culture: An Exhibition at the Newberry Library, August 26, 1994–January 7, 1995*, edited by Richard White, Patricia Nelson Limerick, and James R. Grossman, 6–65. Berkeley: University of California Press, 1994.

Whitt, Laurie Anne. "Cultural Imperialism and the Marketing of Native America." *American Indian Culture and Research Journal* 19 (1995): 1–31.

Wieskamp, Valerie N., and Courtney Smith. "'What to Do When You're Raped': Indigenous Women Critiquing and Coping through a Rhetoric of Survivance." *Quarterly Journal of Speech* 106 (2020): 72–94.

Winchester, Juti A. "Log Cabin Dreams: Women, Domesticity and Museums in the Early Twentieth Century." *Points West: Journal of the Buffalo Bill Historical Center*, Summer 2003. Online.

Windler, Robert. "Museum Is Set Up for Buffalo Bill: Half-Finished Structure in Wyoming Is Dedicated." *New York Times*, July 5, 1968.

Wolfe, Patrick. "Settler Colonialism and the Elimination of the Native." *Journal of Genocide Research* 8 (2006): 387–409.

Wood, Andrew F. "Haunting Ruins in a Western Ghost Town: Authentic Violence and Recursive Gaze at Bodie, California." *Western Journal of Communication* 85 (2020): 449–56.

Woods, Carly S., Joshua P. Ewalt, and Sara J. Baker. "A Matter of Regionalism: Remembering Brandon Teena and Willa Cather at the Nebraska History Museum." *Quarterly Journal of Speech* 99, no. 3 (2013): 341–63.

Wright, Will. *The Wild West: The Mythic Cowboy and Social Theory.* London: Sage Publications, 2002.

Yates, Francis A. *The Art of Memory.* Chicago: University of Chicago Press, 1966.

Zelizer, Barbie. "Reading the Past against the Grain: The Shape of Memory Studies." *Critical Studies in Media Communication* 12, no. 2 (1995): 213–39.

Zontak, Ken. "Hunt, Capture, Raise, Increase: The People Who Saved the Bison." *Great Plains Quarterly* 15, no. 2 (1995): 133–49.

Zukin, Sharon. *Landscapes of Power: From Detroit to Disney World.* Berkeley: University of California Press, 1991.

Index

Page numbers in italics refer to illustrations

Abercrombie, Robert, 15
aboriginal hauntings, 46
absence: as barring of Other in present, 169; and haunt and haunting, 6, 44, 77, 167, 192; historical, and survivance, 75; tension of presence and absence, 135–38; of works and displays portraying or suggesting violence, injustice, and racism, 114–15, 122, 141, 144, 146–47, 148, 182, 219n4
affect: and bodily response, 105; haunting as, 44, 45, 51, 167, 185, 192; of house museum, 53; as way of knowing, 153
affective dissociation, embodied, 152–54
Aiello, Giorgia, 40
Alcoff, Linda, 209n5
Allen, Mary Jester, 53, 54, 55, 206n18
American Indian Movement (AIM), 73
American Museum of Natural History, 124, 134
Amiotte, Arthur (Oglala Lakota), 73, 84–85, 209n14
amnesia, dissociative, 153, 154, 155, 221n27
"amnesiac state of memory," 154, 212n49
amnesiatic looking, 79, 89–93, 171
Anderson, Ben, 205n4
Anderson, Kay, 92
Aoki, Eric, 40, 145, 149, 166, 219n1, 209n5, 219n2
architecture and music, 101

argumentative dissociation, 152, 153, 154
Armada, Bernard J., 214n9
Ashworth, G. J., 200n24
Asma, Stephen T., 122, 208n37
atmosphere: atmospheric awe, 121, 125, 130, 142, 215n1; belonging to perceiving subject or aesthetic object, 205n4; created by light and sound, 80–81, 93, 212nn38–39, 218n36; distinction from function, 205n2
authenticity, museums and, 22, 29, 31
awe and wonder, 19; atmospheric, 121, 125, 130, 142, 215n1; evocation of, 121; nature, 79, 115, 116, 119; and possession, 123–24; reaction to art, 105, 114

barbed wire. *See* fencing, barbed wire
Barthes, Roland, 70, 141, 214n23, 219n51
Bartlett, Richard A., 19–20
Baudrillard, Jean, 135, 218n44
being through there (embodied movement), 7, 106; and bodies affectively moved by rhetorical spaces, 100; experiential approach to study of communication, 40; as method of engaging experiential landscapes, 23, 188; and movement in space and time, 41; and particularities of place, 41–42
Berger, John, 216n17, 217n23
Bierstadt, Albert, 13, 19, 188; *Island Lake*, 113; *The Last of the Buffalo*,

107, 109, 110; *Wind River Range,* 113; *Yellowstone Falls,* 113

Bighorn Basin: and Cody, Wyoming, 20; white settlers in, and treaty abrogation, 11–13

Birmingham Civil Rights Institute, and rhetoric of progress, 84

bison, American, 125; destruction of, 58–61, 65, 69, 107, 113, 116, 186, 192; displays depicting, 57–61, 65, 81, 135–36, 138, 161, 192; economic base of Plains Nations, and government destruction of, 58, 60; in plains ecosystem, 57–58, 207n28; preservation efforts, 58; social associations, 208n36

Biss, Earl, *Gen. Custer in Blue and Green,* 105–6

Black Lives Matter, 149, 180

Blair, Carole, 29, 31, 95, 99

Boehme, Sarah E., 113

Böhme, Gernot: atmospheric awe, 215n1; "attuned spaces," 97; distinction between function and atmosphere, 205n2; light, sound, and music in atmospheres, 212n38, 218n36

Bowman, Michael, 198n5

Brooks, Winthrop, 17

buffalo. *See* bison, American

Buffalo Bill Center of the West (BBCW): authors on, 195n2; changing institutional goals and designs, 98, 188–92; as defense against effects of late modernity, 20; dioramas of nuclear animal families, 208n37; entrance to, 38; entrance to, poster, 5; entrance to, and statue of Buffalo Bill, 1, 2; five museums, 3, 22; location in Wyoming, 15, 29; and NAGPRA, 200n23; as part of western dreamscapes, 38–39; self-defined relationship with nature, 20, 57; "the Spirit of the American West" credo, 4, 5, 20, 42, 48–49, 100, 116, 207n27; and western landscape as static, 37

Buffalo Bill Center of the West (BBCW), haunt and haunting, 6, 7, 42–47; acknowledgment of loss of people, land, and animals while placing losses elsewhere, 94; emplaced and embodied, 43; encompassing fear and comfort, 43, 193; haunted by settler colonialism, 43, 45–47, 116, 171, 184; inclusive of past, present, and future, 43, 45; linked to national identity and "American" values, 184; pleasurable return to painfully lost world system, 43; shifting emphasis from Buffalo Bill to the West as place and ideology, 42; "Spirit of the American West" theme as idealization of West, 4, 5, 20, 42, 47, 69, 116, 183, 184; symbolic and material rhetoric, 4, 185; "the Other does not have to be the Same," 193; and West as Anglo-Saxon place of heroism, individualism, and masculinity, 5–6, 47

Buffalo Bill Historical Center (BBHC). *See* Buffalo Bill Center of the West (BBCW)

Buffalo Bill Memorial Association, 16–17, 53, 54, 55

Buffalo Bill Memorial Remington rifles, and funding for Buffalo Bill Museum, 18, 26, 55

Buffalo Bill Museum (BBM), early forms of: changing attitudes toward the West, and need for revision of, 99, 189; dependence on private financing to date, 197n27; founded as center of the West, 17–21; log cabin as idealized version of Cody's TE Ranch house, 52, 53, 54–55, 206n18; putative scalp of Chief Yellow Hair, 17, 53–54; renamed Buffalo Bill Historical Center in 1969 (BBHC), 18; 1969 version focused on Cody's construction of the story of the cowboy and violent conflicts of western frontier, 30, 51, 55–56

Buffalo Bill Museum (BBM), and ghost of William F. Cody: bison family diorama, and domestication of West, 57, 58–59; completed reinstallation 2012, 48; design principles replicating those in other BBCW museums, 56–57; diorama of Cody overlooking civilizing forces of West, 59–60; display of Cody's show attire from *Buffalo Bill's Wild West*, 67, *68*; display of Game of Buffalo Bill board game, amid life-sized reproduction of game, *63*, 63–65, *65*, 208n41; entrance to ghostly visual image of Buffalo Bill with actor voice-over, 42, 48, *49*, 49–50, 51, 69, 183, 184, 205nEpi; focus on Cody's desire to return to the old West, 60–61, 66–67, 69–70; guiding of visitors through space/time and authenticity/reproduction shifts, 60–65; less emphasis on violent masculinity than in older version of BBM, 50; portrayal of Cody as struggling family man haunted by dreams, 50, 56–57, 69–70; shift in emphasis from Buffalo Bill and *Wild West* to the West as place and ideology, 42, 51; substitution of Cody's life for the history of the West, 70; William F. Cody's camping tent, *67*, *68*; window designs performing contradictions of Cody's life, 61–63; *Window of the West*, 65–67. *See also* Cody, William F. ("Buffalo Bill")

Buffalo Bill's Wild West: audience reception of story as authentic narrative of the history of the West, 14; centrality of buffalo as icon of the West, 58; costumes displayed in early Buffalo Bill Museum, 54, 72; frontier mythology as civilizing of West by white Euro Americans, 14–15; Lakota regalia, 89; launched by Cody in 1883, 14; marketing opportunities from,

208n41; narratives of warlike, disappearing savages, 72, 208n41; recreation of Custer's Last Stand, 111. *See also* Cody, William F. ("Buffalo Bill")

Buffalohead, Julie (Ponca Tribe, Oklahoma), 117

Burgin, Victor, 38, 217n29

Burke, Kenneth: and appeal of form, 103, 114; and embodied practice, 152; and metonymy, 81, 211n37; and transcendence of guilt, 210n20

Burlington Railroad, 11

Burns, Emily, 89

California, admission to Union, 12

Cariou, Warren, 46

Cary, William de la Montagne, *Indian Mother and Child*, 106–7, 110

Catlin, George, 13, 71, 96

Chamberlain, Charles, 5, 32, 44, 121

Cheng, Chris, 159, 161

Christopherson, Ed, 18–19

Clark, Jordin, 221n28

Clemmons, Katherine, 64

Cody, William F. ("Buffalo Bill"), 196n7; destruction of buffalo, 58–60; founding of Cody, Wyoming, 14; image as Buffalo Bill, 14, 205n3; image as the West, 14–15; TE Ranch in Wyoming, 14, 15, 54, 196n18. *See also* Buffalo Bill Museum (BBM), and ghost of William F. Cody; *Buffalo Bill's Wild West*

Cody, Wyoming, 15–17; and Bighorn Basin, 20; and Buffalo Bill Memorial Association, 16–17; as "lost America," 43; success as image of western town founded by Buffalo Bill, 16, 19

Cody Firearms Museum (CFM), early design: absence of history, context, and violence associated with firearms, 146–47, 150, 169; built after Olin Corporation donation of firearms to BBCW, 18, 26, 150;

dedicated in 1991, 18; giant fan or sunburst pattern of guns, 175; as "gunquarium," 150, 175, 220n10; understanding of firearms as inert objects of visual pleasure, 146; wars, lack of contextualization, 163–64

Cody Firearms Museum (CFM), 2019 redesign: absence of association of firearms with mass shootings, injustices, and costs of armed conflict, 146–47, 148, 182, 219n4; approaches to appeal to a variety of audiences, 156–57; contextualizing of firearms as technologies of modernity while dissociating firearms from violence and injustices, 8, 91, 147, 148, 150–52, 155, 157–58, 168–69, 171–72, 182, 186, 189, 190, 192; *The Cost of War* exhibit, and haunting of firearm violence, 24–25, 91, 147, 162–69, *163*; cultural capital of firearms, 178–79; embodied adjustment to colonizing force of firearms, 148; encyclopedic display of firearms as aesthetic goods, 146, 177–78, 219n3; exhibit featuring female sharpshooters, *160*; *Firearms of the West* gallery, 176–77, 222n43; "gunquarium" atmosphere, 178; and haunting of design and of viewers, 148, 179–82; Heart Mountain Relocation Center photograph as example of dissociative contextualization, *163*, 164–68, 181; Native American firearms limited or undisplayed, 151, 222n38; nostalgia associated with firearms, 179; place and time in, 155–58; pointing to Plains Indian Museum for story of guns used in Indian Wars, 170–71; redesigned in 2019, 3, 4, 6, 24, 148, 150–52; role of guns as sporting tools, technological marvels, and objects of play and pleasure, 91, 151, 152, 156, 158–62,

168, 172; self-memorialization of past museum design, 147, 148, 151, 155, 174–79, 191; story of founding, 156; *Time* mural and link to Guns in America website, 172–74; wall commemorating prior installation, 175–77, *176*; Woodruff Modern Shooting Sports Gallery, 158–59, *159*

Cody Memorial Association, 53

Cody Stampede, 16

Coe, William Robertson, 15, 16, 17, 55, 196n18, 207n24, 209n14

collected memory, 7, 23–24, 25–28, 199n6

context and text, 221n26

contextualization, as rhetorical mode to foster dissociation, 154–55

COVID-19, 117, 148, 149, 180

cowboy: Cody's embodiment of, 4, 15, 16, 30, 51, 55–56, 66; "Cowboys and Indians" games and fantasies, 65, 208n41; as embodiment of white individualism and heroism, 13, 14, 105; in frontier of conflict and violence, 14, 188; works deflating heroic image of, 105, 116, 118

Crazy Horse, 111

Cunningham, Ann Pamela, 52

Custer, George, 11, 53–54, 105–6, 111, 114, 118, 192

Daughters of the American Revolution, 53

Daughters of the Republic of Texas, restoration of the Alamo, 53

Dawes Allotment Act, 76

daydreaming, 153, 221n22

de Certeau, Michel: distinction between place and space, 122, 123, 216n15; and eighteenth-century partitioning of land, 130; "saying" of space, 122, 216n14; transformation of spaces into places and vice versa, 213n32, 218n32

Deloria, Philip J. (Dakota Sioux), 107, 210n21

Deloria, Vine: American Indians, and anthropologists, 211n34

Derrida, Jacques, 28, 69

Dickinson, Greg, 31, 40, 99, 146, 149, 153, 181, 204n82, 209n5, 219n2

Dippie, Brian, 71, 111

displayed memory: representation strategies to shape meaning of artifacts, 30; as spatial practices for the purpose of creating a seemingly authentic experience, 29

dissociation: affective, 152–54, 221n24; argumentative, 152, 153, 154; and daydreaming, 153, 221n22

dissociative amnesia, 154, 155, 221n27

dissociative contextualization: as rhetorical mode, 154–55; and settler colonialism of West, 8, 91, 147, 148, 150–52, 155, 157–58, 168–69, 171–72, 182, 186, 189, 190, 192

Domash, Mona, 92

Dorst, John, 39, 59, 188, 219n5

Draper Museum of Natural History: absence of critical examination of present/future, 141; absence of reference to changes in natural world wrought by Euro American invasion of West, 122, 144; absence of reference to evolution, 122; *Bison Jump* (sculpture), 135–36; and dialectical relationship of nature and culture, 121; directed movement from alpine to plains and from scientific observation to control and consumption, 128–31, 212n43, 218n48; efforts to produce "master naturalists" through directed movement and simulated environments, 120–21, 123, 131, 133; embodied experience of place over time, 121–22, 129, 131, 143–44; entrance, 217n31; evocation of (un)natural atmosphere of awe and

wonder, 121; and experiential landscape of Yellowstone, 126, 217n29; exterior view of, *120*; golden eagle exhibit, 140; as history museum, 141, 219n51; map of greater Yellowstone region in tile, 130, 142, *143*; mission of, 119–20; nature as ahistorical object and resource for wealth production, 124–25, 128, 130, 138–40, *139*, 142, 192; nature as a scene of curiosity and fun, 138; nature as method of securing white identity, 124, 144; pedagogical mission, 127, 217n30; scrims providing landscape and skyscape, 129, 132–33, 218n33; Seasons of Discovery Gallery, 130–31; simulated beaver dam exhibit, 138; simulated tensions between real and fake, 133–40; simulation and tension of presence and absence, 135–38; simulation as natural, 131–33, 141–42; taxidermized animals and recorded nature sounds, 132, 134–35; Ware's cabin, and mastering relationship to natural world, 8, 121, *127*, 127–29, 130, 131, 136, 137–38, 140–41, 142, 143; wolf exhibit, *137*

Drinnon, Richard, 210n21

Dunbar-Ortiz, Roxanne: on destruction of buffalo as economic base of Plains Nations, 60; on settler colonialism, and private property, 124, 130; terminology for Plains Indians and residents of US, 209n5

Dyck, Paul, private collection of Indigenous objects, 27

Egyptian burial sites, looting of, 26

Elgin marbles, British theft of, 26

embodied experience, 34–35, 40; affective dissociation, 152–54; and authenticity of museums, 29; and haunting, 6, 43, 44–45; with music, 101; of place over time in Draper

Museum, 121–22, 129, 131, 143–44; and space, 187. *See also being through there* (embodied movement)

ethos: of the BBCW, 4, 7, 8, 20; connection to "haunt," 5, 44, 121; and spatial and material rhetorics, 5, 32

experience: definition, 202n43; as embodied and emplaced, 34–35, 40, 187, 203n52; as individual and social, 35, 188; and past, present, and future, 33–34, 188; and sensation of things, 32–33

experiential landscapes: built environment as, 186, 187–88; directing of particular ways of looking, 39; and experience, 32–35; as interpretive tool for studying memory sites, 23, 47, 154; and landscapes, 35–37. *See also* experience; landscape

fencing, barbed wire: importance of in the West, 130, 139, 140, 218n47; at internment camps, 166Floyd, George, murder of, 149, 189

Fraser, James Earle, *End of the Trail*, 107, *108*, 108–9, 110

Freud, Sigmund, 45, 205n89

frontier myth: Cody's construction of, 30, 51, 55–56; and cowboy, 14, 188; and extermination of savagery by forces of civilization, 14–15; and tensions over race and class, 15

Gallagher, Victoria, 84

Garlow, Fred, 18, 55

Giffords, Gabby, 180

Glasson, June, *Naomi*, 117

gold, discovery of, 12

Golob, Julie, 159, *160*

Gordon, Avery, and critical haunting, 7, 43, 45, 46, 168, 192, 223n8

Grainger Gallery, 117

Greenblatt, Stephen, 115, 123, 124, 141, 217n25

Grey, Zane, 13

Grusin, Richard, 126, 132

guilt: and "imperialist nostalgia," 210n21; transcendence of, 210n20

Gunn, Joshua, 43, 193, 221n24, 222n44

"gunquariums," 150, 175, 178, 220n10

Hansen, Emma L. (Pawnee): on creative works of contemporary Plains Native artists in PIM, 72; on museums' treatment of Native American culture as "dying" and "disappearing," 72, 107; Plains Indian Museum response to NAGPRA, 27; on Plains Indian response to destruction of buffalo, 60; and redesign of PIM in 2000, 73

Haraway, Donna, 124, 134, 217n25, 218n43

Harjo, Joy, 212n47

Harrison, William Henry, 54

Hassrick, Peter, 73

haunt and haunting: affective state involving unsettling presence/absence, 6, 44, 77, 167, 192; critical haunting, 7, 46, 168, 192, 223n8; and demand for something to be done, 45; emplaced and embodied, 6, 43, 44–45, 185, 186; of firearm violence, 24–25, 91, 147, 162–69, *163*; and Heart Mountain Relocation Center photograph, 167–68; inclusive of past, present, and future, 45; as nostalgia, 206n5; and repressed memories, 6, 43–45, 46, 69, 95, 97, 116, 118, 180–86, 186; rhetorical mode for engaging material places, 23; welcoming and homelike and uncanny or unhomelike, 43, 45, 51, 95, 185, 192, 205n89, 206n7; of the West, 192–93. *See also* Buffalo Bill Center of the West (BBCW), haunt and haunting

Heart Mountain Relocation Center, photograph of in Cody Firearms Museum, 165–68, 181

history museums: artifacts perceived as

authentic and objective, 22; rhetorical qualities and characteristics, 22–23

Hlebinsky, Ashley, 155; curator of Cody Firearms redesign, 150, 156, 161; and dissociation of firearms from violence, 150–51, 152, 170; and roundtable discussion of firearm display, 220n11

Hollywood Weapons, 162

house museums, and "Domestic Religion," 53

Hyde, Doug (Nez Perce/Assiniboine/Chippewa), *Coyote Legend*, 109, *109*, 110, 118

Hyde, Michael, 32

"imperialist nostalgia," 77, 94

Indigenous rights movements, and recovery of looted sacred objects and human remains, 26

Irma Hotel, Cody, Wyoming, 19; wheel of fortune game wheel, 64

Japanese Americans, internment in Intermountain West camps, 165–68, 181

Kammen, Michael, 84, 212n49

Kavanagh, Gaynor, 38

Koener, W. H. D., *Madonna of the Prairie*, 106

Kristeva, Julia, 169

Lake, Randall, 86–87

land ordinance maps, and abstraction of land, 124

landscape: being in and through, 188; characterized by relationships, multiplicity, and continuous construction, 37–38; as material and symbolic, 36; as way of theorizing spatiality, 35–37

Lefebvre, Henri, 32, 37, 38, 39, 187, 203n66

Lincoln, Abraham, idealized log cabin birthplace, 54

Lockhart, Caroline: and Cody, Wyoming, image as tourist destination, 16; editor of Cody *Enterprise*, 16; prolific writer, 16, 17; promotion of Cody Stampede, 16

log cabins: Buffalo Bill Museum, original location of, 18, 52, 54, 56; Cody, 206n18; Draper Museum of Natural History, 126–28, *127*, 128–29, 130, 131, 132, 137, 142; linked to "American" values, 54–55

Lonetree, Amy (Ho-Chunk), *Decolonizing Museums*, 71–72, 92, 95

Lyons, Scott Richard (Ojibwe/Mdewakanton Dakota), "Rhetorical Sovereignty," 76

Maldonado, Chandra, 154

Manifest Destiny, 56, 58, 70, 84, 91, 92

Manship, Paul, *Indian and Pronghorn Antelope*, 108–9, 110, 214n23

Mardon, Allan, *The Battle of Greasy Grass*, *110*, 111, 118, 192

Martin, Elizabeth, 101

Massey, Doreen: and space and time, 35–37, 101; transformation of space into surface, 123–24, 189

mass shootings, 180–82

McCracken, Harold, 73

McCracken Research Library, and William F. Cody Archives, 18, 28

McCreary, Miranda, 24

McWhorter, Karen B., 117

memories: "amnesiac state of memory," 154, 212n49; conflicting structures, 95; embodied, 33, 44–45; and meaning making, 154; national, 93–95; repressed, and haunting, 6, 43–45, 46, 69, 95, 97, 116, 118, 167, 180–86. *See also* collected memory; displayed memory

memory sites, and experiential landscapes, 23, 47

Metesh, T. Logan, 220n10

Michael, Danny, curator of the CFM, 24

Michel, Neil, 29, 95
Michener, James, 19
Miller, Dave, 161
Mills, Amy, 36, 37
Moran, Thomas, 96; *Golden Gate*, 113; *Yellowstone National Park*, 113; *Zoroaster Peak (Grand Canyon Arizona)*, 113
Mount Vernon, as house museum, 52
Mount Vernon Ladies' Association, 52–53
Murray, John, 27
Musée d'Orsay, 115
museums: and audience memories, 154; and authenticity, 29, 31; collected memory, 7, 23–24, 25–28, 47; and colonizing of time, 124; decisions about what to collect and preserve, and social authority, 27–28; decolonizing practices, 92; design focus on narrative, immersion, and audience engagement, 155; displayed memory, 29–31, 47; forces of changes, 98–99, 189–92; history museums, 22–23; human remains and sacred objects collected by colonizing countries, 26; interweaving of subject and object to create experience, 39, 40, 97; order of exhibition, and making of meaning, 30, 77; part of larger symbolic or imaginary landscapes, 38; potential for exonerating or eradicating conflictual histories, 25–26; as rhetorical performances, 23–24, 39; selectively valued objects, 25; spaces within a larger physical and psychic environment, 39; structured invitations of, 30, 77
music: and atmosphere, 212n38, 218n36; embodied interaction with, 101

Na'puti, Tiara R. (Chamorus), 76
National Civil Rights Museum, 214n9

National Museum of the American Indian, 211n22
National Park Service, founding in 1916, 125
Native American Graves Protection and Repatriation Act (NAGPRA), 26–27, 31, 200n23
Native Americans: and anthropologists, 211n34; communal responsibility, 75–76; cultural refusal to interact with land as private property, 76; destruction of, 214n22; eighteenth-century removal of from West, 12; government destruction of buffalo as economic base of Plains Nations, 60; non–Native American uses of images of Indianness, 204n74; and nineteenth-century government "treaties," 12–13; nomenclature, 195n6; relationship to museum sites, 71–72; survivance, and resistance to dominant narratives and building of Native identities, 75–76, 89; survivance and sovereignty, and agency, 76; survivance and sovereignty, and experiential landscapes, 77; survivance as active sense of presence over historical absence, 75; violence against, and "American" identity, 210n21; the West as homeland, 5. *See also* Plains Indians
natural history museums: as sites of science pedagogy, 216n10; study and representation of evolutionary change, 122
nature: BBCW self-defined relationship with, 20, 57; as form of private property, 124; nineteenth- and twentieth-century spectacular imaginations of as captured or dead, 124; PIM embeddedness of Plains Indians in, 85–89, 90, 94. *See also* Draper Museum of Natural History
Nesheim, David, 58

Nicholas, Liza, 16
Noë, Alva, 33, 34, 203n53

O'Gorman, Ned, 113
Olick, Jeffrey K., 199n6
Olin Corporation, firearms gift to
BBCW in 1980s, 18, 26, 150
Ott, Brian L., 31, 40, 99, 145, 149, 153,
166, 204n82, 209n5, 219n2

Paxson, Edgar S., *Custer's Last Stand*,
111, 192
Pershing, John J., 17
place and space, distinction between,
122, 216n15
places of public memory, 31, 40, 184;
Places of Public Memory, Dickinson,
Greg, Carole Blair, and Brian L. Ott
(eds.), 99
Plains Indian Museum (PIM): active participation of Plains Natives on board
of, 72–73, 209n14; advisory board,
209n14; amnesiatic mode of looking
at nineteenth century history of conquest of Plains Indians, 90–93, 94,
192, 212n49; anthropological looking,
and professional distancing, 79–80,
82–84, *83*, 121; atmosphere created
with lighting and sound, 80–81, 93,
212n39; and Bill Cody's collection
from *Wild West* show, 72; completed
in 1979 and redesigned and reopened
in 2000, 18, 19, 72; conflicting memory structures, 95; construction of
world culturally distant from most
visitors, 81–82, 84, 90, 94; and discourse of recovery, 90; dreamscape of
non-Native American representations
of indigenous peoples, 38–39; embeddedness of Plains Indians in nature, 85–89, 90, 94; entrance featuring
montage of Plains Indians, *80*; exhibit
of river homes of Plains Indians along
the Missouri in twentieth century,

88, *89*, 213n52; gender stereotypes in
contrast to lived experiences of Plains
Indian women, 86, 212n47; hallway
leading to Museum, and sense of distance, *78*, 78–80, 85, 89–90, 94; and
haunting, 7, 77–78, 94–95; historical
distance and amnesiatic looking, 89–
93, 171; "humanities perspective" and
multicultural sensibility of practices,
73, 210n16; and national memory,
93–95; natural distance and technological looking, 85–89; negotiation for
return of Beaver Medicine Bundle to
Blackfeet Tribe, 27; progress, rhetoric
of, and Othering of Plains Indians, 84,
87, 212n49; reconstruction of Plains
Indian identity to conform with national identity, 93; redesign efforts to
avoid cultural biases of past, 73–74;
reduction of affective and symbolic
engagement with settler colonialism
practices, 77–78, 90–93, 94, 186; and
rhetoric of reverence absolving white
visitors of social guilt, 7, 74–75, 93,
94, 210n19; and rhetoric of survivance and rhetorical sovereignty, 7,
74–78, 88, 93, 129, 171; *Seasons of Life*
multimedia exhibit, 57, *86*, 86–89,
90. *See also* Native Americans; Plains
Indians
Plains Indians: government destruction of buffalo as economic base of,
60; government efforts to turn into
farmers and remake religious practices, 58; introduction of horse culture, 58; nomenclature, 195n6
Points West, 117
possession, desire of, and awe and wonder, 123–24
Prelli, Lawrence J., and rhetorics of display, 219n4
preservation movement, 200n24; nineteenth century, and white women's
role, 53

progress, discourse of, 84, 87, 129–30, 139–40, 142, 212n43, 212n49

Rawhide (TV show), 219n1
Remington, Frederic, 13, 19, 96, 105
rhetorical studies, 201n42; and context, 154; and museums, 198n2, 198n5, 201n36, 212n43; and place, 31–32; rhetorical criticism, 204n82m 221n26, 222n44; rhetorics of display, 219n4; and role of rhetorical critics, 180, 222n44
Rickert, Thomas, 101
Rifkin, Mark, 88
Robbins, Jim, 19
Roll-Preissler, Audrey, *Western Man with Beer and Dog*, 105, 118
Roosevelt, Franklin D., 165
Roosevelt, Teddy, 161–62
Rosaldo, Renato, "imperialist nostalgia," 77, 94, 210n21
Rosenzweig, Roy, 22
Rothstein, Edward, 19, 150
Russell, Charles M., 13, 19, 96; *Making the Chinaman Dance*, 114–15, 215n34

Schneider, Lindsey, 219n6
scholarly criticism, changes in over time, 190–92
Scholder, Fritz (Luiseño), *Custer and 20,000 Indians*, 105–6, 114, 118
settler colonialism: and abstract view of land, 219n6; and destruction of nature, 124; and dissociative contextualization in Cody Firearms Museum, 8, 91, 147, 148, 150–52, 155, 157–58, 168–69, 171–72, 182, 186, 189, 190, 192; reduction of affective and symbolic engagement with PIM, 77–78, 90–93, 94, 186; represented as nation-building, 92; US "national" identity, and narrative contradictions about, 92–93;

violence of as hidden and repressed, 46
Shepard, Matthew, 149
Slotkin, Richard, 14
Smith, Jacqueline, 214n9
South African museums, changes in, 99
space: "attuned," 97; and place, 122, 201n42, 216n15; and surface, 124; and time, 35–36, 101
spatial invention, 32
"Spirit of the American West" credo, 4, 5, 20, 42, 48–49, 100, 116, 118, 184, 207n27; "spirit," definition of, 222n1
St. Germain, Jill, 12, 13
Standing Bear, 84
Starsky and Hutch scene, Cody Firearms Museum, 162
stereographic photographs, 132, 134
Stormer, Nathan, 113, 114, 215n2
sublime: Stormer and, 215n2; western sublimity, 8, 37, 65, 79, 97–98, 103, 104, 112–18

taxidermized animals: in the American Museum of Natural History, 124; in the Buffalo Bill Center of the West, 59; in the Buffalo Bill Museum, 17, 53; in the Cody Firearms Museum, 161; in the Draper Museum of Natural History, 57, 126, 131, 132, 134–35, 137, 138, 141; movement across difference, and ecstasy, 217n25; and transcendence of time, 123, 124
Taylor, Breonna, 149
Thelen, David, 22
Tompkins, Jane, 13
Topperweins, Fabulous, 158–59
trickster practices, and survivance, 75, 89
Trump, Donald, 180, 182; Trumpism, 149
Turner, Frederick Jackson, thesis of, 12

Union Pacific Railroad, 11–12

United States Holocaust Memorial Museum, 30–31
US "national" identity: link to Buffalo Bill Center of the West (BBCW), 184; myth of, 195n3; narrative contradictions about colonization of Native Peoples, 92–93; nomenclature, 195n7; and violence against Native Americans, 210n21

Van Buren, Martin, 54
Vanderbilt, General Cornelius, 17
van Rees, Agnes, 152
Veracini, Lorenzo, 45–46
Vizenor, Gerald (Chippewa), on survivance, 75–76, 85, 87–88, 89

Weiser, Elizabeth, 34
Weiss, Kirsten Joy, 159, *160*, 161
West, Patricia, 53
West, Rebecca, and redesign of PIM in direct consultation with Plains Natives, 73, 200n23
Western Journal of Communication, 4
western sublime, 8, 37, 65, 79, 97–98, 103, 104, 112–18
westward expansion: completion of, 14; and destruction of ties between Plains Indians, bison, and horses, 58; Manifest Destiny as justification for, 92; nineteenth century, 12; violence of, 14–15, 172
Whitney, Cornelius Vanderbilt, 18–19
Whitney, Gertrude Vanderbilt: *Buffalo Bill—The Scout*, 2, *3*, 4, 16–17, 18–19, 26, 55, 99–100; and Cody, Wyoming, as tourist destination, 16; founder of Whitney Museum of American Art, 16, 100
Whitney Gallery of Western Art (later Whitney Western Art Museum): opened in 1958 and dedicated in 1959, 18, 99; traditional western artists shown in conventional manner,

96. *See also* Whitney Western Art Museum
Whitney Western Art Museum: absence of works portraying racism of the West, 114–15; cathedral-like windows looking out at *Buffalo Bill—The Scout* and sublime western landscape, 30, 66–67, 103, 110, 112, *112*, 116, 213n4; changes over time and call for more complex ways of seeing the West, 117, 189; commitment to vision of Spirit of the American West, 116, 118; design as sacred hymn that resolves discordant images and narratives into western sublime, 97–98, 101–3, 112, 213n4; *First Peoples of the West* installation, 106–10; *Heroes and Legends* installation, 105–6, 110; inclusion of works by white and Native women, 117; *Inspirational Landscapes* installation, 113; landscape paintings, and western sublime, 37, 91, 113–14; layout of staggered walls ending with elevated open space, 102–3, 110; and the rebranded Buffalo Bill Historical Center (BBHC), 99–100; renovation and reopening in 2009, 96; repeated movement between affective dissonance and resolution, 104, 105–13, 115 (*See also specific works*); representations expressing belief that Plains Indians ought to be destroyed to make way for modern civilization, 107–8, 214n22; thematic organization into five subjects built upon structured rhythms and harmonies, 96–97, 102, 114; and western sublimity, 112–18
Whitt, Laurie Anne, 210n21
Winchester, Juti A., 54, 206n18
Winchester, Oliver, 150
Winchester Company, donation of firearms for Cody Firearms Museum.

See Olin Corporation, firearms gift to BBCW in 1980s

Wister, Owen, 13

Wright, Will, 14

Wyoming: experiential landscape, 79; as idealized western landscape representing "American" values, 15; promotion of as imaginative heart of the West, 13. *See also* Cody, Wyoming

Yellow Hair, Chief, Cheyenne warrior, 17, 53–54, 62

Yellowstone National Park, 11, 15, 31, 85, 91–92, 100, 114, 119; and BBCW within experiential landscape of, 120, 122, 125–27, 130, 133, 140–44, *143*, 187, 188; *Golden Gate, Yellowstone National Park* (Thomas Moran painting), 113; technologies introducing the park to mass audiences in nineteenth century, 132, 134; and Teddy Roosevelt, 162; and tourism, 125, 217n27; wolves in region, 136–37, *137*

Zelizer, Barbie, 29

zoos, 124, 217n23

Zukin, Sharon, 36, 37